HOORAY FOR HEROES!
Books and Activities Kids Want to Share with Their Parents and Teachers

by
DENNIS DENENBERG
and
LORRAINE ROSCOE

The Scarecrow Press, Inc.
Lanham, Md., & London

Library of Congress Cataloguing-in-Publication data available

Library of Congress Cataloging-in-Publication Data

Denenberg, Dennis, 1947-
    Hooray for heroes! : books and activities kids want to share with their parents
and teachers / by Dennis Denenberg and Lorraine Roscoe.
     p. cm.
    Includes bibliographical references and indexes.
    ISBN 0-8108-2846-4 (alk. paper)
    1. Education--Biographical   methods.   2. Education, Preschool--Activity
programs. 3. Education, Primary--Activity programs. 4. Children--Books and
reading. I. Roscoe, Lorraine, 1955- . II. Title.
LB1029.B55D46 1994
372.83--dc20   93-48983

DEDICATION

Frequently we think only of famous people when we use the terms "hero" and "heroine." But many of us are fortunate enough to live side by side with individuals who have made positive contributions to our lives. They are heroes and heroines, too.

Among those individuals are our family members: Lorraine's husband, Michael, and her daughters, Allison and Bethany; Dennis's parents, his sister, Diana, and her husband, Don.

To those special people, we say "thank you" for helping us become who we are. We dedicate this book of heroes and heroines to you.

TABLE OF CONTENTS

ACKNOWLEDGEMENTS

In the final stages of this book, two special elementary school teachers added their insights to our work. Wanda Helmuth and Joy Rice proof-read the manuscript and edited/rewrote some of the activities. Their efforts were an invaluable contribution to bringing this book to fruition. **THANK YOU** Wanda and Joy.

We also want to thank David Bird, Jr., whose initial efforts to compile the lists of biographies enabled us to begin this work.

For ideas we thank Sandy Peters, Carol Miller, Cathy Gust, Deb Marko, Linda Fogg, Nancy Stevens and Christopher Hostetter; for technical assistance, Mike Roscoe and Dr. Fritz Erikson; and for help in putting it all together, Diana Durand, Fay Deibert, Lisa Shannon, Traci Fatzinger, Karen Hollman and Bill Pennewill.

To others who have influenced our work directly or indirectly, we offer our sincere gratitude. They include numerous librarians at Ganser Library (Millersville University) and public libraries, as well as individuals from various publishing companies.

WHY AND HOW TO USE THIS BOOK

Why don't we teach our children about great men and women anymore?

We used to. Not so many years ago, every school child knew that Abe Lincoln grew up in a log cabin and courageously freed the slaves. Parents and teachers eagerly shared the stories of Helen Keller, Anne Frank and others who overcame adversity to make a difference.

By hailing the accomplishments of modern-day pioneers like Martin Luther King, Jr. and John Glenn, we gave substance to the dreams of our children and encouraged young people to reach for the stars.

Lately, though, we have lost our way in our search for heroes. Our youngsters are surrounded with cartoon icons, some virtuous, others not. These figments of creative imagination seem to help us motivate our children. We read stories about them and we decorate our homes and schools with them.

We ask them to help us make learning fun. And they do! But we have allowed them to take over. Their importance has been inflated in our own minds and the minds of our children. Consequently, the child of the '90's knows all about Mickey Mouse, but has never heard of Walt Disney. The exploits of Wonder Woman provide a theme for playground games, while the real-life adventures of Sally Ride are merely yesterday's news.

Some creatures from the animated world are also having a less than desirable effect on children today. For instance, a '90's cartoon character associated with a brand of cigarettes has achieved as much recognition among kids as the venerable Mouse itself. As a result, teenagers beginning to smoke select that brand of cigarette over its competition. We can only surmise in what other ways cartoon creatures are affecting our children.

Do our kids admire *any* "real people" heroes? Just whom do they seek to emulate? Look at rock videos or the sports page for the answer. The latest, the hottest, the coolest, capture their attention.

So, wasn't that always the case? Haven't kids in this century always looked up to sports figures, movie idols and, yes, even cartoons and superheroes? So, why raise the issue?

The problem today is a lack of balance. Children and young people have little opportunity to *engage* in learning about great men and women. Occasionally, they are passive recipients of information about an exceptional person, but they don't really get to know that individual or be influenced by his/her greatness. They don't realize that exploring the worlds of real-life heroes and heroines can be fun and fascinating.

That is why we wrote this book. We believe children can aspire to ride in a space shuttle like real people have done, but they cannot fly like superheroes. Real people are real role models. *Hooray for Heroes!* will provide you, as parents and teachers, with a treasure trove of ideas that link children with famous people who have made positive contributions to humankind. We have combined a list of biographies written for children with many activities that will enhance the impressions those biographies make on the young people who read them. The books make excellent reading for adults, too!

Obviously, we had to make some decisions about which heroes to highlight in this volume. Names of additional positive role models can be found in the Series Index (pages 219-233).

Most of the books we have chosen are listed in *Books in Print* as currently available. Some especially good children's books are no longer in print, but can still be found in many local libraries. We have arranged the books according to four age groups:

pre-school (ages 3 to 5)
primary (ages 6 to 8)
intermediate (ages 9 to 11)
young people (ages 12 to 14).

Of course reading abilities vary and often do not correlate with chronological age. We urge you not to restrict your children or yourself to one particular list. After reading a primary-age book on

Ben Franklin, your eight-year-old may want to read an intermediate-age book on the inventor/statesman. READ, READ, READ!

The books listed are divided into two categories:

Ordinary People in Extraordinary Situations - real-life stories of individuals who found themselves in very special circumstances; and

Biographies - chronological accounts of the lives of famous individuals.

Each year, the National Council for the Social Studies (NCSS) designates a number of biographies as part of its listing of "Notable Children's Trade Books in the Field of Social Studies." We have chosen to review most of these special books, and have boxed our comments for your attention. (As this book went to press, the NCSS released its 1993 listing; those books are cited in Appendix A, pages 217-218.) In addition, other books are briefly annotated and marked with an "*" indicating that they have received favorable reviews in various publications.

If a book is part of a publisher's series, the series' name, in parentheses, is included in the listing and in a special index. If you like a particular book, you may want to read others in the same series.

We provide imaginative activities at the beginning of the two major divisions. Because age distinctions are often unimportant in terms of children's talents and interests, pre-school and primary activities are combined, as are those for intermediate and young people.

The activities are arranged into four groups:

Imagine That!
Arts, Crafts and Food
Music and Drama
Reading and Writing

This should help you find the right approach for each famous person you read about. Your judgment, as well as the child's own inclinations, can guide you in selecting appropriate activities.

You will notice that we have written the activities so that grown-ups and children can read them together, do them together, and enjoy them together.

Although the work of great men and women is often serious business, learning about them can be exciting. That is why we have woven humor into many of the activity descriptions. Meeting new people (especially famous ones) is a joy!

So, have a good time. Interact with a few exceptional citizens of the world. Offer a child you know a chance to be influenced by some of the most admirable people who ever lived. For who knows? Perhaps one day we will learn from that child's life story as well.

PRE-SCHOOL/PRIMARY ACTIVITIES

Introduction

You are never too young to begin learning about great people, and the best way to learn about them is to get involved with them!

Have FUN with famous men and women. Read stories about them, then pick an activity to help make those people part of your world.

We've written some "FUN-tastic" ideas here, and there are even more you may want to try in the Intermediate/Young People section of this book.

So, "FUNnel" your energies and talents into becoming friends with your heroes and heroines. We guarantee it will be

Full of
fab **U** lous
adve **N** tures!

Imagine That!

Imagine That...the television died!

Try something new. Turn off the television for one week! You have just rewarded yourself with a wonderful week of free time. Now, dive into a good book about a famous person chosen from the hundreds of books presented here. In addition to the time to read, you'll have time to enjoy some of the fun activities we've invented.

Did you know there was a time, and not too long ago, when no one watched TV because there were no televisions? Here's your chance to discover the good times you and friends can share by meeting real heroes and heroines. You'll open up a whole new world for yourself.

1

Imagine That...you have been challenged to run a race, but you'll be running while blindfolded!

How would you feel being different from the other racers? Would you still want to run? Would your goal be to win, or would it be more important just to cross the finish line?

Learn about famous people, like Louis Braille, who didn't let their disabilities stop them from becoming great people. Then pretend to be your hero. If you are Louis Braille, who was blind, put on a blindfold and have a grown-up help you walk from your bedroom to the kitchen. If your hero is Joni Eareckson Tada, have a grown-up tie your hands behind your back. Now carefully put a pencil between your teeth and try to draw a picture.

Talk about how you felt while you were doing these activities and after you were finished. It's a good feeling to finish a tough job, isn't it?

Imagine That... your grandparents knew your hero.

Did you ever ask? It's too bad, but sometimes we're too busy to take the time to talk about our heroes. But maybe your grandparents, or a friend's grandparents, have exciting stories to share about famous people and important events.

Ask older people you know where they were or what they were doing when man first landed on the moon, or when President John F. Kennedy was shot, or when Pearl Harbor naval base was attacked. As you listen to the stories, close your eyes and pretend that you are there when the story really happened...a long time ago! When the story is over, draw a picture of how you imagined the whole adventure.

Imagine That...you can BE your hero for a day!

Think about what your day would be like? How would you spend your time? Who would you talk to? What would you like about being that person? What wouldn't you like? We can't really become someone else for a day or for even an hour, but we can choose to live our lives like great people.

Here is one idea--pretend your treehouse is Valley Forge. You are a hungry, cold soldier who wants to help make America free. One of your friends can be George Washington. Playing "Valley Forge" for an afternoon can help you learn some of the same lessons that General Washington learned. Be sure to talk about how you felt and what you were thinking as you were pretending.

Imagine That... Once upon a time, every great person was a child-- just like you!

And, in fact, your hero was.

Find out what kinds of toys were popular when your hero or heroine was young. The library has special books that show pictures of toys and tell about them.

Do you think your hero played with toys like yours? Maybe the stories you've read mention some of your hero's favorite playthings. Now separate your own toys into two groups--toys that your hero might have had when he or she was a child, and toys that your hero would not have had. Which group of toys is bigger?

Next time you build a block tower or bounce a ball, pretend you are your hero. Maybe you'll be famous someday, too!

Arts, Crafts and Food

Up, up, and away!

What kid doesn't like to make paper airplanes? Actually, grown-ups love to make them also, especially when they're stuck in a boring meeting.

And what better way to honor the Wright Brothers than to make paper airplanes? Fold a piece of paper into a flying machine (a grown-up can help). Have a Kitty Hawk Jamboree in your backyard with paper airplane building contests. You could give awards for the biggest airplane, the smallest, the prettiest and the best flyer.

So, have a great time imagining you are the Wright Brothers. Throw on some old caps and goggles (sunglasses will do fine) and PRETEND. No fancy directions or lessons on aerodynamics are needed. This activity is "trial and error"--some will fly, others won't. Wasn't that exactly how it was at Kitty Hawk?

Let's build it higher and higher.

Okay, let's make our famous people totem pole go up to the ceiling.

Using old milk cartons, cereal boxes, oatmeal containers or other empty packages, decorate each one to look like a famous person from a book you've read or a book someone read to you. Your totem pole can show 5 people, 10 people, or however many you want, depending on your ceilings and how much you read! If you don't have enough oatmeal boxes, flat pictures taped on a door frame from the floor to the ceiling will look the same as a totem pole. What a wonderful rainy day or snowy weekend pastime. And you thought only videos could keep you busy!

Start saving things like containers, paper, crayons, odds and ends to add special touches, and wait for bad weather.

Red and yellow and pink and blue.

All the colors of the rainbow--and more--can be in your own coloring book about your hero. There are many different ways to make your book. You might start with blank papers or a blank scrapbook and make pencil drawings first. Then you and your friends can add color to your drawings. Won't your friends think it's great when you start telling them what you know about your hero?

Try using words about your hero to make a word find puzzle for use in your coloring book. Or how about scrambling up some famous words your hero once said. "A nnyep vdesa si a ypnen darene." Did you know Ben Franklin said that? Sure! "A penny saved is a penny earned." Puzzles like these, along with some nice drawings of your hero, his or her family, house or important objects your hero owned, will make a very special homemade coloring book. Perhaps you'll want to give your book to a friend for a special occasion.

Whatever ideas you choose, you'll have a great time. It's your own special coloring book, so let it show how wonderful you think your hero is.

Take a famous person out to lunch

Whether you take your lunch to school in a bag or a lunch box, here's a way to show everyone that you know a famous person. Paint over the cartoon character on your store-bought lunch box and design your own, using somebody famous. If you use paper bags, make a stencil, such as a profile of your favorite famous person, and trace it on lots of bags. Make each one slightly different if you want to by using different colors. Just think, you'll always have somebody important sharing your lunch with you!

Put those refrigerator magnets to good use.

All sorts of good things are in the refrigerator, so put some good things on the outside of the refrigerator, too! Refrigerator magnets can hold up: pictures of famous people that you draw, find in magazines, or buy in stores; or sayings by famous people. You can even hang pictures of "mystery" objects belonging to famous people and give a prize to the person who figures out the hero that matches the mystery object.

In fact, the refrigerator can be used to display "mystery" people. You might give clues to help others learn who the famous person is.

By the way, take a look at those magnets you're using! Yes, yes, yes--redecorate the boring ones to look like someone famous.

Please, please, please--can I dress up like Thomas Jefferson?

Of course you can. In fact, let's have a costume party where all your friends come dressed as their favorite *real* person hero. No reptiles or phony super heroes allowed. Costumes are easy to put together; you do not need to rent a fancy historical one or spend hours making one. You can take old clothing and make it look like a famous character's outfit. Or visit a thrift shop and you're likely to find what you need.

What to do at your party? Have everyone tell why he/she chose to be that particular hero/heroine. Play games like "pin the beard on Abraham Lincoln." Or eat Dolley Madison ice-cream sundaes.

Here's the real bonus for this activity--you now have your next "trick or treat" costume.

Watching heroes grow!

It's great fun seeing something you planted grow. So, plant a Heroes garden either indoors or outdoors.

Since heroes come in all colors and sizes, you want your garden to show those differences too. So choose at least five or six different types of plants--flowers or vegetables. In some cases a particular plant, such as the peanut, might represent a special hero, such as Jimmy Carter. Otherwise you can name your plant after anyone you admire.

In our Heroes Garden all of our plants are labeled with fancy signs we made and covered with plastic wrap. We have Jackie Robinson marigolds, George Washington carrots, Jane Addams hollyhocks, and Laura Ingalls Wilder wildflowers-- what a colorful way to honor great men and women.

1,001 ways to make PUPPETS!

Minus 995, which leaves six ways we're going to tell about. Many wonderful hours can be spent making and playing with puppets of famous people. These puppets can act out your hero's life--or live entirely new, imaginary adventures. So let Florence Nightingale meet Madame Curie, because to six-year-olds, both those famous women lived "a long time ago."

Our six favorite fun-filled puppet creations are:
- old light bulbs, covered with papier maché (make sure a grown-up helps you with this one)
- paper bags (use buttons, yarn for hair, and fabric scraps to make these look like your hero)
- milk cartons (use a 1/2 gallon size, cut off the bottom 1/3, the spout becomes the mouth)
- fingers (decorate your own fingers or make small puppets to fit on the end of your fingers)
- stick puppets (use odds and ends to decorate popsicle sticks)
- sock puppets (use an old sock and buttons, yarn, and odds and ends to make the sock become your favorite famous person)

Experiment and have fun. You'll be amazed how these six, and the 995 we didn't mention, can lead you to having fun with puppets.

Barbie and Ken are missing!

They've disappeared, and in their places are the Babes! Babe
Didrikson Zaharias and Babe Ruth, that is!

Yes, just take some dolls or toy figures you have and change them
into real people. You can create a whole display of famous people--
you could even open a museum.

Do you have to spend a lot of money on historical costumes? Of
course not. Use your imagination and cloth scraps. It doesn't matter
if the outfit isn't exactly like the one your hero wore. What does
matter is whether you learn about the great person and can teach a
friend about your hero.

Just think how unique your toys will become--everybody will want
to know about them. You'll be as special as the new toys you made!

Class, did everyone notice Arthur's new book bag, the one with Leonardo on it?

Yes, the one with Leonardo da Vinci on it--the book bag you
made!

By taking a store-bought one and covering it with other materials,
you can have your very own special book bag. Because book bags
have to last through all types of weather and a lot of handling, we
recommend using a piece of canvas on which you can draw your
design with waterproof markers or fabric paint. Ask someone to sew
it over your old book bag for you.

There are lots of good things about making your own hero's book
bag. First, it will show everyone whom you admire. And second, it
will be easy to find when all of the group's book bags are lined up in
the classroom!

Molly Pitcher wasn't really green, was she?

No, but it's the only color balloon you had, so for today at least her
face is green. Why?

Because you made a balloon person. After carefully blowing up the
balloon, and using a bread bag twister to keep it inflated instead of
a knot, you can draw your hero's face by using permanent markers
gently. Imagine making a whole collection of balloon people.

And by using the twister instead of a knot, you can deflate your "hero heads" and take them on a trip or to school. When you arrive, you blow up the balloon again, and your "hero heads" come back to life!

Concrete canvas captures community's curiosity!

Try saying that five times quickly! Well, that's what will happen when you and friends take out *chalk* and turn your sidewalks and driveways into giant art shows. Make chalk drawings of your heroes and important things about them for others to see and read. Just think of how people will smile and slow down as they walk past your chalk drawings of Robert Fulton and his steamboat. You could even list a good book or two for them to learn more about the subject. Make sure you sign your work, because you deserve the credit.

By the way, it's important to use chalk, not paint. Sidewalks are public places. It's okay to decorate them temporarily, but it's not okay for you to mark them permanently.

[Special note: Sometimes construction companies will permit you to paint on their fences at building sites, so ask them for permission to present your hero to the public there.]

Stick 'em up!

Or stick 'em on--on envelopes, paper bags, or school papers you have written. Yes, make your own stickers. Show other people that stickers don't just have to be cartoonish figures or dinosaurs; they can be heroes too! Get some plain labels from any stationery store and begin. We made lots of different people stickers; sometimes we didn't draw pictures, we only wrote "Abe Lincoln is our hero" on the label. Every letter you send will have a famous person's picture on it.

So, don't stick solely to store-bought stickers, start making self-designed stickers instead! Try saying that sentence six times swiftly.

Is that Louis Pasteur on your cereal box?

How appropriate that you're going to pour pasteurized milk over his cereal!

Take your favorite cereal and redo the box. Rename the cereal in honor of your favorite famous person, then make the box tell the story of the important events in his/her life. Use bright colors, catchy phrases, and a clever name. After all, you want other people to "buy" your hero.

Please, please, please, may we have a party?"

YES, you may have a party--to celebrate George Washington Carver's birthday on July 14th. Everybody loves a fun party, so plan lots of activities and games to go along with that famous person's life and achievements. For Carver, have a peanut scramble, a peanut butter tasting test (to pick the best), and of course peanut butter icing on the cake! Someone should definitely become Dr. Carver for the party, and everyone should sing "Happy Birthday" to him after he talks to the party guests about his great work. So, send out the invitations, in the shape of peanuts, and have FUN!

New York Times headline: PEOPLE CRACKERS REPLACE ANIMAL ONES!

Think of the fun you have biting off the leg of a llama animal cracker; well now you can bite off Charles Lindbergh's nose!

With the help of someone who enjoys baking, make a whole bunch of famous PEOPLE CRACKERS. Use one of your favorite holiday cookie recipes.

Maybe your PEOPLE CRACKERS will have a theme, such as "Famous Flyers." So in addition to Lindbergh, you could have Wilbur and Orville Wright, Amelia Earhart, Chuck Yeager, and many others. You need to draw simple outlines of their profiles that can be easily copied when you cut the figure out of the cookie dough. They may not look exactly like the person you have in mind, but that's okay. It's the idea, and the fun you'll have making them, that is important.

One final warning please--don't grab a glass of milk and eat all of them at one time! Save some to share.

So, who have you been hanging around with lately?

Well, from the looks of that mobile in your room, we guess it's Roberto Clemente. Once you've read about a great person, create a mobile using a coat hanger, string, and paper. Draw scenes from his life, inventions, or other things that remind you of your hero. Or write words that tell about why your hero was great. When you're finished, your mobile should show many different parts of your hero's life. So, when you and he are just hanging loose together, you'll be reminded, and hopefully inspired, by his greatness.

By the way, if you don't have space to hang a mobile, make a collage for one of your walls. Better yet, do both!

"Wear" ever you go, take somebody famous with you.

You can never have enough tee-shirts! So, design your own special tee-shirt showing everyone your favorite famous person. Take any plain tee-shirt and use waterproof pens, or fabric paint. We recommend you do several designs on paper first, then pin your final design to the tee-shirt and check it out in a mirror. Ask others for their ideas before you "copy" it on the shirt. To "transfer" your design from paper to shirt, simply poke small holes following the lines of your drawings, place the "holey" design over a flat, tightly stretched tee-shirt, and trace over the design, using the special pens. When you lift the paper, your design's outline--in dots--will be on the shirt. Now, fill in the lines, add color, and "tee hee!," you have your OWN designer tee-shirt. Besides drawing faces, you may want to copy some famous words your hero once said, or some objects that go with your hero (like Alexander Graham Bell and the telephone). It's your shirt with your hero--wear it PROUDLY.

Move over, Charlie Brown and Calvin--

Make room for some comic strips about real people. They might be "comic" or they might be somewhat serious. Who says Christopher Columbus can't have words in a bubble over his head, just because he was a real person?

But why stop with only one comic strip? Create a whole "comic" book about your hero or heroine. It's quite a job, but it will be fun! Use lots of bright colors so your characters jump off the pages and excite your readers.

How long should you make your comic book? You're the author so you decide. You'll know what works best for you.

Even 200 years later, John Chapman (whom we call Johnny Appleseed) is helping save the environment!

We hope you're saving trees by using those canvas shopping bags,
if not for your big grocery orders then at least for times when you
stop at a convenience store for only a few items.

So, decorate the bag or bags with someone famous--maybe
someone who even became famous because of his/her work to save
the environment. The bag will remind you of that person's great
work, and that person will remind you to use your bag. "Oh, I've got
to take Johnny Appleseed into the store with me."

P.S. If you can't find any plain canvas bags, simply dye the ones
with words already on them. Or turn them inside out and make the
blank inside the new outside!

Create a cardboard castle

Use large boxes that once had major appliances in them to make
places and things you read about in a biography. You might make
John Glenn's spaceship, Squanto's tepee, or even Narcissa Whitman's
covered wagon. All it takes are scissors, paint, tape, and lots of
imagination.

Some day, your prints may be famous!

Ben Franklin spent many years as a printer's apprentice. Try *your*
hand at print-making. Using tempera paint, you can make hand
prints, finger prints, and potato prints (cut a potato in half, cut shapes
into the flat sides, then use the potato pieces as stampers).

Or, glue a design on a piece of paper using string, buttons, paper
clips, noodles--whatever. Then, using a special roller called a "brayer,"
found at art supply stores, roll tempera paint onto the collection of
objects. Lay a piece of clean paper on the painted design. Rub
carefully with the back of a spoon, lift off, and enjoy your print.

Hey, with a little effort and some imagination, you can even make
your print look like your hero!

Music and Dramatics

"Somewhere over the rainbow . . ."

It's one of our favorite songs, and maybe one of yours too.
Now, take one of your favorite tunes and make up new words about
your hero. Think of the many different songs you can write:

(To the tune of "Old McDonald Had a Farm")
Young Tom Edison had an idea, ei, ei, o
And his invention was a light bulb, ei, ei, o
With a bright light here, a bright light there
Here a light, there a light, everywhere a bright light . . .

Well, you get the point.
Once you and your friends have made up new songs, have fun
moving and dancing to them. Come up with special hand motions
too.
You'll have a great time showing off your new song and dance.

Time to try moon walking!

If Neil Armstrong and other astronauts can walk on the moon, so
can you! How? All through the magic of PM!
Pretend to Move like you are walking on the moon, where there is
less gravity.
Or Pretend to Move like some other famous person doing
something important. You can Pretend to Move like Rosa Parks by
walking onto an imaginary bus and sitting in a front seat.
There are as many possibilities as there are famous people. Get
busy and learn about a new hero, then imagine, imitate and act out
their movements.
So, have fun with PM--Pretend to Move like great men and women.

Hero charades!

Write on small slips of paper the names of ten or more of your
family's heroes. Put these names in a hat. Now take turns picking
a name out of the hat and acting out what that hero did. If you pick
the name "Paul Revere", gallop yourself across the living room

pretending to shout "The British are coming!" Remember, in the game of charades, the person doing the acting may not say one single word. Now your audience can guess who they think you are.

Hurry, hurry, hurry—there goes another chair!

We're sure you have played musical chairs before, so here's a new way to play the game with your heroes. All players will wear a name tag on which they have written the name of their favorite famous person. When a player gets "out," he or she must tell the others about the person whose name is on the tag. All players must listen carefully to learn about their friends' heroes, because the second time you play the game you must switch name tags!

With each round you play, you'll learn more and more heroes. And you'll be having a great time too.

Musical fun and games to entertain YOUR hero!

Pretend your hero is coming to your birthday party, and you want to make sure he or she has a fun time. Here are some ideas for you to try:

- Make up a new dance to music by a great composer like Beethoven or Mozart, and plan on teaching it to your hero.
- Using rhythm instruments, like rhythm sticks, tambourines, drums, or triangles, make up a new song and dance to it. You might play a special tune to honor a Native American hero like Chief Joseph.
- Cover flashlights with colored cellophane and take your hero and your friends into a dark room. Have a grown-up play some patriotic music by George M. Cohan and pretend to create a fireworks display!

Remember, heroes like to have fun just like you do.

Reading and Writing

"We need a new holiday to get another day off from school!"

Whom do you think we should honor by a new holiday? When would it be? How would we celebrate it?

If you think people should miss school or their job for this new holiday, you need to have very good reasons for choosing your hero and wanting a special day in his or her honor. Write a plan for the special day, including your reasons for wanting it to be made an official holiday. Don't leave any of your ideas out!

Then, send it to your Governor! Or, better yet, write a very convincing letter to your local legislator--they are always happy to help future voters! Wait a minute, you're saying: "That's really stupid." Well, it isn't. It is because of the ideas of citizens like you and us that heroes and causes become well-known. Days, or even whole weeks, are set aside to honor them.

Okay, maybe we won't get the day off like you want, but think how proud you'll be if your hero gets the recognition she/he deserves.

Ode to My Hero

As we sit and ponder,
Our thoughts begin to wander
To the days of yesteryear
When young Lafayette knew no fear.

His desire to lend a hand
To this new freedom-loving land,
Showed he was a caring man
And that is why we are his fans.

Poetry! You can have so much fun playing with words, creating rhymes, figuring out new phrases, and most of all, writing about your favorite famous person.

Poems are special ways for you to share your special thoughts.

And so, without delay
Don't wait for any other day
Start writing now and you will see
Just how special you and words can be!

P.S. Remember, sometimes the best poems don't rhyme!

Write a rebus!

"Okay," you say, "but first tell me what it is."

Well, it's a picture story. You draw pictures in place of some of the words. For instance, instead of just writing "Thomas Edison invented the light bulb," you take out the words "light bulb" and put in a picture of one instead.

Children of early American settlers often wrote and read rebuses. So, write one today! If you want to, make your rebus a letter to your hero.

PRE-SCHOOL BOOKS

Biographies

JOHNNY APPLESEED (Pioneer)
Aliki. *The Story of Johnny Appleseed.* Simon & Schuster, 1987.
32 pp. Ill.

GEORGE WASHINGTON CARVER (Scientist)
Aliki. *A Weed Is a Flower: The Life of George Washington Carver.*
Simon & Schuster, 1988. 32 pp. Ill.

CHRISTOPHER COLUMBUS (Explorer)
Lillegard, Dee. *My First Columbus Day Book.* Childrens Press,
1987. 32 pp. Ill.
Parker, Margot. *What Is Columbus Day?* Childrens Press, 1985.
64 pp. Ill.
Richards, Dorothy F. *Christopher Columbus, Who Sailed On!*
Child's World, 1979. 32 pp. Ill.

BENJAMIN FRANKLIN (Inventor, Statesman)
Aliki. *The Many Lives of Benjamin Franklin.* Simon & Schuster,
1988. 32 pp. Ill.

HELEN KELLER (Humanitarian)
Graff, Stewart. *Helen Keller.* Dell, 1991. 32 pp. Ill.

JOHN F. KENNEDY (U.S. President)
Adler, David A. *A Picture Book of John F. Kennedy.* Holiday
House, 1991. 32 pp. Ill.

MARTIN LUTHER KING, JR. (Civil Rights Leader)

Lillegard, Dee. *My First Martin Luther King Book.* Childrens Press, 1987. 32 pp. Ill.

McKissack, Patricia. *Our Martin Luther King Book.* Child's World, 1986. 32 pp. Ill.

Parker, Margot. *What Is Martin Luther King, Jr. Day?* Childrens Press, 1990. 48 pp. Ill.

Schlank, Carol H., and Barbara Metzger. *Martin Luther King, Jr.: A Biography for Young Children.* Gryphon House, 1990. 32 pp. Ill.

GEORGE WASHINGTON (U.S. President)

Richards, Dorothy F. *George Washington, a Talk with His Grandchildren.* Child's World, 1978. 32 pp. Ill.

Roop, Peter and Connie. *Buttons for General Washington.* Carolrhoda, 1986. 48 pp. Ill.

PRIMARY BOOKS

Ordinary People in Extraordinary Situations
Real-life stories of individuals who found themselves in very special circumstances

PRISCILLA ALDEN
Boynton, Alice B. *Priscilla Alden and the First Thanksgiving.* Silver, 1990. 32 pp. Ill. (Let's Celebrate)

LOUIS BLERIOT
Provensen, Alice and Martin. *The Glorious Flight: Across the Channel with Louis Bleriot.* Viking, 1983. 40 pp. Ill.

EL CHINO

Say, Allen. *El Chino.* Houghton Mifflin, 1990. 32 pp. Ill.
Bill Wong, the bullfighter--sound improbable? Perhaps, but that is often true of a hero's tale. Allen Say has written an easy-to-read story of Chinese-American Bill Wong, who pursued an unusual dream--to become a famous bullfighter in Spain. Colorful illustrations augment the simple prose in introducing the world of the matador and "El Chino's" rise to fame.

TERRY FOX
Johnson, Ann D. *The Value of Facing a Challenge: The Story of Terry Fox.* Oak Tree, 1983. 64 pp. Ill. (The ValueTales)

CHRISTA McAULIFFE
Martin, Patricia S. *Christa McAuliffe: Reach for the Stars.* Rourke, 1987. 24 pp. Ill. (Reaching Your Goal)

Naden, Corinne, and Rose Blue. *Christa McAuliffe: Teacher in
Space.* Millbrook, 1990. 48 pp. Ill. (Gateway Biography)

MOLLY PITCHER
Gleiter, Jan, and Kathleen Thompson. *Molly Pitcher.* Raintree,
1987. 32 pp. Ill. (Biographical Stories)

POCAHONTAS
Accorsi, William. *My Name Is Pocahontas.* Holiday House, 1992.
32 pp. Ill.
Adams, Patricia. *The Story of Pocahontas, Indian Princess.* Dell,
1987. 32 pp. Ill.
Benjamin, Anne. *Young Pocahontas: Indian Princess.* Troll, 1992.
32 pp. Ill. (First Start Biographies)
D'Aulaire, Ingri and Edgar Parin. *Pocahontas.* Dell, 1985. 48 pp.
Ill.
Gleiter, Jan, and Kathleen Thompson. *Pocahontas.* Raintree, 1984.
32 pp. Ill.
Greene, Carol. *Pocahontas: Daughter of a Chief.* Childrens Press,
1988. 48 pp. Ill.
Richards, Dorothy F. *Pocahontas, Child Princess.* Child's World,
1978. 32 pp. Ill.

DEBORAH SAMPSON
Stevens, Bryna. *Deborah Sampson Goes to War.* Carolrhoda, 1984.
47 pp. Ill.

SAMANTHA SMITH
Martin, Patricia S. *Samantha Smith: Young Ambassador.* Rourke,
1987. 24 pp. Ill. (Reaching Your Goal)

JONI EARECKSON TADA
Tada, Joni Eareckson. *Joni's Story.* Harper Collins Children's
Books, 1992. 112 pp. (Today's Heroes)

Primary Biographies

JANE ADDAMS (Humanitarian)
Gleiter, Jan, and Kathleen Thompson. *Jane Addams.* Raintree,
1987. 32 pp. Ill. (Biographical Stories)
Johnson, Ann D. *The Value of Friendship: The Story of Jane
Addams.* Oak Tree, 1979. 64 pp. Ill. (The ValueTales)
Klingel, Cynthia, and Dan Zadra. *Women of America: Jane
Addams.* Creative Education, 1987. 32 pp. Ill. (We the People)

HANS CHRISTIAN ANDERSEN (Author)
Cote, E. *Hans Christian Andersen.* Rourke, 1989. 24 pp. Ill.
(Reaching Your Goal)
Greene, Carol. *Hans Christian Anderson: Prince of Storytellers.*
Childrens Press, 1991. 48 pp. Ill. (Rookie Biographies)
Johnson, Spencer. *The Value of Fantasy: The Story of Hans
Christian Andersen.* Oak Tree, 1979. 64 pp. Ill. (The
ValueTales)
Moore, Eva. *The Fairy Tale Life of Hans Christian Anderson.*
Scholastic, 1992. 80 pp. Ill.

MARIAN ANDERSON (Singer)
McKissack, Patricia and Fredrick. *Marian Anderson: A Great
Singer.* Enslow, 1991. 32 pp. Ill. (Great African Americans)
*A thorough biography geared toward younger readers; this
remarkably talented woman became a role model for many black
children.

SUSAN B. ANTHONY (Women's Rights Leader)
Klingel, Cynthia, and Dan Zadra. *Women of America: Susan B.
Anthony.* Creative Education, 1987. 32 pp. Ill. (We the People)

JOHNNY APPLESEED (Pioneer)
Gleiter, Jan, and Kathleen Thompson. *Johnny Appleseed.* Rain-
tree, 1986. 32 pp. Ill. (Biographical Stories)
Greene, Carol. *John Chapman: The Man Who Was Johnny
Appleseed.* Childrens Press, 1991. 48 pp. Ill. (Rookie Biogra-
phies)

Johnson, Ann D. *The Value of Love: The Story of Johnny Appleseed.* Oak Tree, 1979. 64 pp. Ill. (The ValueTales)
Kellogg, Steven. *Johnny Appleseed.* Morrow, 1988. 48 pp. Ill.
Kellogg, Steven. *Johnny Appleseed: A Tall Tale Retold.* Scholastic, 1988.
Lindbergh, Reeve. *Johnny Appleseed.* Little, 1990. Ill.
Moore, Eva. *Johnny Appleseed.* Scholastic, 1990. 48 pp. Ill.

LOUIS ARMSTRONG (Musician)
McKissack, Patricia and Fredrick. *Louis Armstrong: Jazz Musician.* Enslow, 1991. 32 pp. Ill. (Great African Americans)

JOHN J. AUDUBON (Artist)
Gleiter, Jan, and Kathleen Thompson. *John James Audubon.* Raintree, 1987. 32 pp. Ill. (Biographical Stories)

JOHANN SEBASTIAN BACH (Composer)
Greene, Carol. *Johann Sebastian Bach: Great Man of Music.* Childrens Press, 1992. 48 pp. Ill. (Rookie Biographies)
Rachlin, Ann. *Bach.* Barron's, 1992. 24 pp. Ill. (Famous Children)

ROBERT BADEN-POWELL (Humanitarian)
Brower, Pauline. *Baden-Powell: Founder of the Boy Scouts.* Childrens Press, 1989. 32 pp. Ill. (Picture-Story Biographies)

CLARA BARTON (Medical Leader, Humanitarian)
Klingel, Cynthia, and Dan Zadra. *Women of America: Clara Barton.* Creative Education, 1987. 32 pp. Ill. (We the People)

LUDWIG VAN BEETHOVEN (Composer)
Greene, Carol. *Ludwig van Beethoven: Musical Pioneer.* Childrens Press, 1989. 48 pp. Ill. (Rookie Biographies)
Johnson, Ann D. *The Value of Giving: The Story of Ludwig van Beethoven.* Oak Tree, 1979. 64 pp. Ill. (The ValueTales)

ALEXANDER GRAHAM BELL (Inventor)
Johnson, Ann D. *The Value of Discipline: The Story of Alexander Graham Bell.* Oak Tree, 1985. 64 pp. Ill. (The ValueTales)

Quackenbush, Robert. *Ahoy. Ahoy. Are Ya There? A Story of Alexander Graham Bell.* Prentice, 1981. 36 pp.

HENRY BERGH (Humanitarian)

Hoff, Syd. *The Man Who Loved Animals.* Coward, 1983. 48 pp. Ill.
Question: Who founded the American Society for the Prevention of Cruelty to Animals? Answer: Henry Bergh, "the man who *loved* animals." Here is a simple, informative story that can teach many adults as well as children something new. In a clear, straightforward style, the author points out incidents that raised Bergh's consciousness regarding the humane treatment of animals. He relates Berg's courageous, single-minded, and somewhat unpopular effort to protect animals.

MARY McLEOD BETHUNE (Educator)
Greenfield, Eloise. *Mary McLeod Bethune.* Harper Collins Children's Books, 1977. 40 pp. Ill.
Keslo, Richard. *Building a Dream: Mary Bethune's School.* Raintree, 1992. 58 pp. Ill. (Stories of America)
McKissack, Patricia and Fredrick. *Mary McLeod Bethune: A Great Teacher.* Enslow, 1991. 32 pp. Ill. (Great African Americans)

ELIZABETH BLACKWELL (Medical Leader)
Greene, Carol. *Elizabeth Blackwell: First Woman Doctor.* Childrens Press, 1991. 48 pp. Ill. (Rookie Biographies)
Klingel, Cynthia. *Women of America: Elizabeth Blackwell.* Creative Education, 1987. 32 pp. Ill. (We the People)

NELLIE BLY (Journalist)
Carlson, Judy. *"Nothing Is Impossible," said Nellie Bly.* Raintree, 1989. 32 pp. Ill.
Kendall, Martha E. *Nellie Bly: Reporter for the World.* Millbrook, 1992. 48 pp. Ill. (Gateway Biography)
Quackenbush, Robert. *Stop the Presses: Nellie's Got a Scoop.* Simon & Schuster, 1992. 40 pp. Ill.

SIMON BOLIVAR(Freedom Fighter)
> Adler, David A. *A Picture Book of Simon Bolivar.* Holiday House, 1992. 32 pp. Ill.
> DeVarona, Frank. *Simon Bolivar: Latin American Liberator.* Millbrook, 1993. 32 pp. Ill. (Hispanic Heritage)

DANIEL BOONE (Pioneer)
> Gleiter, Jan, and Kathleen Thompson. *Daniel Boone.* Raintree, 1984. 32 pp. Ill. (Biographical Stories)
> Greene, Carol. *Daniel Boone: Man of the Forests.* Childrens Press, 1990. 48 pp. Ill. (Rookie Biographies)
> Zadra, Dan. *Frontiersmen of America: Daniel Boone.* Creative Education, 1987. 32 pp. Ill. (We the People)

LOUIS BRAILLE(Inventor)
> Birch, Beverly. *Louis Braille: Bringer of Hope to the Blind.* Gareth Stevens, 1989. 64 pp. Ill. (People Who Made A Difference)
> Davidson, Margaret. *Louis Braille, The Boy Who Invented the Books for the Blind.* Scholastic, 1991. 80 pp. Ill.

RALPH BUNCHE (Statesman)
> Johnson, Ann D. *The Value of Responsibility: The Story of Ralph Bunche.* Oak Tree, 1978. 64 pp. Ill. (The ValueTales)
> McKissack, Patricia and Fredrick. *Ralph J. Bunche: Peacemaker.* Enslow, 1991. 32 pp. Ill. (Great African Americans)

BEN CARSON (Medical Leader)
> Carson, Ben. *Ben Carson.* Harper Collins Children's Books, 1992. 112 pp. (Today's Heroes)

RACHEL CARSON (Environmentalist)
> Greene, Carol. *Rachel Carson: Friend of Nature.* Childrens Press, 1992. 48 pp. Ill. (Rookie Biographies)
> Ring, Elizabeth. *Rachel Carson: Caring for the Earth.* Millbrook, 1992. 48 pp. Ill. (Gateway Biography)

GEORGE WASHINGTON CARVER(Scientist)
> Benitez, Mirna. *George Washington Carver: Plant Doctor.* Raintree, 1989. 32 pp. Ill.

Epstein, Sam and Beryl. *George Washington Carver: Agricultural Scientist*. Dell, 1991. 80 pp. Ill. (Easy-to-Read Biographies)
Greene, Carol. *George Washington Carver: Scientist and Teacher*. Childrens Press, 1992. 48 pp. Ill. (Rookie Biographies)
McKissack, Patricia and Fredrick. *George Washington Carver: The Peanut Scientist*. Enslow, 1991. 32 pp. Ill. (Great African Americans)

MARY CASSATT (Artist)
Venezia, Mike. *Mary Cassatt*. Childrens Press, 1990. 32 pp. Ill. (Getting to Know the World's Greatest Artists)

CESAR CHAVEZ (Labor Leader)
Cedeno, Maria E. *Cesar Chavez: Labor Leader*. Millbrook, 1993. 32 pp. Ill. (Hispanic Heritage)
Franchere, Ruth. *Cesar Chavez*. Harper Collins Children's Books, 1986. 48 pp. Ill.
Roberts, Naurice. *Cesar Chavez and La Causa*. Childrens Press, 1986. 32 pp. Ill. (Picture Story Biographies)

WINSTON CHURCHILL (World Leader)
Johnson, Ann D. *The Value of Leadership: The Story of Winston Churchill*. Oak Tree, 1987. 64 pp. Ill. (The ValueTales)

HENRY CISNEROS (Government Official)
Martinez, Elizabeth C. *Henry Cisneros: Mexican-American Leader*. Millbrook, 1993. 32 pp. Ill. (Hispanic Heritage)
Petrucelli. *Henry Cisneros: A Hard Working Mayor*. Rourke, 1989. 24 pp. Ill. (Reaching Your Goals)
Roberts, Naurice. *Henry Cisneros: A Leader for the Future*. Childrens Press, 1988. 32 pp. Ill. (Picture Story Biographies)

BEVERLY CLEARY (Author)
Martin, Patricia S. *Beverly Cleary: She Makes Reading Fun*. Rourke, 1987. 24 pp. Ill. (Reaching Your Goals)

ROBERTO CLEMENTE (Athlete)
Greene, Carol. *Roberto Clemente: Baseball Superstar*. Childrens Press, 1991. 48 pp. Ill. (Rookie Biographies)

West, Alan. *Roberto Clemente: Baseball Legend*. Millbrook, 1993.
32 pp. Ill. (Hispanic Heritage)

COCHISE (Native American Leader)
Johnson, Ann D. *The Value of Truth and Trust: The Story of Cochise*. Oak Tree, 1977. 64 pp. Ill. (The ValueTales)

CHRISTOPHER COLUMBUS (Explorer)
Adler, David A. *A Picture Book of Christopher Columbus*. Holiday House, 1991. 32 pp. Ill.
*Columbus is brought to life for the reader through the use of many illustrations.
Bourne, Russell. *The Big Golden Book of Christopher Columbus and Other Early Adventurers*. Goldencraft, 1991. 64 pp. Ill.
Carpenter, Eric. *Young Christopher Columbus: Discoverer of New World*. Troll, 1992. 32 pp. Ill. (First Start Biographies)
D'Aulaire, Ingri and Edgar Parin. *Columbus*. Dell, 1987. 64 pp. Ill.
DeKay, James T. *Meet Christopher Columbus*. Random House, 1989. 72 pp. Ill. (Step-Up Biographies)
Durio, Alice, and James Rice. *Cajun Columbus*. Pelican, 1975. 32 pp. Ill.
Fradin, Dennis B. *Columbus Day*. Enslow, 1990. 48 pp. Ill. (Best Holiday Books)
*An excellent biography of Columbus for young readers that makes use of photos, engravings, and maps.
Gleiter, Jan, and Kathleen Thompson. *Christopher Columbus*. Raintree, 1986. 32 pp. Ill. (Biographical Stories)
Greene, Carol. *Christopher Columbus: A Great Explorer*. Childrens Press, 1989. 48 pp. Ill. (Rookie Biographies)
Gross, Ruth B. *A Book about Christopher Columbus*. Scholastic, 1991. 32 pp. Ill.
Johnson, Spencer. *The Value of Curiosity: The Story of Christopher Columbus*. Oak Tree, 1977. 64 pp. Ill. (The ValueTales)
Knight, David. *I Can Read about Christopher Columbus*. Troll, 1979. 48 pp. Ill.
Krensky, Stephen. *Christopher Columbus: A Step Two Book*. Random House, 1991. 48 pp. Ill.

Lawson, Robert. *I Discover Columbus: A True History of the Great Admiral by One Who Sailed with Him.* Little, Brown, 1969.

Liestman, Vicki. *Columbus Day.* Lerner, 1993. 56 pp. Ill.

McGovern, Ann. *Christopher Columbus.* Scholastic, 1993. 64 pp. Ill.

Murphy, Carol. *Christopher Columbus.* ARO Publishing, 1991. Ill. (Famous People)

Sis, Peter. *Follow the Dream: The Story of Christopher Columbus.* Random House, 1991. 40 pp. Ill.

Spencer, Eve. *Three Ships for Columbus.* Raintree, 1992. 32 pp. Ill. (Stories of America)

Weisman, JoAnne B., and Kenneth M. Deitch. *Christopher Columbus and the Great Voyage of Discovery.* Discovery Enterprises, Ltd., 1990. 40 pp. Ill.

Young, Robert. *Christopher Columbus and His Voyage to the New World.* Silver, 1990. 32 pp. Ill. (Let's Celebrate)

Zadra, Dan. *Explorers of America: Columbus.* Creative Education, 1988. 32 pp. Ill. (We the People)

CAPTAIN JAMES COOK (Explorer)

Johnson, Ann D. *The Value of Boldness: The Story of Captain Cook.* Oak Tree, 1986. 64 pp. Ill. (The ValueTales)

BILL COSBY (Entertainer)

Martin, Patricia S. *Bill Cosby: Superstar.* Rourke, 1987. 24 pp. Ill. (Reaching Your Goal)

JACQUES COUSTEAU (Environmentalist)

Greene, Carol. *Jacques Cousteau: Man of the Oceans.* Childrens Press, 1990. 48 pp. Ill. (Rookie Biographies)

CRAZY HORSE (Native American Leader)

Zadra, Dan. *Indians of America: Crazy Horse.* Creative Education, 1987. 32 pp. Ill. (We the People)

DAVY CROCKETT (Frontiersman)

Quackenbush, Robert. *Quit Pulling My Leg! A Story of Davy Crockett.* Simon & Schuster, 1987. 40 pp. Ill.

Trotman, Felicity, and Shirley Greenway. *Davy Crockett.* Raintree, 1986. 32 pp. Ill. (Biographical Stories)

Zadra, Dan. *Frontiersmen of America: Davy Crockett.* Creative Education, 1987. 32 pp. Ill. (We the People)

MARIE CURIE (Scientist)

Birch, Beverly. *Marie Curie: Pioneer in the Study of Radiation.* Gareth Stevens, 1990. 68 pp. Ill. (People Who Made a Difference)

Johnson, Ann D. *The Value of Learning: The Story of Marie Curie.* Oak Tree, 1978. 64 pp. Ill. (The ValueTales)

Lepscky, Ibi. *Marie Curie.* Barron's, 1993. 24 pp. Ill. (Famous People)

FATHER DAMIEN (Humanitarian)

Brown, Pam. *Father Damien: Missionary to a Forgotten People.* Gareth Stevens, 1990. 64 pp. Ill. (People Who Made a Difference)

CHARLES DARWIN (Scientist)

Quackenbush, Robert. *The Beagle & Mr. Fly Catcher: A Story of Charles Darwin.* Simon & Schuster, 1983. 40 pp. Ill.

LEONARDO DA VINCI (Inventor, Artist)

Lepscky, Ibi. *Leonardo da Vinci.* Barron's, 1983. 28 pp. Ill. (Famous People)

Provensen, Alice and Martin. *Leonardo da Vinci: The Artist, Inventor, Scientist in Three Dimensional Moveable Pictures.* Viking, 1984. 12 pp. Ill.

What a delightful book! The work of da Vinci comes to life in this intricate, three-dimensional picture book. There are stars and planets, drawings of inventions, flying machines--all representative of the brilliant man's wide-ranging talents and interests. We even peek in on the "Mona Lisa" in progress!

Although any three-dimensional book should be handled with care, this one seems to hold up well to considerable manipulation.

Raboff, Ernest. *Leonardo da Vinci*. Harper Junior Books Group, 1987. 32 pp. Ill. (Art for Children)

Venezia, Mike. *Da Vinci*. Childrens Press, 1989. 32 pp. Ill. (Getting to Know the World's Greatest Artists)

CHARLES DICKENS (Author)

Johnson, Spencer. *The Value of Imagination: The Story of Charles Dickens*. Oak Tree, 1977. 64 pp. Ill. (The ValueTales)

Stanley, Diane, and Peter Vennema. *Charles Dickens: The Man Who Had Great Expectations*. Morrow, 1993. 48 pp. Ill.

FREDERICK DOUGLASS (Abolitionist)

Adler, David A. *A Picture Book of Frederick Douglass*. Holiday House, 1993. 32 pp. Ill.

McKissack, Patricia and Fredrick. *Frederick Douglass: Leader Against Slavery*. Enslow, 1991. 32 pp. Ill.

DAVE DRAVECKY (Athlete)

Dravecky, Dave, and Tim Stafford. *Dave Dravecky*. Harper Collins Children's Books, 1992. 112 pp. (Today's Heroes)

AMELIA EARHART (Aviator)

Alcott, Sarah. *Young Amelia Earhart: A Dream to Fly*. Troll, 1992. 32 pp. Ill. (First Start Biographies)

Parlin, John. *Amelia Earhart: Pioneer of the Sky*. Dell, 1991. 80 pp. Ill. (Easy-to-Read Biographies)

Quackenbush, Robert. *Clear the Cow Pasture, I'm Coming in for a Landing! A Story of Amelia Earhart*. Simon & Schuster, 1990. 40 pp. Ill.

*A fine portrait of this female aviator that is enhanced by its illustrations.

Wade, Mary Dodson. *Amelia Earhart: Flying for Adventure*. Millbrook, 1992. 48 pp. Ill. (Gateway Biography)

THOMAS ALVA EDISON (Inventor)

Adler, David A. *Thomas Alva Edison, Great Inventor*. Holiday House, 1990. 48 pp. Ill.

*A concise biography that traces Edison's life and career, incorporating anecdotes about his unique character.

Davidson, Margaret. *The Story of Thomas Alva Edison, Inventor: The Wizard of Menlo Park*. Scholastic, 1990. 64 pp. Ill.

Guthridge, Sue. *Thomas A. Edison: Young Inventor*. Macmillan Children's Book Group, 1986. 192 pp. Ill.

Johnson, Ann D. *The Value of Creativity: The Story of Thomas Edison*. Oak Tree, 1987. 64 pp. Ill. (The ValueTales)

Keller, Jack. *Tom Edison's Bright Idea*. Raintree, 1989. 32 pp. Ill.

Quackenbush, Robert. *What Has Wild Tom Done Now? A Story of Thomas Edison*. Prentice Hall, 1981. 36 pp. Ill.

Weinberg, Michael. *Thomas Edison*. Longmeadow Press, 1988. 48 pp. Ill.

ALBERT EINSTEIN (Scientist)

Lepsky, Ibi. *Albert Einstein*. Barron's, 1987. 28 pp. Ill. (Famous People)

Smith, Kathie B., and Pamela Bradbury. *Albert Einstein*. Simon & Schuster, 1989. 24 pp. Ill. (Great Americans)

FRANCIS OF ASSISI (Saint, Religious Leader)

Cole, Joanna. *A Gift from Saint Francis: The First Creche*. Morrow, 1989. 40 pp. Ill.

DePaola, Tomie. *Francis: The Poor Man of Assisi*. Holiday House, 1982. 48 pp. Ill.

BENJAMIN FRANKLIN (Inventor, Statesman)

Adler, David A. *A Picture Book of Benjamin Franklin*. Holiday House, 1990. 32 pp. Ill.

*This beginner's biography contains full-color line and watercolor illustrations highlighting Franklin's accomplishments throughout his life.

D'Aulaire, Ingri and Edgar Parin. *Benjamin Franklin*. Dell, 1950. 48 pp. Ill.

Greene, Carol. *Benjamin Franklin: A Man with Many Jobs*. Childrens Press, 1988. 48 pp. Ill. (Rookie Biographies)

Johnson, Spencer. *The Value of Saving: The Story of Benjamin Franklin*. Oak Tree, 1978. 64 pp. Ill. (The ValueTales)

Lawson, Robert. *Ben and Me: An Astonishing Life of Benjamin Franklin by His Good Mouse, Amos*. Dell, 1973.

Quackenbush, Robert. *Benjamin Franklin and His Friends*. Simon & Schuster, 1991. 32 pp. Ill.

Scarf, Maggi. *Meet Benjamin Franklin*. Random House, 1989. 64 pp. Ill. (Step-Up Biographies)

Weinberg, Lawrence. *Benjamin Franklin*. Longmeadow Press, 1988. 48 pp. Ill.

ROBERT FULTON (Inventor)

Quackenbush, Robert. *Watt Got You Started, Mr. Fulton? A Story of James Watt and Robert Fulton*. Prentice Hall, 1982. 39 pp. Ill.

MAHATMA GANDHI (World Leader)

Rich, Beverly, and Michael Nicholson. *Mahatma Gandhi: Champion of Human Rights*. Gareth Stevens, 1990. 64 pp. Ill. (People Who Made a Difference)

GERONIMO (Native American Leader)

Wheeler, Jill. *The Story of Geronimo*. Abdo and Daughters, 1989. 32 pp. Ill.

Zadra, Dan. *Indians of America: Geronimo*. Creative Education, 1987. 32 pp. Ill. (We the People)

JANE GOODALL (Scientist)

Birnbaum, Betty. *Jane Goodall and the Wild Chimpanzees*. Raintree, 1989. 32 pp. Ill.

Lucas, Eileen. *Jane Goodall: Friend of the Chimps*. Millbrook, 1992. 48 pp. Ill. (Gateway Biography)

CHARLES GOODYEAR (Entrepreneur)

Quackenbush, Robert. *Oh, What an Awful Mess: The Story of Charles Goodyear*. Simon & Schuster, 1983. 40 pp. Ill.

MIKHAIL GORBACHEV (World Leader)

Bennett, Charles R., and Anna Sproule. *Mikhail Gorbachev: Changing the World Order*. Gareth Stevens, 1992. 68 pp. Ill. (People Who Made A Difference)

JOHN HANCOCK (Colonial American)
Fritz, Jean. *Will You Sign Here, John Hancock?* Putnam, 1982. 48
pp. Ill.

GEORGE FRIDERIC HANDEL (Composer)
Rachlin, Ann. *Handel.* Barron's, 1992. 24 pp. Ill. (Famous
Children)
Stevens, Bryna. *Handel and the Famous Sword Swallower of Halle.*
Philomel, 1990. 32 pp. Ill.

JOSEPH HAYDN (Composer)
Rachlin, Ann. *Haydn.* Barron's, 1992. 24 pp. Ill. (Famous
Children)

JIM HENSON (Entertainer)
Gikow, Louise. *Meet Jim Henson.* Random House, 1993. (Step-
Up Biographies)
Petrucelli. *Jim Henson: Creator of the Muppets.* Rourke, 1989. 24
pp. Ill. (Reaching Your Goal)

MATTHEW HENSON (Explorer)
Gleiter, Jan, and Kathleen Thompson. *Matthew Henson.* Raintree,
1988. 32 pp. Ill. (Biographical Stories)

"WILD BILL" HICKOCK (Frontiersman)
Weidt, Maryann. *Wild Bill Hickock.* Lothrop, Lee & Shepard,
1992. 48 pp. Ill.

LANGSTON HUGHES (Poet)
McKissack, Patricia and Fredrick. *Langston Hughes: Great
American Poet.* Enslow, 1992. 32 pp. Ill. (Great African
Americans)

ZORA NEALE HURSTON (Author)
McKissack, Patricia and Fredrick. *Zora Neale Hurston: Writer and
Storyteller.* Enslow, 1992. 32 pp. Ill. (Great African Americans)

ANDREW JACKSON (U.S. President)

Quackenbush, Robert. *Who Let Muddy Boots into the White House? A Story of Andrew Jackson.* Simon & Schuster, 1986. 40 pp. Ill.

JESSE JACKSON (Civil Rights Leader)

Martin, Patricia S. *Jesse Jackson: A Rainbow Leader.* Rourke, 1987. 24 pp. Ill. (Reaching Your Goal)

THOMAS JEFFERSON (U.S. President)

Adler, David A. *Thomas Jefferson: Father of Our Democracy.* Holiday House, 1987. 48 pp. Ill.
*A concise biography of Jefferson highlighting his many accomplishments, concentrating on his political career.

Adler, David A. *A Picture Book of Thomas Jefferson.* Holiday House, 1990. 32 pp. Ill.

Barrett, Marvin. *Meet Thomas Jefferson.* Random House, 1989. 72 pp. Ill. (Step-Up Biographies)

Greene, Carol. *Thomas Jefferson: Author, Inventor, President.* Childrens Press, 1991. 48 pp. Ill. (Rookie Biographies)

Johnson, Ann D. *The Value of Foresight: The Story of Thomas Jefferson.* Oak Tree, 1979. 64 pp. Ill. (The ValueTales)

Quackenbush, Robert. *Pass the Quill, I'll Write a Draft: A Story of Thomas Jefferson.* Pippin, 1989. 32 pp. Ill.

Smith, Kathie B., and Pamela Bradbury. *Thomas Jefferson.* Simon & Schuster, 1989. 24 pp. Ill. (Great Americans)

JOAN OF ARC (Saint, Military Leader)

Nottridge, Harold. *Joan of Arc.* Bookwright/Watts, 1987. 32 pp. Ill.

Storr, Catherine. *Joan of Arc.* Raintree, 1985. 32 pp. Ill. (Biographical Stories)

Windeatt, Mary F. *St. Joan of Arc.* TAN Books, 1989. 32 pp. Ill.

JOHN PAUL JONES (Military Leader)

Zadra, Dan. *Statesmen in America: John Paul Jones.* Creative Education, 1988. 32 pp. Ill. (We the People)

CHIEF JOSEPH (Native American Leader)
Zadra, Dan. *Indians of America: Chief Joseph.* Creative Education, 1987. 32 pp. Ill. (We the People)

BENITO JUAREZ (Freedom Fighter)
DaVarona, Frank. *Benito Juarez, President of Mexico.* Millbrook, 1993. 32 pp. Ill. (Hispanic Heritage)
Palacios, Argentina. *Viva Mexico! The Story of Benito Juarez and Cinco de Mayo.* Raintree, 1992. 32 pp. Ill. (Stories of America)

HELEN KELLER (Humanitarian)
Adler, David A. *A Picture Book of Helen Keller.* Holiday House, 1990. 32 pp. Ill.
Benjamin, Anne. *Young Helen Keller: Woman of Courage.* Troll, 1992. 32 pp. Ill. (First Start Biographies)
Davidson, Margaret. *Helen Keller.* Scholastic, 1989. 64 pp. Ill.
Graff, Stewart and Polly Anne. *Helen Keller: Crusader for the Blind and Deaf.* Dell, 1991. 80 pp. Ill. (Easy-to-Read Biographies)
Johnson, Ann D. *The Value of Determination: The Story of Helen Keller.* Oak Tree, 1976. 64 pp. Ill. (The ValueTales)
Polcovar, Jane. *Helen Keller.* Longmeadow Press, 1989. 48 pp. Ill.

JOHN F. KENNEDY (U.S. President)
Donnelly, Judy. *Who Shot the President? The Death of John F. Kennedy.* Random House, 1988. 48 pp. Ill.
*A well-written account of the events surrounding Kennedy's death especially designed for young readers.
Graves, Charles. *John F. Kennedy.* Dell, 1991. 80 pp. Ill. (Easy-to-Read Biographies)
Smith, Kathie B., and Pamela Bradbury. *John F. Kennedy.* Simon & Schuster, 1987. 24 pp. Ill. (Great Americans)
*With many photos and illustrations, this book presents a solid portrait of Kennedy's life.
Stein, R. Conrad. *The Story of the Assassination of John F. Kennedy.* Childrens Press, 1985. 32 pp. Ill.

MARTIN LUTHER KING, JR. (Civil Rights Leader)

Adler, David A. *Martin Luther King, Jr.: Free at Last.* Holiday House, 1986. 48 pp. Ill.

Free At Last ably conveys Martin Luther King's ability to handle with dignity the ugliness of bigotry. Adler stresses the non-violence of Dr. King's quest for civil rights, specifically pointing out Mahatma Gandhi's influence on the civil rights leader. Dr. King is presented as a calming influence in a world filled with violence and suspicion. Frequent references to the Jim Crow laws remind the reader of the unspeakable injustices African-Americans faced not so many years ago.

Adler, David A. *A Picture Book of Martin Luther King, Jr.* Holiday House, 1989. 32 pp. Ill.

Through simple language and fine watercolors, Adler and illustrator Casilla provide young readers with an excellent introduction to the life of Dr. King. Elements of black history are presented along with details of Dr. King's personal history. In just 32 pages, the reader learns about the beginnings of the civil rights movement, the March on Washington, riots and protests as well as highlights in Martin Luther King's personal and professional life.

A list of important dates completes this useful and important book.

Behrens, June. *Martin Luther King, Jr.: The Story of a Dream.* Childrens Press, 1979. 32 pp. Ill.

Birch, Beverly, and Valerie Schloredt. *Martin Luther King, Jr.: Leader in the Struggle for Civil Rights.* Gareth Stevens, 1990. 68 pp. Ill. (People Who Made a Difference)

Cauper, Eunice. *Martin Luther King, Jr. and Our January 15th Holiday for Children.* E. Cauper, 1991. 32 pp. Ill.

Davidson, Margaret. *I Have a Dream: The Story of Martin Luther King.* Scholastic, 1986. 128 pp. Ill.

DeKay, James T. *Meet Martin Luther King, Jr.* Random House, 1989. 72 pp. Ill. (Step-Up Biographies)

Greene, Carol. *Martin Luther King, Jr.: A Man Who Changed Things.* Childrens Press, 1989. 48 pp. Ill. (Rookie Biographies)

Jones, Margaret. *Martin Luther King, Jr.* Childrens Press, 1968. 32 pp. Ill. (Picture-Story Biographies)

Livingston, Myra Cohn. *Let Freedom Ring: A Ballad of Martin Luther King, Jr.* Holiday House, 1992. 32 pp. Ill.

Lowery, Linda. *Martin Luther King Day.* Carolrhoda, 1987. 56 pp. Ill.
*This book traces the life of Dr. King and the events leading up to the creation of a holiday in his honor.

MacMillan, Dianne M. *Martin Luther King, Jr. Day.* Enslow, 1992. 48 pp. Ill. (Best Holiday Books)

Mattern, Joanne. *Young Martin Luther King, Jr.: "I Have a Dream."* Troll, 1992. 32 pp. Ill. (First Start Biographies)

McKissack, Patricia and Fredrick. *Martin Luther King, Jr.: Man of Peace.* Enslow, 1991. 32 pp. Ill. (Great African Americans)

Murphy, Carol. *Martin Luther King, Jr.* ARO Publishing, 1991. Ill. (Famous People)

Myers, Walter Dean. *Young Martin's Promise.* Raintree, 1992. 32 pp. Ill. (Stories of America)

Smith, Kathie B., and Pamela Bradbury. *Martin Luther King, Jr.* Simon & Schuster, 1989. 24 pp. Ill. (Great Americans)

Thompson, Margurite. *Martin Luther King, Jr.: A Story for Children.* Gaus, 1983. 24 pp. Ill.

Woodson, Jacqueline. *Martin Luther King, Jr. and His Birthday.* Silver, 1990. 32 pp. Ill. (Let's Celebrate)

ROBERT E. LEE (Military Leader)

Greene, Carol. *Robert E. Lee: Leader in War and Peace.* Childrens Press, 1989. 48 pp. Ill. (Rookie Biographies)

Zadra, Dan. *Statesmen of America: Robert E. Lee.* Creative Education, 1988. 32 pp. Ill. (We the People)

MERIWETHER LEWIS AND WILLIAM CLARK (Explorers)

Zadra, Dan. *Explorers of America: Lewis & Clark.* Creative Education, 1988. 32 pp. Ill. (We the People)

ABRAHAM LINCOLN (U.S. President)

Adler, David A. *A Picture Book of Abraham Lincoln.* Holiday House, 1989. 32 pp. Ill.
*This book presents Lincoln's achievements through the use of many illustrations.

Barkan, Joanne. *Abraham Lincoln and President's Day.* Silver, 1990. 32 pp. Ill. (Let's Celebrate)

Bennett, Charles R., and Anna Sproule. *Abraham Lincoln: Healing a Divided Nation.* Gareth Stevens, 1992. 68 pp. Ill. (People Who Made a Difference)

Bulla, Clyde R. *Lincoln's Birthday.* Harper Collins Children's Books, 1965. 144 pp. Ill.

Cary, Barbara. *Meet Abraham Lincoln.* Random House, 1989. 72 pp. Ill. (Step-Up Biographies)
*In this book, Lincoln's love of books and studying is emphasized. Also, it does not ignore his willingness to take unpopular stands on the issue of slavery.

D'Aulaire, Ingri and Edgar Parin. *Abraham Lincoln.* Dell, 1987. 64 pp. Ill.

Fradin, Dennis B. *Lincoln's Birthday.* Enslow, 1990. 48 pp. Ill. (Best Holiday Books)
*A concise biography that describes the creation of the holiday honoring Lincoln.

Greene, Carol. *Abraham Lincoln: President of a Divided Country.* Childrens Press, 1989. 48 pp. Ill. (Rookie Biographies)

Carol Greene's biography of Lincoln speaks to the child in each of us. Her style is refreshing and clear; her messages, simple.

Greene tells us that rain washed away young Abe's newly planted pumpkin seeds. "That was hard," writes Greene, and we feel the disappointment.

Greene touches on all the highlights of Lincoln's life without over-explaining them. The simple text and numerous photos and illustrations make this a wonderful introduction to our 16th President.

Gross, Ruth B. *If You Grew Up with Abraham Lincoln*. Scholastic, 1985. 80 pp. Ill.

Gross, Ruth B. *True Stories about Abraham Lincoln*. Lothrop, Lee and Shepard, 1989. 48 pp. Ill.

Johnson, Ann D. *The Value of Respect: The Story of Abraham Lincoln*. Oak Tree, 1977. 64 pp. Ill. (The ValueTales)

Kunhardt, Edith. *Honest Abe*. Greenwillow, 1993. 32 pp. Ill.

McGovern, Ann. *If You Grew Up with Abraham Lincoln*. Scholastic, 1985. 64 pp. Ill.

Miller, Natalie. *Story of the Lincoln Memorial*. Childrens Press, 1966. 32 pp. Ill.

Smith, Kathie B., and Pamela Bradbury. *Abraham Lincoln*. Simon & Schuster, 1989. 24 pp. Ill. (Great Americans)

Wallower, Lucille. *My Book about Abraham Lincoln*. Penns Valley, 1967.

Weinberg, Lawrence. *Abraham Lincoln*. Longmeadow Press, 1988. 48 pp. Ill.

Woods, Andrew. *Young Abraham Lincoln: Log-Cabin President*. Troll, 1992. 32 pp. Ill. (First Start Biographies)

CHARLES LINDBERGH (Aviator)

Stein, R. Conrad. *The Story of the Spirit of St. Louis*. Childrens Press, 1984. 32 pp. Ill.

JACK LONDON (Author)

Gleiter, Jan, and Kathleen Thompson. *Jack London*. Raintree, 1987. 32 pp. Ill. (Biographical Stories)

JULIETTE LOW (Humanitarian)

Behrens, June. *Juliette Low: Founder of the Girl Scouts of America*. Childrens Press, 1988. 32 pp. Ill. (Picture-Story Biographies)
*With many historical photographs, this book provides the reader with great insight into Low's life and her founding of the Girl Scouts.

Steelsmith, Shari. *Juliette Gordon Low: Founder of the Girl Scouts*. Parenting, 1990. 24 pp. Ill.

DOLLEY MADISON (U.S. First Lady)
Klingel, Cindy. *U.S. First Ladies: Dolley Madison.* Creative
Education, 1987. 32 pp. Ill. (We the People)

NELSON MANDELA (Political Activist/Leader)
Daniel, Jamie, and Benjamin Pogrund. *Nelson Mandela: Speaking
Out for Freedom in South Africa.* Gareth Stevens, 1992. 68 pp.
Ill. (People Who Made a Difference)

THURGOOD MARSHALL (U.S. Supreme Court Justice,
Civil Rights Leader)
Greene, Carol. *Thurgood Marshall: First Black Supreme Court
Justice.* Childrens Press, 1991. 48 pp. Ill. (Rookie Biographies)

MAYO BROTHERS (Medical Leaders)
Johnson, Spencer. *The Value of Sharing: The Story of the Mayo
Brothers.* Oak Tree, 1978. 64 pp. Ill. (The ValueTales)

MARGARET MEAD (Anthropologist)
Johnson, Spencer. *The Value of Understanding: The Story of
Margaret Mead.* Oak Tree, 1979. 64 pp. Ill. (The ValueTales)

MICHELANGELO (Artist)
Raboff, Ernest. *Michelangelo.* Harper Junior Books Group, 1987.
32 pp. Ill. (Art for Children)
Venezia, Mike. *Michelangelo.* Childrens Press, 1991. 32 pp. Ill.
(Getting to Know the World's Greatest Artists)

WOLFGANG AMADEUS MOZART (Composer)
Brighton, Catherine. *Mozart: Scenes from the Childhood of the
Great Composer.* Dell, 1990. 32 pp. Ill.
Downing, Julie. *Mozart Tonight.* Macmillan Bradbury, 1991. 40
pp. Ill.
*This beautiful book is a wonderful introduction to the great
composer.
Lepsky, Ibi. *Amadeus Mozart.* Barron's, 1983. 28 pp. Ill.
(Famous People)
Rachlin, Ann. *Mozart.* Barron's, 1992. 24 pp. Ill. (Famous
Children)

JOHN MUIR (Environmentalist)
Greene, Carol. *John Muir: Man of the Wild Places*. Childrens
Press, 1991. 48 pp. Ill. (Rookie Biographies)
Naden, Corinne J., and Rose Blue. *John Muir: Saving the Wilder-
ness*. Millbrook, 1992. 48 pp. Ill. (Gateway Biography)

RALPH NADER (Consumer Advocate)
Peduzzi, Kelli. *Ralph Nader: Crusader for Safe Consumer Products*.
Gareth Stevens, 1991. 68 pp. Ill. (People Who Made a Differ-
ence)

FLORENCE NIGHTINGALE (Medical Leader)
Adler, David A. *A Picture Book of Florence Nightingale*. Holiday
House, 1992. 32 pp. Ill.
Johnson, Ann D. *The Value of Compassion: The Story of Florence
Nightingale*. Oak Tree, 1986. 64 pp. Ill. (The ValueTales)
Tolan, Mary, and Pam Brown. *Florence Nightingale: The Founder
of Modern Nursing*. Gareth Stevens, 1991. 68 pp. Ill. (People
Who Made A Difference)
Turner, Dorothy. *Florence Nightingale*. Bookwright/Watts, 1986.
32 pp. Ill.

ANNIE OAKLEY (Frontierswoman)
Gleiter, Jan, and Kathleen Thompson. *Annie Oakley*. Raintree,
1986. 32 pp. Ill. (Biographical Stories)
Quackenbush, Robert. *Who's That Girl With the Gun? A Story of
Annie Oakley*. Prentice, 1988. 39 pp. Ill.

SANDRA DAY O'CONNOR (U.S. Supreme Court Justice)
Greene, Carol. *Sandra Day O'Connor: The First Woman on the
Supreme Court*. Childrens Press, 1982. 32 pp. Ill. (Picture-Story
Biographies)

GEORGIA O'KEEFFE (Artist)
Lynes, Barbara B. *Georgia O'Keeffe*. Rizzoli, 1993. 24 pp. Ill.
(Art)

OSCEOLA (Native American Leader)
Zadra, Dan. *Indians of America: Osceola.* Creative Education, 1987. 32 pp. Ill. (We the People)

JESSE OWENS (Athlete)
Adler, David A. *A Picture Book of Jesse Owens.* Holiday House, 1992. 32 pp. Ill.
McKissack, Patricia and Fredrick. *Jesse Owens, Olympic Star.* Enslow, 1992. 32 pp. Ill. (Great African Americans)

SATCHEL PAIGE (Athlete)
McKissack, Patricia and Fredrick. *Satchel Paige: The Best Arm in Baseball.* Enslow, 1992. 32 pp. Ill. (Great African Americans)

ROSA PARKS (Civil Rights Leader)
Greenfield, Eloise. *Rosa Parks.* Harper Collins, 1973. 40 pp. Ill.

LOUIS PASTEUR (Scientist)
Angel, Ann, and Beverly Birch. *Louis Pasteur: Leading the Way to a Healthier World.* Gareth Stevens, 1992. 68 pp. Ill. (People Who Made a Difference)
Greene, Carol. *Louis Pasteur: Enemy of Disease.* Childrens Press, 1990. 48 pp. Ill. (Rookie Biographies)
Johnson, Spencer. *The Value of Believing in Yourself: The Story of Louis Pasteur.* Oak Tree, 1976. 48 pp. Ill. (The ValueTales)

PABLO PICASSO (Artist)
Lepscky, Ibi. *Pablo Picasso.* Barron's, 1983. 28 pp. Ill. (Famous People)
Raboff, Ernest. *Pablo Picasso.* Harper Junior Books Group, 1987. 32 pp. Ill. (Art for Children)
Venezia, Mike. *Picasso.* Childrens Press, 1988. 32 pp. Ill. (Getting to Know the World's Greatest Artists)

MARCO POLO (Explorer)
Ceserani, Gian P. *Marco Polo.* Putnam, 1982. 40 pp. Ill.
Reynolds, Kathy. *Marco Polo.* Raintree, 1986. 32 pp. Ill. (Biographical Stories)

PONTIAC (Native American Leader)
Zadra, Dan. *Indians of America: Pontiac.* Creative Education, 1987. 32 pp. Ill. (We the People)

COLIN POWELL (Military Leader)
Blue, Rose, and Corinne Naden. *Colin Powell: Straight to the Top.* Millbrook, 1990. 48 pp. Ill. (Gateway Biography)

RONALD REAGAN (U.S. President)
Behrens, June. *Ronald Reagan: All-American.* Childrens Press, 1981. 32 pp. Ill.
Lawson, Don. *The Picture Life of Ronald Reagan.* Don Lawson. Watts, 1985. 48 pp. Ill.

REMBRANDT VAN RIJN (Artist)
Raboff, Ernest. *Rembrandt Van Rijn.* Harper Junior Books Group, 1988. 32 pp. Ill. (Art for Children)
Venezia, Mike. *Rembrandt.* Childrens Press, 1988. 32 pp. Ill. (Getting to Know the World's Greatest Artists)

PAUL REVERE (Colonial American)
Gleiter, Jan, and Kathleen Thompson. *Paul Revere.* Raintree, 1986. 32 pp. Ill. (Biographical Stories)
Lawson, Robert. *Mr. Revere and I: An Account of Certain Episodes in the Career of Paul Revere, Esq., As Revealed by His Horse, Scheherezade.* Dell, 1953/Little, Brown, 1988. 152 pp. Ill.
Longfellow, Henry Wadsworth. *Paul Revere's Ride.* Mulberry, 1993. 48 pp. Ill.
Weinberg, Lawrence. *Paul Revere.* Longmeadow Press, 1988. 48 pp. Ill.
Zadra, Dan. *Statesmen of America: Paul Revere.* Creative Education, 1988. 32 pp. Ill. (We the People)

SALLY RIDE (Astronaut)
Behrens, June. *Sally Ride, Astronaut: An American First.* Childrens Press, 1984. 32 pp. Ill. (Picture-Story Biographies)

DIEGO RIVERA (Artist)

Winter, Jonah. *Diego*. Knopf, 1991. 40 pp. Ill.
This book is a work of art. Through magnificent miniature paintings, it tells the tale of Mexico's Diego Rivera, one of the greatest muralists in the world. The simplicity of the prose intensifies the impact of the illustrations.
An additional page of biographical information appears at the book's conclusion.
Diego is magnificent to look at, a fine tribute to the artist and to the people of Mexico.

PAUL ROBESON (Singer, Actor)

Greenfield, Eloise. *Paul Robeson*. Harper Collins, 1975. 40 pp. Ill.
McKissack, Patricia and Fredrick. *Paul Robeson: A Voice to Remember*. Enslow, 1992. 72 pp. Ill. (Great African Americans)

JACKIE ROBINSON (Athlete)

Adler, David A. *Jackie Robinson: He Was the First*. Holiday House, 1990. 48 pp. Ill.
Farrell, Edward. *Young Jackie Robinson: Baseball Hero*. Troll, 1992. 32 pp. Ill. (First Start Biographies)
Golenbock, Peter. *Teammates*. Harcourt Brace Jovanovich, 1990. 23 pp. Ill.
*The focus of this book is not Robinson's life or career, but rather his first season with Brooklyn and how his teammates accepted him when others would not.
Greene, Carol. *Jackie Robinson: Baseball's First Black Major Leaguer*. Childrens Press, 1990. 48 pp. Ill. (Rookie Biographies)
Johnson, Spencer. *The Value of Courage: The Story of Jackie Robinson*. Oak Tree, 1977. 64 pp. Ill. (The ValueTales)
O'Connor, Jim. *Jackie Robinson and the Story of All-Black Baseball*. Random House, 1989. 48 pp. Ill.
Weinberg, Lawrence. *Jackie Robinson*. Longmeadow Press, 1988. 48 pp. Ill.

WILL ROGERS (Entertainer)
Anderson, Peter. *Will Rogers: American Humorist.* Childrens
Press, 1983. 32 pp. Ill. (Picture-Story Biographies)
Johnson, Spencer. *The Value of Humor: The Story of Will Rogers.*
Oak Tree, 1976. 64 pp. Ill. (The ValueTales)

ELEANOR ROOSEVELT(Humanitarian, Diplomat, U.S. FirstLady)

Adler, David A. *A Picture Book of Eleanor Roosevelt.* Holiday
House, 1991. 32 pp. Ill.
For years, picture books have introduced our children to bears
that care, fairies that sing, and cows that jump over the moon. Now,
thanks to David Adler, they introduce great people as well.
A Picture Book of Eleanor Roosevelt is one of Adler's many easy-
to-understand biographies for children. His text and Robert
Casilla's illustrations work together to offer a young reader (or
listener) a glimpse into Eleanor's busy life. Adler skillfully blends
fact and personality to bring this great lady to life.

Johnson, Ann D. *The Value of Caring: The Story of Eleanor
Roosevelt.* Oak Tree, 1977. 64 pp. Ill. (The ValueTales)

THEODORE ROOSEVELT(U.S. President)
Kay, Helen. *The First Teddy Bear.* Stemmer House, 1985. 40 pp.
Ill.
Quackenbush, Robert. *Don't You Dare Shoot that Bear! A Story of
Theodore Roosevelt.* Simon & Schuster, 1990. 36 pp. Ill.

BETSY ROSS (Colonial American)
Spencer, Eve. *A Flag for Our Country.* Raintree, 1992. 32 pp. Ill.
(Stories of America)

SACAJAWEA (Native American Leader)
Gleiter, Jan, and Kathleen Thompson. *Sacajawea.* Raintree, 1987.
32 pp. Ill. (Biographical Stories)
Johnson, Ann D. *The Value of Adventure: The Story of Sacajawea.*
Oak Tree, 1980. 64 pp. Ill. (The ValueTales)

ALBERT SCHWEITZER (Humanitarian)

Bentley, James. *Albert Schweitzer: The Doctor Who Devoted His Life to Africa's Sick.* Gareth Stevens, 1991. 68 pp. Ill. (People Who Made a Difference)

Johnson, Spencer. *The Value of Dedication: The Story of Albert Schweitzer.* Oak Tree, 1979. 64 pp. Ill. (The ValueTales)

SEQUOYA (Native American Leader)

Gleiter, Jan, and Kathleen Thompson. *Sequoya.* Raintree, 1988. 32 pp. Ill. (Biographical Stories)

Peterson, David. *Sequoya: Father of the Cherokee Alphabet.* Childrens Press, 1991. 32 pp. Ill. (Picture-Story Biographies)

DR. SEUSS (THEODOR GEISEL) (Author)

Martin, Patricia S. *Dr. Seuss: We Love You.* Rourke, 1987. 24 pp. Ill. (Reaching Your Goal)

SHAKA (World Leader)

Stanley, Diane, and Peter Vennema. *Shaka, King of the Zulus.* Morrow, 1988. 40 pp. Ill.

Here is a wonderful book for the reader who wants to explore a world completely different from his or her own. Through easy-to-read prose and dazzling illustrations, Vennema and Stanley present the well-researched story of a Zulu warrior who persevered through hard times to become a leader among his people. Although the non-violent among us might question the admiration of Shaka's gifts as a warrior, the author encourages us to accept the Zulu leader in the context of his society.

This biography also includes a helpful guide to pronouncing the many African words found in the story.

WILLIAM SHAKESPEARE (Author)

Lepscky, Ibi. *William Shakespeare.* Barron's, 1989. 28 pp. Ill. (Famous People)

Stanley, Diane, and Peter Vennema. *Bard of Avon: The Story of William Shakespeare.* Morrow, 1992. 48 pp. Ill.

SITTING BULL (Native American Leader)
  Smith, Kathie B., and Pamela Bradbury. *Sitting Bull*. Simon &
  Schuster, 1989. 24 pp. Ill. (Great Americans)

SQUANTO (Native American Leader)
  Celsi, Teresa. *Squanto and the First Thanksgiving*. Raintree, 1989.
  32 pp. Ill.
  Kessel, Joyce K. *Squanto and the First Thanksgiving*. Carolrhoda,
  1983. 48 pp. Ill.
  Zadra, Dan. *Indians of America: Squanto*. Creative Education,
  1987. 32 pp. Ill. (We the People)

ELIZABETH CADY STANTON (Women's Rights Leader)
  Gleiter, Jan, and Kathleen Thompson. *Elizabeth Cady Stanton*.
  Raintree, 1988. 32 pp. Ill. (Biographical Stories)
  Schlank, Carol H., and Barbara Metzger. *Elizabeth Cady Stanton:
  A Biography for Young Children*. Gryphon House. 32 pp. Ill.

PETER STUYVESANT (Colonial American)
  Quackenbush, Robert. *Old Silver Leg Takes Over: A Story of Peter
  Stuyvesant*. Prentice Hall, 1986. 40 pp. Ill.
  *A humorous work that traces the life of Stuyvesant, this book
  relates how the governor of New Amsterdam (New York) forged
  a city out of the frontier.

MOTHER TERESA (Humanitarian)
  Greene, Carol. *Mother Teresa: Friend of the Friendless*.
  Childrens Press, 1983. 32 pp. Ill. (Picture-Story Biographies)
  Jacobs, William Jay. *Mother Teresa: Helping the Poor*. Millbrook,
  1992. 48 pp. Ill. (Gateway Biography)
  Ullstein, Susan, and Charlotte Gray. *Mother Teresa: Servant to the
  World's Suffering People*. Gareth Stevens, 1990. 68 pp. Ill.
  (People Who Made a Difference)

SOJOURNER TRUTH (Abolitionist)
  McKissack, Patricia and Fredrick. *Sojourner Truth: A Voice for
  Freedom*. Enslow, 1992. 32 pp. Ill. (Great African Americans)

Tolan, Mary, and Susan Taylor-Boyd. *Sojourner Truth: The Courageous Former Slave Who Led Others to Freedom.* Gareth Stevens, 1991. 68 pp. Ill. (People Who Made a Difference)

HARRIET TUBMAN (Abolitionist)

Adler, David A. *A Picture Book of Harriet Tubman.* Holiday House, 1992. 32 pp. Ill.

Benjamin, Anne. *Young Harriet Tubman: Freedom Fighter.* Troll, 1992. 32 pp. Ill. (First Start Biographies)

Carter, Polly. *Harriet Tubman and Black History Month.* Silver, 1990. 32 pp. Ill. (Let's Celebrate)

Johnson, Ann D. *The Value of Helping: The Story of Harriet Tubman.* Oak Tree, 1979. 64 pp. Ill. (The ValueTales)

Klingel, Cindy. *Women of America: Harriet Tubman.* Creative Education, 1987. 32 pp. Ill. (We the People)

Meyer, Linda D. *Harriet Tubman: They Called Me Moses.* Parenting, 1992. 32 pp. Ill.

Polcovar, Jane. *Harriet Tubman.* Longmeadow Press, 1988. 48 pp. Ill.

Smith, Kathie B., and Pamela Bradbury. *Harriet Tubman.* Simon & Schuster, 1989. 24 pp. Ill. (Great Americans)

DESMOND TUTU (Political Activist/Leader)

Greene, Carol. *Desmond Tutu: Bishop of Peace.* Childrens Press, 1986. 32 pp. Ill. (Picture-Story Biographies)

Winner, David. *Desmond Tutu: Religious Leader Devoted to Freedom.* Gareth Stevens, 1991. 68 pp. Ill. (People Who Made a Difference)

MARK TWAIN (Author)

Greene, Carol. *Mark Twain: Author of Tom Sawyer.* Childrens Press, 1992. 48 pp. Ill. (Rookie Biographies)

Quackenbush, Robert. *Mark Twain? What Kind of Name Is That? A Story of Samuel Langhorn Clemens.* Simon & Schuster, 1984. 40 pp. Ill.

VINCENT VAN GOGH (Artist)

Raboff, Ernest. *Vincent van Gogh.* Harper Junior Books Group, 1987. 32 pp. Ill. (Art for Children)

Venezia, Mike. *Van Gogh*. Childrens Press, 1988. 32 pp. Ill.
(Getting to Know the World's Greatest Artists)
Zemel, Carol. *Vincent van Gogh*. Rizzoli, 1993. 24 pp. Ill. (Art)

LECH WALESA(Freedom Fighter)

Angel, Ann, and Mary Craig. *Lech Walesa: Champion of Freedom
for Poland*. Gareth Stevens, 1992. 68 pp. Ill. (People Who
Made A Difference)

RAOUL WALLENBERG (Humanitarian)

Daniel, Jaime, Michael Nicholson, and David Winner. *Raoul
Wallenberg: One Man against Nazi Terror*. Gareth Stevens, 1992.
68 pp. Ill. (People Who Made a Difference)

BOOKER T. WASHINGTON (Educator)

Gleiter, Jan, and Kathleen Thompson. *Booker T. Washington*.
Raintree, 1987. 32 pp. Ill. (Biographical Stories)
McKissack, Patricia and Fredrick. *Booker T. Washington: Leader
and Educator*. Enslow, 1992. 32 pp. Ill. (Great African
Americans)

GEORGE WASHINGTON (U.S. President)

Adler, David A. *George Washington: Father of Our Country*.
Holiday House, 1988. 48 pp. Ill.
*Washington's childhood is emphasized, so the reader learns of
how his love of mathematics led him to surveying, then soldiering,
then greatness.
Adler, David A. *A Picture Book of George Washington*. Holiday
House, 1989. 32 pp. Ill.
Bulla, Clyde R. *Washington's Birthday*. Harper Collins, 1967. 40
pp. Ill.
D'Aulaire, Ingri and Edgar Parin. *George Washington*. Dell, 1987.
64 pp. Ill.
Fradin, Dennis B. *Washington's Birthday*. Enslow, 1990. 48 pp.
Ill. (Best Holiday Books)
Fritz, Jean. *George Washington's Breakfast*. Putnam, 1984. 48 pp.
Ill.
Giblin, James C. *George Washington: A Picture Book Biography*.
Scholastic, 1992. 40 pp. Ill.

Greene, Carol. *George Washington: First President of the United States*. Childrens Press, 1991. 48 pp. Ill. (Rookie Biographies)

Gross, Ruth B. *If You Grew Up With George Washington*. Scholastic, 1982. 64 pp. Ill.

Heilbroner, Joan. *Meet George Washington*. Random House, 1989. 72 pp. Ill. (Step-Up Biographies)

Hoobler, Dorothy and Thomas. *George Washington and President's Day*. Silver, 1990. 32 pp. Ill. (Let's Celebrate)

Johnston, Johanna. *A Birthday for General Washington*. Childrens Press, 1976. 32 pp. Ill.

McGovern, Ann. *If You Grew Up with George Washington*. Scholastic, 1985. 64 pp.

Quackenbush, Robert. *I Did It With My Hatchet: A Story of George Washington*. Pippin, 1989. 32 pp. Ill.

Smith, Kathie B., and Pamela Bradbury. *George Washington*. Simon & Schuster, 1989. 24 pp. Ill. (Great Americans)

Tunnell, Michael O. *The Joke's on George*. Tambourine Books, 1993. 32 pp. Ill.

Weinberg, Lawrence. *George Washington*. Longmeadow Press, 1988. 48 pp. Ill.

Woods, Andrew. *Young George Washington: America's First President*. Troll, 1992. 32 pp. Ill. (First Start Biographies)

ELIE WIESEL (Humanitarian)

Greene, Carol. *Elie Wiesel: Messenger from the Holocaust*. Childrens Press, 1987. 32 pp. Ill. (Picture-Story Biographies)

LAURA INGALLS WILDER (Author)

Greene, Carol. *Laura Ingalls Wilder: Author of the Little House Books*. Childrens Press, 1990. 48 pp. Ill. (Rookie Biographies)

WRIGHT BROTHERS (Inventors)

Johnson, Spencer. *The Value of Patience: The Story of the Wright Brothers*. Oak Tree, 1976. 64 pp. Ill. (The ValueTales)

Marquardt, Max. *Wilbur, Orville and the Flying Machine*. Raintree, 1989. 32 pp. Ill.

Woods, Andrew. *Young Orville and Wilbur Wright: First to Fly*. Troll, 1992. 32 pp. Ill. (First Start Biographies)

INTERMEDIATE/YOUNG PEOPLE ACTIVITIES

Introduction

YES, there are ways to interest preteens and teenagers in real people! After all, these young minds are genuinely curious about people--look at their intense interest in "popular personalities." So what if many famous people aren't regulars on television, the sports pages, or rock videos; they still have fascinating lives. With the right hook, that interest can be caught.

These activities are designed to provide you with ways to help "reel 'em in." Enough of the fish metaphor, already--let's get to the "porpoise" (sorry, we couldn't resist it!).

Imagine That!

Imagine That...the television died! (It's so important we repeated it!)

As an experiment, turn off the television for one week! You have just rewarded yourself with a wonderful week of free time. Now, jump into a good biography or two, chosen from the hundreds of books presented here. In addition to the time to read, you'll have time to become involved with some of the entertaining activities we've invented.

Remember, there was a time, and not too long ago, when no one watched television. Here's your chance to discover the good times you and friends can share by meeting real heroes and heroines. You'll open up a whole new world for yourself.

If you really miss your television set, get a large cardboard box and cut it to look like a TV screen. With your family or friends helping you, perform a show about your favorite famous person. Maybe

51

you'll even want to make a soundtrack for the show. Be creative and have fun!

Imagine That...you get to take your hero to the mall!

Yes, you are the guide for your hero to your local shopping mall.

What stores would your hero like to visit? If he is an inventor, like Henry Ford, maybe a hardware store would be of interest. John Muir the environmentalist would definitely want to go to a shoe store, so he could buy a new pair of hiking boots for his next nature walk.

Here's a special bonus for you as the guide. You have been given a gift certificate to choose three books for your hero at the mall's largest bookstore. What books would you pick, and why? Remember to consider any special needs of your hero, such as books in braille for Helen Keller.

P.S. Wouldn't this activity be a great creative writing activity? Just a thought!

Imagine That...you can peek inside Albert Einstein's fanny pack!

Okay, so he didn't own one, since they're a fairly recent addition to modern life. But imagine that he did! What would the great thinker carry in there? Why? Do you have similar things in your fanny pack?

For fun, you could actually rummage through your attic or garage and "find" Mr. Einstein's belongings. Share your discovery with your classmates. In fact, your class could have a "Fanny Pack Festival" centered around what heroes may carry with them.

(P.S. We're certain Al did not carry a comb in there--just take one look at his hair!)

Imagine That...she's a he, or he's a she!

What would happen if Charles Lindbergh would suddenly become Charlotte Lindbergh, or Amelia Earhart were Harry Earhart. Think about how being a different gender might have changed that person's career.

Did you know that Elizabeth Cochrane signed her newspaper articles with the name Nellie Bly to avoid some of the problems of gender bias? Read a book about her to learn more details of her difficulties.

Is there still "gender bias" today in certain careers? That means, are some jobs thought of as being only for women and other jobs only for men? Make a list of these jobs. Take this a step further and interview a man or woman in a nontraditional job. How is that person being a trailblazer in getting rid of gender bias?

Imagine That...Rosa Parks is YOUR MOTHER!

That's right, your Mom would then be a well-known heroine, a person who made a difference. Think about how you would feel, how your life might be different, and how it might influence your career plans.

Of course, many parents are still heroes because they sacrifice so much to help their children. When's the last time you said "THANK YOU" to those who are doing their best to look out for you?

For a special surprise, make a thank-you card for your parents or grandparents or someone else who uses their time and energy to make your life better.

Imagine That...our school's hallways have names!

That's right, name your school hallways after your favorite famous people. In fact, the school and the playground could also be named to honor great men and women. So, here's what you do. Organize! Yes, form a committee, talk to your teacher and principal, and then present a plan to name the hallways, playground, and maybe even the school! We want you to think about a unique idea here--these names could change every three months, so that many heroes and heroines can be honored. In January, the second floor could be Roberto Clemente Avenue, then in March it could become Mother Teresa Boulevard. You and your "street committee" would be in charge of name signs and displays telling about the person and why he/she is being honored.

Perhaps you could name the rooms of your house, too. How about the Stonewall Jackson Room for a room with a fireplace or brick wall, or the Dolley Madison Room for the place where guests are entertained.

Hmm, maybe there's even a street in your community that could actually use a new name...! "Hello, may I please talk to the Mayor?"

Imagine That...YOU are in charge...

... of teaching your family, relatives, friends, church group, or class about your hero or heroine. What would you do? How would you do it? What are absolutely the most important points you want them to learn and remember?

Wouldn't it be exciting to plan and present a heroes' puppet show or write a new song about a famous person? A bright, colorful poster could teach information too. Or maybe you want to go all out and plan a Heroes' Fair. Get some people to help you set up booths where visitors can have fun and learn about famous people. Then as guests are tossing a bean bag into Abe Lincoln's stovepipe hat, tell them why you think President Lincoln is a hero.

Be CLEVER, be CREATIVE, and be CONVINCING!

Imagine That...the world's food supply has been suddenly depleted!

Or, worse yet, all the chocolate on earth has vanished. How would your hero or heroine solve that problem--or other problems you and your friends conceive? Think about problems, serious ones or crazy ones, and then think how your particular hero might suggest solving them. Would it be the same way you would try to solve it? Are the solutions practical; will they work?

Set up a panel discussion or council meeting. You and your friends can each pretend to be a different hero. Discuss the problems from your heroes' points of view and try to solve these situations.

Now, share the problems and solutions at dinnertime, because they'll be wonderful *food for thought*. (We could not resist this pun!)

Imagine That...you have been chosen to teach a group of visiting Japanese students about American heroes!

Think about it: they have probably never heard about many of our heroes. So decide carefully who you would include in your presentation. How would you teach them? We hope you wouldn't just "lecture" to them; try to come up with imaginative, fun ways to teach.

Here's a fun idea. Choose several heroes to introduce to the Japanese visitors. Now find one object or piece of clothing to represent each of those heroes. For example, you could have a mustache for Teddy Roosevelt, eye glasses for Ben Franklin, or a nurse's hat for Clara Barton. After you introduce the visitors to these people, play a little game. Let the visitors dress up as the heroes and see if they can recognize facts that you read about their characters. Ask who started the American Red Cross. Sure, it was Clara Barton!

Perhaps you'll enjoy this so much that you could give your name as a volunteer to organizations like People-to-People and Youth for Understanding. Just maybe they'll actually invite you to make your presentation to visiting students.

Imagine That...Franklin D. Roosevelt had given up after he was stricken by polio.

Think about how great men and women have persevered even when bad times have struck.

What does it mean to persevere, to refuse to give in or give up? How can family and friends--and heroes--help you to persevere?

Think of three things that are hard for you to do...but you want to try to persevere. Stick with your goals and don't give up! Someday your perseverance may be an inspiration to someone else.

Imagine That...Eleanor Roosevelt had given up because she lacked self-confidence.

Think about how important it is to believe in yourself! Have confidence in your abilities, and try to do your best in everything you do. You can achieve like Eleanor did.

No one is perfect, so don't hide your talents because of being afraid to make mistakes. Make a list of five things you are good at doing. It may be things like being polite, or it may be specific talents like drawing. Now, hang your list somewhere you look at every day.

How can you use your individual abilities to help people? Why not start with a plan to make your home or school or neighborhood a better place?

Imagine That...you started The Albert Schweitzer Foundation!

Well, there already is one, and it was started by an individual who, as a child, learned all about Dr. Schweitzer by reading of the great man. Start a "foundation" or charity to honor your hero. You can create a name, design a logo (symbol for your organization), and plan how your organization would raise and use money. In fact, you may even want to do jobs, save the money you earn, and give it to help people or causes. You could give the money in honor of your hero, and you would feel great helping a worthy cause.

Imagine That...you have adopted the motto: I CAN DO THAT!

Yes, YOU CAN. Dorothea Dix became involved in helping people less fortunate than herself, and so can you. VOLUNTEER. Spend time with older people who would love to have your friendship and company. Help a handicapped person go grocery shopping once a week. Call your local hospital, nursing home, or the Red Cross to see if they could use your volunteer help. Begin a lifetime of service while you are young, and your entire life will be richer for it.

Imagine That...you can actually talk to your hero!

What would you say to this individual you admire? How would you introduce yourself? What one or two questions would you ask? What one or two things about yourself would you most like to tell him/her?

If your hero is alive, you could write to him/her and ask if there is any way you could talk over the telephone or even meet. Sometimes, if your letter is very persuasive, and very honest, the encounter may occur. But please remember two important items: first, famous people are very busy and may not have time to answer your request; and secondly, everyone has a right to privacy, so you shouldn't contact that individual too often.

If your hero isn't alive, pretend! Tape record yourself asking interview questions; then have a parent or someone special to you answer the questions from your hero's point of view. Who knows... after learning about your hero, your parents or special friend may adopt him or her as their hero, too.

Imagine That... you can compare yourself to your hero!

Make two silhouettes out of white paper--one of yourself and one of your hero.

Find some old magazines or newspapers. Cut out at least ten words that describe important positive character traits of your hero. Glue them on his or her silhouette. For example, you might admire Harriet Tubman's determination or Jackie Robinson's courage.

Then, have a family member or special friend list at least ten positive adjectives on your silhouette, describing your character traits. How many match? How are you like your hero? How are you different? What did you learn about yourself?

Imagine That... you can arrange a family vacation around your hero!

That's right, you ask the other people in your household if you can plan a trip to a place associated with your favorite famous person.

Maybe there is a museum dedicated to your hero or a place or building associated with that special person. If the individual is living, maybe you can visit where he/she works!

Obviously, you have many decisions to make and many factors (such as cost, distance, places to stay) to consider. But the hard work for you could pay off, for it will be a trip you'll always remember!

And even if you don't actually go on the trip, you'll learn many things by planning it. You have lots of time later in your life to make the trip become a reality!

Imagine That... you won a trip to Michelangelo World!

Hey, why should only Walt Disney have a wonderful place on earth named after him? Design a theme park around your hero, like we did for the great Renaissance artist.

At Michelangelo World, there is a special roller coaster to take you through the marble quarries from which the stone was cut for his sculptures. In the haunted house, figures from his famous paintings come alive and talk to you. And, in our favorite attraction, you get to dress up like the great artist and help paint a ceiling.

Create your own major theme park where kids and adults can learn about your hero while still having fun. You might even build models of some of the rides.

Then send your ideas to the creative "imagineers" at the Disney Studios with a persuasive letter. Maybe, just maybe, your hero will end up in a new attraction!

Imagine That...you were suddenly "beamed" over to your hero's home!

What do you imagine his or her home to look like? Did your reading provide you with any description of the house? If not, from what you've learned about your hero, what do you suppose is hanging on the walls, found on top of mantels and bureaus, and kept in secret places (we all have secret places!)?

Would you see paintings and sculptures by the great masters, such as Rembrandt or van Gogh? Or would you see modern art by Picasso? What kind of music would you hear? Classical, by Mozart or Beethoven? Or jazz, by Duke Ellington?

Some of us are lucky enough to be able to actually visit our hero's home. For example, touring Monticello in Charlottesville, Virginia, is being able to spend special time with Thomas Jefferson in his special home. Maybe your hero's home, office, or laboratory is a public shrine that you can actually go to--WOW!

Before you go to visit, predict what your hero's place, museum or house will look like. Make a sketch of what you might see. If you are able to visit, take your sketch along and compare the real building to what you imagined.

If you can't really visit your hero's home, perhaps you could make a model or shoebox scene of what you imagine it to be like.

Imagine That...you could have saved President Lincoln from the assassin's bullet!

Imagine yourself in a different time and place. You have been given the opportunity to change one event in your hero's life. What would you choose to change? Why? How would you do it? What would be the consequences of the change in your hero's life? In history?

The human mind enjoys imaginary journeys; it's a way we have of leaving the "here and now." Through reading and then thinking "What if I had. . .," you can learn to see new possibilities not only for your hero, but for yourself as well.

Maybe these ideas will get you started. What if Sacajawea had refused to lead Lewis and Clark on their expedition? Or what if Rosa Parks had given up her seat on the bus? Hey, what if you would write a story about one of these imagined events? What do you think might happen?

Imagine That... Mary McLeod Bethune and Dr. Seuss were trapped in an elevator together!

That's right, they're stuck between the 72nd and 73rd floors of the Empire State Building, and they could be stuck there for hours.

Role play what you think they would talk about. Would most of their conversation be about education, or would they talk about happy times in their lives? Would they become bored? Are they scared? Would they play a word game like "20 Questions" to pass the time? Suppose you were trapped in there with them--how would you react?

Okay, so you hate closed-in spaces (that means you're claustrophobic). Instead of being trapped in an elevator, imagine you are stranded on a small tropical island with a wonderful sandy beach. Now, that might be lots of fun for you and your hero.

Arts, Crafts and Food

Guess who's coming to dinner?

That's right, your hero is! So get busy and plan the menu. Does he/she have a favorite food mentioned in a biography, or are there special foods from your hero's country or geographical region? Foods may be related to an historical time, too. You must also consider religion, because certain foods are off-limits to some followers.

Once it is planned, share the menu with the cooks in your home. If you agree to help, maybe they'll even make it! And share it too with your school's cafeteria staff--because sometimes they prepare special meals. You could persuade them to have a lunch in honor of your special hero! Why not decorate the table by making a center-piece or place cards that illustrate a part of your hero's life.

Give some thought to inviting someone else to this unique dinner, and be prepared to tell them all about your favorite famous person.

By the way, you can add some funny lines to your menu by thinking of clever names for some of the food items. You might have Benjamin Frankfurters or Molly Brownies! It's not often you could have so many famous people all at the same dinner.

What time is it? It's *Howdy Doody* time!

At least it was way back in the 1950's, but now it can be Jim Abbott's time . . . or any great person's time!

Design a watch dial with your hero's face and name on it, and attach it to your real watch. There are even companies, with ads in popular magazines, which would make your design into a real watch for you. But at no cost, you can make your own watch--or maybe a bigger dial face for your bedroom clock.

You and your favorite famous person will then be sharing a lot of time together.

I found the missing puzzle piece. It was on top of the computer.

Jigsaw puzzles are fun to put together and simple to make. Design, draw and color a "people picture"; remember, action pictures make the neatest puzzles. We drew Sally Ride on a space walk outside the shuttle.

Glue your drawing onto a piece of lightweight cardboard. On the other side, draw the shapes of your puzzle pieces. Don't make them too small, or they might get lost! *Carefully* cut out the pieces and challenge someone to put them back together.

We guarantee you'll enjoy making a puzzle so much that you'll make an entire series. Just don't get the different pieces mixed up-- or Sally Ride's head could end up in Dr. Elizabeth Blackwell's office!

Ring around the rosy, a parking lot full of . . . heroes!

Picture your mall's parking lot. On every car's windshield is an autoshade reflecting the sun's heat. On each of those car "sunglasses" is a drawing of a hero or a heroine. WHAT AN INSPIRING SIGHT!

Take a commercial cardboard sunshade and redo it. Cover the boring advertising message or cartoon figure with paper or paint. Then create your own heroic message so your family car will reflect your ideas on an important real person. Remember to sign your work because you're the artist and you deserve full credit.

P.S. "But we don't have a car!" That's okay--make one for someone who does, maybe a relative, teacher, a friend, someone you really like. What a great gift, and inexpensive, too.

Let's go fly a kite . . . or an airplane . . . or a telephone!

Okay, so you can't fly a telephone. But you can make one--you can make a replica of Alexander Graham Bell's first telephone. You can build lots of things used by famous people from your reading--the canoe Sacajawea used to guide Lewis and Clark, or Laura Ingalls Wilder's "little house."

Imagine making your OWN collection of famous objects--your OWN museum in your OWN bedroom or basement. Maybe you'll choose a theme, such as famous transportation vehicles, or select six people famous in different fields--then make things associated with them. Next, invite people to your museum and give them a guided tour.

Of course, we definitely recommend making a Benjamin Franklin kite (directions are easily found in a library book). On a wonderfully beautiful windy day, close your museum and do what Ben did--"go fly a kite." But be sure never to fly your kite in stormy weather. That could be a shocking experience!

You have been asked to design a new money system!

What a great job that would be! What coins and bills would you create? What heroes would you picture on the paper money; on the coins?

While you're busy thinking, try drawing your designs. You might want to use some colors other than green for your money. We think a wallet full of rainbow colors would certainly brighten everyone's financial picture!

Can you come closer? I can't read your button.

"Sure can--cause I'm proud to be wearing my 'Harriet Tubman is my Hero' button. I made it myself!" That alone should start an interesting conversation, and it will give you a great opportunity to tell someone all about your hero. After all, you'll be the expert!

Simply take an old campaign or rock star button and redo it. Or make one out of cardboard and glue a safety pin on the back. It's so easy to do. Decorate your button with a drawing or photo if your button is large enough. And wear it everywhere. You'll probably meet other Harriet Tubman fans too!

[Note: If you like buttons a lot, you could start a collection of political campaign buttons--and visit the Smithsonian's marvelous display of them.]

A cup of flour, 1 teaspoon of salt, 1/2 cup water--and suddenly you have Mahatma Gandhi!

Well, with a little work you can--by making a papier-mache' sculpture of him. Take an oval shaped balloon and carefully cover it with newspaper strips (1" wide by about 10" long) dipped in the above mixture. Form important facial features like ears, nose, lips, eyebrows, chin by molding some paper strips. You'll have to experiment and play around a bit to become comfortable and confident with papier-mache'.

Once Gandhi's features are shaped, allow him to dry thoroughly. Now he's ready to be painted or colored with markers--and then proudly displayed in a prominent place.

A world of heroes!

Do you have an old world map or globe around the house? You can use it to create a very special display--a "World of Heroes." Using pins with small color triangles attached (like a sports pennant), color code famous people by their type of contribution, such as yellow for inventors, blue for humanitarians and so on. Place their initials on the pennants and match them with the countries where the famous people live. Fill your map or globe with a rainbow of colored pins.

If all or most of your heroes are from one area of the world, try to learn about others from different parts of the world.

You'll be amazed at the number and variety of great people who have contributed so much to humankind.

Hey Martha, isn't that Mark Twain over there in our neighbor's yard?

Well, it certainly is the distinguished Samuel Clemens, who is also known as Mark Twain. And he's decorating the yard just like a blue crystal ball or some silly lawn animal does. The big difference is that his presence gives an important message about you and your family.

So let the whole neighborhood--and the entire community--see who your real heroes are. Make a wooden cut-out (don't hesitate to ask someone to help) in the shape of your hero. Then paint it to look realistic. It'll take some effort to do a good job on this project, but believe us, your work will not go unnoticed. Our guess is the local papers will even do a feature story on you and your "lawn" hero!

Maybe your family will be so impressed with your "heroic" efforts that they will want you to paint another hero's picture on your mailbox (if you have one). We're sure that Patrick Henry would be proud to raise your mailbox's flag.

Excuse me, Betsy Ross, will you hold my place for me?

Of course she will, because she is so delighted you put her image on your bookmark. Simple to make, bookmarks are very useful--and they make wonderful gifts. They can range from a very simple cardboard one, usually 1 1/2" wide and 6" long, to a fancy cloth or leather one, which you can make or buy in a craft store. Decorate the bookmark with sequins, puffy paint, or by sewing on your favorite famous person's name, birthday, significant achievements, and maybe even a silhouette.

You'll never lose your place again, thanks to Betsy. We were going to use that old saying "heavens to Betsy," but we don't have the slightest idea what it means.

Thirty days has September, April, June, and -- wait a minute, who's that in November?

It's Marie Curie, because she was born November 7, 1867. And since she's one of your heroes, her picture replaced that month's regular photograph.

Maybe you'll want to have an entire "Year of Heroes." Making a calendar is really easy. You'll need to look at a real one so you have the right dates on the right weekdays. Then, with drawings or pictures, put together a year-long flip calendar.

In addition to saving money, you'll be looking at something you made--and that alone makes it worth much more than any store-bought calendar. And what a great gift this would be for someone else who enjoys famous people!

A mighty oak from a tiny acorn grows.

Trees are wonderful--to sit under, to look at, to climb safely, and even to measure time. So make a tree--a family tree--for the Adams family (not the monster one, the real one). Find a dead branch (please don't break off a live one from a healthy tree) or make one out of old sticks by wiring them together. Decorate it with paper portraits of the famous family--oldest members near the bottom, the newest "growth" in the family at the top! Or use some kind of ornament on which you've placed names and maybe something special about that family member. The tree will remind you that families grow and branch out.

By the way, your famous family tree might lead you to do one of your own family. Be sure to display them side-by-side!

You want to do WHAT to your bedroom wall?

Okay, so use the basement or garage wall instead! That's right, do a wall mural in honor of your hero. The possibilities are almost endless--drawings, photos, symbols, famous quotes, words expressing your admiration--anything you can imagine to bring him/her to life.

We'll bet it will be so wonderful the others in your home will say, "Okay, you can do another one in your bedroom, if you promise to do one on our bedroom walls too!"

"I stand for motherhood, America, and a hot lunch for orphans. . ."

That's what a character in a famous American musical comedy*
stood for. So what does you hero "stand for?" What *values* does
your hero represent? Show them in a colorful, exciting collage.
Using pictures from old magazines before they're put in the recycle
bin, you can create a VALUERAMA!

It can be a cardboard box, or a mobile hanging from the ceiling, or
even a three dimensional pyramid. Let your imagination go wild.
Cover the outside with pictures showing values. For example, if your
hero is a caring person, look for pictures of people who are caring
for injured or sick people, or caring for the environment. Then, atop
these pictures--on real bright, wild paper--put the word CARING.
When others see your VALUERAMA, they'll know instantly the
most important values associated with your hero. Maybe--just
maybe--your hero's VALUERAMA will also be YOURS!!

If a famous athlete is one of your heroes, such as Joe DiMaggio or
Althea Gibson, the VALUERAMA can become a SPORTSMAN-
SHIPORAMA. Now that's a cool word, isn't it? Make a collage or
pyramid of the qualities of good sportsmanship, and try to copy those
traits whenever you play a sport.

* P.S. In case you were really curious, the show was *Hello Dolly!*

Timelines--yes timelines--can be FUN!

Not the boring ones you too often see in classrooms--but creative,
fun-to-look-at timelines. Make a list of items and/or events
important to your favorite famous person, then put the list in a
sequence. You might order it chronologically from his/her birth to
death, or you may decide on some other clever sequence, such as
things in order of importance to your hero's work. Now--think *BIG*.
Using lots of yarn, string, or ribbon, or whatever you have around,
hang your time line in your bedroom or basement or garage. Hang
pictures and maybe lightweight items from it, in sequence. Use some
labels--but not a lot of dates or names. Your time line should
feature *key ideas* about your hero--and whoever sees it will be
impressed with your hero and your ability to create a FUN time line.

WOW! Where did you get that cool hat? No way, you didn't make it!

Oh, YES YOU DID! You took an old baseball cap, or some other style hat you really like, and you made it into a real "HAT"--Heroes Are Tops! Just use a dark dye to cover whatever design or ad is on the old hat or buy a new, plain one. Then, using whatever materials you want (cloth, cardboard, foil) make your own HAT. One that we made shows Dr. Martin Luther King, Jr., saying "I have a dream," then the words "Me too" underneath. The HAT isn't completely water-proof, but if you're more clever than we are--and we are sure you are--you can make it so. Hey, no excuses about "I can't sew." We can't either, but our friends can, and they even taught us a few simple sewing steps. Our HATS get great comments wherever we wear them.

Someday they could be worth money.

So get busy designing your own set of great people trading cards. It's a big project, so we recommend you and friends do it together. You may decide to draw pictures or use some you photocopied from books. Keep the size small (usually 3" x 3 1/2"), and write short, meaningful descriptions about the people to fit on the back.

If your group is really ambitious, why not contact one of the leading card companies, such as TOPS. It could lead to a whole new series to sell.

Let's play Jeopardy!

Or any hero's game you can create! Maybe it will be like one of your television favorites or a popular board game. For the clues, use biographical data from the books you've read.

An easy game to make is a version of *Concentration*. Make identical pairs of clue cards (about 15 sets), scramble them, lay them face down and then try to find matches by turning them over two at a time. You could make it very tough by having the two clues relate to one person but not be exactly the same. For example, one card could read Christopher Columbus, and its matching partner could be the Nina, Pinta, and the Santa Maria. You'll really have to "concentrate" to make a match!

Be creative and come up with an entirely new game idea. That's how *Trivial Pursuit* started!

Should it be the young Dwight Eisenhower or President Ike?

Hey, if the Postal Service can create that debate over an Elvis stamp, why not raise the same discussion when you design a stamp about your hero or heroine. How do you want her/him portrayed? Maybe a series of four stamps is needed to honor your great individual.

We suggest you do some research on stamps too, because they are a great way to learn about famous people. And, if there is no U.S. stamp for your hero, send your design to the Postal Service. Of course, the Postal Service has requirements for people honored on stamps. Check this out before you mail in your design.

Do us one favor, please. Try to keep the stamp's cost the same as the current rate--even though your design may be worth a million!

Here's your chance to send the very best.

Make your own greeting cards, because no store-bought cards could possibly be better! And use your hero on your cards. Imagine your relatives and friends getting a card from you saying something like: Maya Angelou, my hero, and I wish you a great big HAPPY BIRTHDAY. Then, on the card, you could write a sentence or two explaining why she is your hero. For special holidays when you send several cards, you could easily do a stencil, or make photo copies and then color them. Others will show and save those original cards designed by you and focusing on your hero. They're special--and you will be too for taking the time and effort to make them!

Wish you were here. I'm getting a good earth tan!

That's what Neil Armstrong wrote on the postcard he sent you from the moon. So, design postcards from some of the places associated with your favorite famous person. You might want to draw the pictures or use some from magazines. Some postcards even use animated drawings instead of realistic ones.

If you make them U.S. Postal Service regulation size (3" by 5"), you can actually use them. Imagine how surprised your favorite aunt will be when she gets your handmade postcard showing Jonas Salk's birthplace.

It's a Grand "New" Flag!

Flags are symbols of things we hold dear. They are usually seen as symbols of countries, but they don't have to be. Our heroes and heroines can be represented by flags too. On the banner there could be a picture of the great person, along with words and symbols honoring his/her contributions. Imagine Helen Keller's image on a flag!

You can make your Hero's Flag out of paper or cloth. Use your creativity to make it attractive and colorful. Remember flags are made to be displayed with honor. We expect to see your flag flying high!

Why, her hair alone has over 200 pieces!

Wrong, it's not another puzzle idea--it's a mosaic. An ancient, beautiful art form, a mosaic creates a picture by using many small pieces.

Tear colored paper into a variety of sizes and shapes (usually no larger than 1/2" x 1/2"), then piece together a portrait or scene of your hero. It may be easier to start with a basic sketch, but sometimes you'll get a mosaic idea as you work with the pieces. Once you're satisfied, glue the pieces onto cardboard for a permanent display.

Want an "all-natural" mosaic? Use flower petals and leaves to create a very unique one which you can save by spraying with a special product found in crafts stores.

Wouldn't Rachel Carson, a famous environmentalist, look wonderful in an all-natural mosaic?

"Look at it, look what it says. Courage! Ain't it the truth?"

So spoke the "Cowardly Lion" when the Wizard of Oz pinned the medal on his chest. It's a wonder he didn't say "ouch" first!

What about designing a Medal of Courage on behalf of that brave pilot, Amelia Earhart? Or a Medal of Bravery for Molly Pitcher?

You can think of a medal in honor of your hero, focusing on a key trait he/she exhibited. Design and make the medal, and then award it to someone you know who is worthy of that honor.

Won't Mom be surprised when you present her with the Medal of Hard Work showing Florence Nightingale's picture on it!

Wild, wild hair and a real bushy mustache--what a character!

Actually, what a caricature! Take your famous person, as we did with Albert Einstein, and draw a portrait in which you exaggerate some outstanding physical feature of the individual. Caricatures are not meant to poke fun at people; rather, they emphasize the features which make people unique and interesting.

Have some fun and do a caricature of yourself. Do you and your hero share any of the same special physical features?

Our guess is you'll enjoy doing caricatures so much you'll make an entire album of them--some of famous men and women and some of you and your friends.

Look up at the Mother Teresa window--I designed it.

And it is beautiful. Imagine your hero honored in a stained glass window, shimmering brightly as the sunlight filters through. What a magnificent sight.

No, we're not describing real stained glass windows, which are made by expert crafts people and cost lots of money. We're talking about the one you made using colored cellophane paper, available in art stores. And it is every bit as spectacular!

Another way is to cut a stained glass window shape from aluminum foil. Draw a design and color in the sections with bright permanent markers. Carefully crumple the foil window, then open it up and smooth it out. Your design will now look like a shimmering stained glass window!

We recommend actually examining some stained glass windows first, either by visiting some churches or looking at photos in books.

We guarantee you will create a work of art you will be proud to hang in a window. You'll smile radiantly as the sun's rays illuminate your hero.

A license to be creative.

Did you ever wonder what your heroes would put on their vanity license plates if they had them? Would Dr. Martin Luther King, Jr.'s say "I EQL U" or Christopher Columbus' "NU WORLD"?

Design a license plate commemorating your favorite famous person and make it out of cardboard or cookie dough. Decorate the cardboard with markers or the cookie dough with chocolate chips. License plates are a standard size ("10"x 6") and usually there may not be more than seven identification letters and/or numbers.

Sometimes a state chooses to honor a particular person or place on its license plates. For example, Illinois is the Land of Lincoln and Arizona is the Grand Canyon state. You could try a state slogan and design on your license plate along with your hero's personalized identification number. How about "Mississippi--Home of Jim Henson" as the slogan and "MUP-PET" as the ID letters. Or "Ohio--Home of John Glenn" and "TAKE OFF" for his ID letters.

Can you actually use your license plate? Well, it can't replace the official plate or plates on your car, but you can certainly display it in a side window, being careful not to interfere with the driver's view.

Tonight let's use the Robert E. Lee place mats since we're having Southern Fried Chicken!

Now there's the ultimate coordinated meal--the place mats match the menu!

It's quite simple to design place mats, and maybe even matching paper napkins, to honor your hero. Generally, (or General Lee), place mats are 11" wide by 17" long, but they don't have to be the standard rectangular type. Be creative and make them round, star-shaped or maybe in the shape of your hero's hat! To protect them so they are reusable, you can have them laminated at a crafts store, or you can cover them carefully with cellophane or clear contact paper.

You may also want to include a crossword puzzle or dot-to-dot silhouette on your placemat. Your family could solve these with a crayon or wipe-off marker before or after your special meal.

Your special place mats will make meal time just a bit more special for everyone, especially when guests join you. They'll give you the perfect chance to talk about your hero--in between bites, of course.

There he is--made of 20,000 red roses, 45,000 white chrysanthemums, and 30,000 bluebells.

It's a giant George M. Cohan, and he's leading off the annual Rose Parade in Pasadena, California, or Portland, Oregon--take your pick.

Those floats are truly spectacular, and year after year the designers need new ideas. That's where you come in. Think up clever ways to present your hero on a float made entirely of flowers and plants. Provide a detailed description of the float; if you can, include dimensions or draw it to scale. Many of the floats have wonderful mechanical devices making parts move.

Send your ideas, along with a persuasive letter outlining the reasons that your hero should be in the parade, to the organizing committee (c/o Rose Parade, either or both cities).

Maybe the right person will see your idea. Maybe you'll even be invited to help build the float and watch the parade in person!

For an idea closer to home, decorate your wagon or bike to "show off" your hero. Join the neighborhood July 4th parade and honor those who made our nation great.

This is a great book--why haven't more people read it?

Why? Because nobody knew about it! So, it's your job to promote the book you have just read about your hero. Since you loved it, that will be an easy job for you. Maybe you'll design a new book cover for it, or an advertising poster or special in-store display. In fact, if you're a real go-getter, a local book store might use your work and even give you a "commission" if they sell extra copies because of your promotion.

Hey, why stop there? Work on a television or radio commercial, send it to the book's publisher, and share it with the local book store.

Maybe, just maybe, your positive review will spark interest in the book. Your advertisement could make you famous just like the person in the book you promoted!

That's the most beautiful and unique holiday tree I've ever seen! Tell me about those people.

"Those people" are on the ornaments you made.

Whether or not you celebrate Christmas by decorating a tree, most people have some special occasion during the year when ornaments are displayed. It may be a party, or a national holiday of some significance, or just a desire to make the home look different for a while.

Whatever the reason, make your own decorations and ornaments using your heroes' pictures, drawings, and words of wisdom. Check around the house for supplies. Lids from frozen juice cans are great for making tin punch ornaments. Small scraps of wood can be painted with a design. Use colorful paper, pipe cleaners, fabric and ribbons, too.

You'll be surrounded by famous people, and you'll have a chance to tell all the curious visitors who they are.

Did you invent that whatchamacallit? Well, what does it do?

George Westinghouse was just a kid when he created his first invention. So what are *you* waiting for?

Always forgetting your books at school? Invent a gadget to help you remember! Is feeding the family pet your job? Why not come up with an automatic distributor of doggy delights?

Bring your friends together for an *Invention Convention*. Throw your imaginations into high gear and dream up something new. Have a neighborhood or classroom contest. Parents or teachers can be the judges. Who knows? Your thingamajig might be the invention America's been waiting to have!

I read and reread those two pages--they were written so beautifully.

So, SHARE them with other people! How? We'll give you several ideas, but we're sure you can think of others.

Find a famous quotation or descriptive paragraph from a book that you enjoyed. In your best printing or writing, copy the words to give to a friend or relative. Or, make a poster-size display, complete with fancy borders. Or, make gift wrapping paper using copies of these special pages (so your gift takes on an extra-special significance).

Great words about great people should be shared; they're much too wonderful to be kept sealed away in books.

Music and Dramatics

Who's that rapping at my door?

(Read to a steady rap beat)
Now there's a style that's fun to do,
And that's why we rap all day through.
To tell you of our number one dudes,
People of many shades and hues.

Hey, when you're more than 16-years-old, rapping does not come naturally, but we gave it our best shot. So can you, and you'll probably find it a breeze. A good rap can breathe life and interest into any famous man or woman:

So if your hero's George, Hank, or Susan
Start writing that rap and keep on cruisin'

"The hills are alive, with the sound of music."

Actually your school cafeteria is the place that's alive with music, and its music you selected to honor your hero.

Why? Because your hero decided to visit you at your school. That's right, Juliette Low will eat lunch with you.

To set the right mood, you've decided to choose some special songs to have played during her visit. What kind of music would you choose, classical or country? Why? You might even select one musical piece as your heroine's theme song.

See if you can find the music and ask your principal if you can have a special musical tribute to her in the cafeteria. If that is not possible, maybe your music teacher can give you some class time to showcase your efforts.

Only 50 cents to enter our Wax Museum of Heroes.

Okay, charge a dollar, but your museum better be worth it.

It's really quite simple to stage the museum. After reading biographies, you and your friends can gather articles of clothing. Thrift shops are great places to buy old clothing for appropriate costumes. Next, prepare short talks about your heroes. When you set up your museum, complete with name signs, you'll be frozen like statues as the customers are admitted.

When they "push your button," such as a make-believe one on your name sign, you unfreeze and begin to talk about who you are. It's a LIVING wax museum! Your guests will be so impressed, and you and your friends will be known as the local experts on those great persons.

BONUS! Take your show on the road. That's right, next Hallow-een, use your costumes. Instead of some boring old stupid witch or ghost, you will be SOMEBODY IMPORTANT.

Time for some tunes.

Get to know Duke Ellington, Marian Anderson, Leonard Bernstein, or some other well-known musician by listening to his or her music. Check out the record collection at your local library. Play the songs and experience the melodies. How do they make you feel? Would you like to listen to other similar musicians?

Share this listening time with a fan of the musician or composer. Find out why they like him or her so much.

You might choose your favorite piece of music and paint a picture of the mood you feel as you listen to it.

And maybe you can even be lucky enough to attend a concert to hear some of this great music performed live.

Shakespeare said it best: "The play's the thing."

You guessed it--write a play! Maybe you'll begin with a brief skit; you and several friends might decide to work on this project as a team. Your local librarian can even show you sample one-act plays. Books like *Act Out* or *Let's Make a Play* can be helpful.

It might focus on a particular day in the life of your favorite famous person. Or it may unravel some mystery in his/her life. Let your imagination soar!

How long should your skit or play be? How many characters? What about costumes? These are only a few of the many decisions you'll have to make as a group.

Of course, once your masterpiece is written, PERFORM IT!

And, like Shakespeare, you may want to have your efforts published; there's always a market for works by new, young, talented playwrights. The publication known as *Writer's Market*, available in a library's reference section, will give you valuable information on how to submit your work to publishing companies.

"Live, from New York, it's Saturday Night."

Actually, "Taped, from Your Hometown, It's Your Hero." Tape recorders are really wonderful devices, and we don't use them nearly as often as we should. So, be creative--get together with some friends and make a tape about your favorite famous people. You could use a skit format or a talk show routine to bring your hero to life. You can add sound effects for extra excitement.

What about adding to the book you've read by placing your hero in a different situation and describing how he/she would respond. Thomas Jefferson landing on the moon--great material for a talk show interview!

By the way, these tapes can be shared with senior citizens, blind persons, or other students. SHARE YOUR WORK.

Stop singing the "I'd be too nervous to do that" song!

We bet you didn't know that in every community--from tiny towns to major cities--there are local service clubs, such as the Lions, Rotary, or Kiwanis, who have monthly meetings. And they are always looking for people to make presentations--and sometimes they even pay speakers! So become a speaker--yes, YOU! Talk about your favorite famous person, show them some objects you have or made about the person, ask them questions to see if they know about your hero, and read a short inspirational passage about the person. What's that--you couldn't possibly speak to a group of adults by yourself? Well, develop a panel, in which you and two or three friends make a presentation together on your heroes. Believe us, there are many adult groups which would love to hear young people talk about real heroes. *DO IT!*

Lights, camera, ACTION!

Disney Studios has called you to direct a movie on the life of your hero. But before you get the job, you need to prepare a plan for the film. The producers want to know whom you would choose to play the important roles, especially *the hero*, and why. Also, you must tell them where it would be filmed, and describe special items relating to the movie. Finally, you must convince them that you are the right person to direct the movie because of what you know about this great person.

Remember--the more clever and creative your plan, the greater the chance that you'll get the job. Include some information about yourself and maybe a photo and send your plan to Disney-MGM Studios, Orlando, Florida.

"Has anybody here seen my old friend Abraham?"

Abraham, Martin, and John--famous names mentioned in a very touching song. You can learn about a lot of famous people by doing some fun research in the musical section of your local public library. Look for songs about the presidents, the Underground Railroad, war songs, or transportation in America.   Or ask a music teacher to share his/her wealth of knowledge on such songs.

What next? You could build a collection of such songs, or if you and your friends sing or play an instrument, you could plan a marvelous concert honoring great people. If you charge a small admission fee, this would be a great way to raise some money for a charity!

America's most heroic home videos.

Okay, they may qualify for funniest too, depending on you and your camera crew! If you or someone you know has a camcorder, you can make a video about your hero or heroine. It takes lots of planning; you must decide on such important elements as the script, characters, location, costumes... Hey, wait a minute--it doesn't have to be a major venture, unless you want it to be.

KISS--keep it short and simple--can be your motto. One person can do a wonderful job simply by telling interesting stories about a great man or woman; or two people can carry on a wonderful conversation between their favorites.

So don't be camera-shy. Bring your hero to life.

Reading and Writing

Star Wars, Star Trek, Starfighter, Stars of Your Future!

Technology. It solves problems, but creates others. Our world depends more and more on it. Will technology create new heroes?

Movies and television offer examples of technological heroes, many of them quite violent. Now it is your turn, and we think you can be more creative than the professional script writers.

Create a new technology-age hero by combining at least three characteristics of famous people you admire. For instance, we created Thomas Chuck Schweitzer. The brains of Thomas Jefferson, the courage of Chuck Yeager, and the caring of Dr. Albert Schweitzer--WOW, what a hero for the future!

Write about your new hero, draw him/her, and act out this new marvelous individual. Edit and rework your ideas, then be bold, like the U.S.S. *Enterprise*, and forge ahead. Send your idea to a movie or television production company, and maybe your new hero will catch the attention of a Hollywood producer.

"I'm going to sit right down and write myself a letter."

Instead of doing that, write a letter to your hero or heroine instead! "But my hero lived over a hundred years ago" is your reply.

So, write to one of the descendants! First, you'll have to do some serious detective work, which in itself could prove to be fascinating. Once you've tracked down the family line, write and tell them of your admiration for their famous relative, and of your research to find them.

Guarantee (well, we're pretty sure): you will receive a reply. We sure did when we wrote to Walt Disney's daughter!

Somebody once said: "Truth is stranger than fiction"!

Well, not always, especially if you decide to undertake this zany creative writing activity. Think about the kinds of transportation your hero might have used. Maybe it was primarily animal, or boat, or airplane. Now, change your hero's way of getting around. That's right, let Paul Revere have a moped! Or give Christopher Columbus a private jet, before airplanes were even invented. Sure, it's a bit crazy, but it can lead to a very clever story. And, besides, you'll have fun "transporting" vehicles from their correct time period to a different one. We hope you'll also be inspired to illustrate your crazy story!

Dearly beloved, we are gathered together to pay tribute to our departed hero.

Even if the famous person we admire has died, we can honor the memory of his/her contributions with a monument. If our hero is alive, we can offer ideas on how to honor him/her when death comes. What saying or epitaph would best honor this person? What kind of monument or marker would you design? Where would your memorial be? By thinking about these questions, you will remember the outstanding characteristics of the person.

Using clay or blocks, make a model of your monument.

Share your ideas with parents, teachers, friends--and maybe even send a special letter to the honoree.

Your deadline is Monday, the 31st. It must be in the mail.

Your publisher can't wait, because the magazine must go to press. "What in the world are we talking about?" you wonder.

Quite simply, we're telling you to write an article about your hero or heroine for a publication. Yes, YOU! The local newspaper, your school newspaper, your church/synagogue/mosque's bulletin, a local service club's newsletter, and zillions of magazines provide you with plenty of places to publish your writing. You'll have to write, rewrite and have friends, teachers, or parents read and critique your work. And then you'll need to contact editors and publishers and convince them that your work is valuable. *Writer's Market*, found in a library, can help you on the national level; check with newspaper editors and journalism teachers for local ideas.

Writing is hard work, and getting published is sometimes even harder. But the reward of seeing your writing in print makes all of the hard work worthwhile. DO IT! We did!

My Bolivian friend Maria just wrote to me about Simon Bolivar!

Why not learn about great men and women in other countries while making new friends at the same time? Pen pals are special people you learn to know through writing letters. One of the topics you could share in your letters are your heroes, great people in your homelands who have made the world a better place. You might even find out you have some heroes in common, or that someone you admire becomes your pen pal's new hero.

By the way, if you're wondering how you can find a foreign pen pal, simply write to the embassy of that country in Washington, D.C., and tell them you would like a pen pal your age from their country.

I would give it three thumbs up.

Hey, you must have really liked the book, to give it three thumbs up in your review.

That's right, you're now the reviewer, which means you'll be making lots of decisions. First, you will need a system for rating the book such as thumbs up and down, or stars, or whatever--be creative! Next, after reading a biography, list its good and bad features. You may want to guide yourself by asking key questions, such as:

Was the book interesting?

What was the quality of the writing? of the illustrations?

What was the book missing?

Now, write your review, and assign it a rating based on your system. Remember--your review may influence other people on whether or not to read this book, so be honest and be fair.

Imagine that a committee is deciding whether to give this book an award. Write a speech to present before the committee in which you persuade them to honor the book in this way.

Rent a movie about your hero!

Instead of the most recent thriller or comedy, see if your local video store has a movie about your hero. The clerk can probably check a master computer listing to see if such a movie was ever made, and if it was, how you can obtain it.

Once you have watched it, compare it to the book or books you've read about the person. Keep track on a chart of ways that the movie and book are alike and ways they are different. Was the movie accurate, or did the Hollywood moviemakers portray your hero in a very different way? How would you change the movie if you could?

If you can't find a movie about your hero, maybe you could write a play or movie script.

Go look him up in the encyclopedia.

Okay, we did--and were we ever surprised to see your name listed as the author of the entry!

Did you think encyclopedia entries magically appear? Or that a little troll at its computer wrote them? NO! People like you and us write them, based on our research and knowledge.

So, work on an entry about your favorite famous person. You'll need to include only the most important information, because encyclopedias cover so many topics in limited space. You may want to see what is already written about the person you have in mind, but we recommend you wait until you've written your version and then compare them.

We think your entry will be better than the one currently being used, and we want you to send it to the publisher and suggest it replace the current entry when the encyclopedia set is revised.

One caution--you'll probably be asked by the publisher to research and write more entries, so you may end up a full-time employee.

Is it live, or is it on tape?

Well, either way, you can become a reader of books--an out loud reader. We'll call you a R.O.L.E. model--that's someone who "Reads Out Loud to Everyone." Visit a senior citizens' home and share your favorite biography with some of the residents. Or read the book onto a cassette tape for the benefit of blind persons, or for younger children in your school or your home. Tape-recorded books are popular among busy people who like to read, so make and share some tapes about your favorite heroes and heroines.

By the way, when you visit a senior center, you'll make lots of new friends--and we are sure some of them will become your ROLE MODELS!

Beam me over, Scotty--over to another culture.

Become familiar with a great person from another culture, or explore the ethnic background of your favorite person. Learn about different customs, foods, folktales, holidays, clothing, music, art, religion, theater, toys, weather, and heroes. Find books that will help you. For example, reading a book about Sadako Sasaki will help you learn a lot about her country, Japan.

You might want to make a scrapbook of another culture. Or you could learn about special musical instruments of that culture and maybe even learn to play one.

By the way, foreign embassies will send you lots of free materials on their countries; all you do is write to the embassy in Washington, D.C. (e.g., Embassy of Thailand).

How about having your family or circle of friends adopt a custom from that other culture? Trying new ideas will help you understand other people better.

Walk a mile in my shoes.

EMPATHY--trying to understand the world through another person's eyes. You have just read this marvelous book about Franklin Roosevelt and you're thinking about how his life is different from your life. Write down everything you did yesterday--from the time you got out of bed until the time you went to sleep. Don't skip anything; include daily personal routines. Now think about what it would be like to be Franklin Roosevelt. Make a second list by taking your first list and commenting about how each activity would change or stay the same if you had the same disability as F.D.R. had. For at least half of the activities that would change, write a sentence or two on how your life would be different and how you think that would make you feel.

If you wish, share your writing with a special friend or relative. You'll learn a lot about yourself and your own life by "walking in someone else's shoes."

Try another idea: buy a pair of plain canvas shoes and decorate them to honor your hero. Use craft paint, puffy paint or permanent markers. Be creative...and then you can really walk in your hero's shoes!

Be a poet--and know it!

We wish that we could meet,
Those famous people we think are neat
Because we know it sure would beat
Sitting here staring at our own feet.

Hey, we don't pretend to be great poets like Langston Hughes or Emily Dickinson. But so what--we had fun writing that verse. And it's even in a book! Your poems about your hero can be published too. Where? Lots of places--such as church bulletins, school bulletin boards, in-school handouts, letters to relatives and friends--wherever you print that poetry for others to read, *you've published it*. And yes, there are lots of places to send poetry, written by people of any age, to be published in magazines and books. Refer to the *Writer's Market* in your local library.

And when you write about a person of fame
Remember, please, to sign your name!

Remember: poems don't have to rhyme. Just be sure to use lots of descriptive words.

"Brave"--be brave and create a crossword puzzle about your special hero. You probably think they're really hard, but you'll be surprised how easily you can do it if you do one simple step first. Make a list as long as you can of adjectives that describe your famous person. Then, add to your list names of people and places important in that person's life. Once you have your list in front of you, building a crossword puzzle becomes much easier. Use graph paper and keep the clues simple, because you don't want to trick your friends and relatives who are going to try to solve your puzzle.

Don't forget to be careful when numbering the "across" and "down" words.

By the way, local newspapers, school newspapers, and kids' magazines are always looking for material to print. So, be brave and send it in!

I've read every book Jean Fritz has written--and I've told her so!

Now that's an accomplishment of which you should be proud.

Select an author of biographies whose work you really like and read *everything* published by her/him. Keep a journal on the books--your thoughts about each one, their similarities and differences, and your feelings about the author's writing style.

Then, write a letter to your favorite author and send a copy of your journal. You might even want to suggest a particular person either from the past or present for her/his next book.

Wouldn't you be surprised--ASTOUNDED--if your idea is accepted and the book is dedicated to you?

HEROES!

Heroes (noun)
Awesome, Real (two adjectives)
Accomplish, Inspire, Motivate (three verbs)
Doers, Thinkers, Changers, Believers (four thoughts/feelings)
Role Models (synonym)

Write a cinquain, a five line poem, about your favorite famous person. The format is simple; it starts with a noun, the name of your hero, and has four additional lines to describe the person. Line two gives two adjectives to describe him/her, line three has three words telling actions of the person, line four contains four words giving thoughts or feelings about that person, and the final line is a synonym. For example, if Matthew Henson was on line one, line five could be Explorer.

Once you've written it, why not learn some simple calligraphy (fancy writing) and make your cinquain into a poster for your wall or an 8" x 10" "picture" you can frame.

What a marvelous work of art you'll own--unless you decide to give it as a special gift to a special person in your life!

She often took me to the beach, and I loved to fetch a stick from the breaking waves.

Who in the world would do that? It's actually a what--it's Katharine Hepburn's golden retriever.

Write a story pretending you are your hero's pet. First, you have to find out from your reading what kind of pet, if any, your hero had. If you can't find out, use your imagination. Then, think about what kind of life you as that pet would have. Would you see other famous people? For example, Thomas Jefferson always had guests at Monticello, his home. Would you meet their pets? Would you get to travel? What do you like, and dislike, about your master? Maybe you'll even want to design a cage or house for this pet. Be sure that it reflects your hero's tastes.

Let your imagination run wild!

Pick a day and pay attention!

In her writing, Beverly Cleary captured every sight, sound, smell and feeling that surrounded her. Spend the day doing that yourself!

What do you hear when you wake up in the morning? How does your bed feel? Is breakfast crunchy or smooshy? Whom do you talk to? Is it sunny or cloudy outside?

Carry a note pad and pen or, if you have one, a small tape recorder. Record *everything* about your day. The next morning, read your notes or listen to your tape. You'll be amazed at how full your day was!

Make a chart of the five senses and sort words about your day into five categories. Then use these sensory words as you write a poem or paint a picture to capture your experiences.

Did Frank Lloyd Wright ever play with Legos building blocks?

Maybe that famous architect did. Perhaps that's how he became interested in creating new and unique buildings.

Look at the interesting buildings in your community. Why not find out who designed them, and when? The local historical society would be a good source of information.

If you were in charge, would you have designed any of these buildings differently? Draw a picture of a house, school, church, even a sports stadium that you would like to see built some day. You might even want to make a model out of Legos! Did you know there are Lego building contests for kids just like you? Keep working on your original ideas and then...get ready, get set, build!

INTERMEDIATE BOOKS

Ordinary People in Extraordinary Situations
Real-life stories of individuals who found themselves in very special circumstances

MOLLY BROWN
Blos, Joan. *The Heroine of the Titanic: A Tale Both True and Otherwise of the Life of Molly Brown.* Morrow, 1991. 40 pp. Ill.

VIRGINIA DARE
Hooks, William. *The Legend of the White Doe.* Macmillan Children's Book Group, 1988.

EMMA EDMONDS

Reit, Seymour. *Behind Rebel Lines: The Incredible Story of Emma Edmonds, Civil War Spy.* Gulliver, 1988. 112 pp.

Did you know that over 400 women posed as men in order to take part in the Civil War?

In *Behind Rebel Lines*, Seymour Reit tells the tale of one of those brave women: Emma Edmonds, soldier, nurse and spy. Known to her comrades on the battlefield as "Franklin Thompson," Edmonds lived an adventure full of danger and intrigue. Reit attests to the authenticity of Edmonds' story, although he has improvised dialogue and some "minor events."

This is an engrossing story that provides much food for thought.

DONN FENDLER
Fendler, Donn. *Lost on a Mountain in Maine.* Beech Tree, 1992. 128 pp. Ill.

AMOS FORTUNE

Yates, Elizabeth. *Amos Fortune, Free Man.* Puffin, 1989. 192 pp. Ill.

Thank goodness Amos Fortune lived to be 91 years old. His long life allowed him to touch scores of people with his gentleness and strength, his sensitivity and simple wisdom.

Born a prince in Africa, Amos was a teenager when he was snatched from his land and the life he knew. *Amos Fortune* is the story of his life as a slave, a free man, a talented tanner, and a generous counselor and caretaker.

Noted children's author Elizabeth Yates takes us inside Amos' mind, sharing his thoughts and motivations. She even offers details on the technique of tanning leather! Yates researched Fortune's own papers, and consulted experts on his life to ensure the authenticity of her work.

ANNE FRANK

Andur, Richard. *Anne Frank.* Chelsea House, 1993. 112 pp. Ill. (Library of Biography)

Bull, Angela. *Anne Frank.* Harnish Hamilton, 1984. 60 pp. Ill.

Hurwitz, Johanna. *Anne Frank: Life in Hiding.* Jewish Publication Society, 1988. (and Beech Tree, 1993) 68 pp. Ill.

This is a straightforward treatment of a story that needs no embellishment. In her celebrated diary, Anne Frank told us of the years she spent hiding from the Nazis with her family and she shared the hopes and dreams that sustained her.

Johanna Hurwitz's book puts Anne's diary in context, describing the Franks' world before the horrors began, and relating events occurring in Germany as Anne's family keeps vigil in their hiding place. Hurwitz also describes the events that led to the publication of the famous diary.

This excellent biography adds to our appreciation of the joy and optimism that young Anne brought to her troubled world.

Tames, Richard. *Anne Frank*. Watts, 1989. 32 pp. Ill. (Lifetimes)

Tyler, Laura. *Anne Frank*. Silver Burdett, 1990. 104 pp. Ill. (What Made Them Great)

Verhoeven, Rian, and Ruud vander Rol. *Anne Frank: Beyond the Diary (A Photographic Remembrance)*. Viking Children's Books, 1993. 150 pp. Ill.

RON KOVIC

Moss, Nathaniel. *Ron Kovic*. Chelsea House, 1993. 112 pp. Ill.

SYBIL LUDINGTON

Brown, Drollene P. *Sybil Rides for Independence*. Whitman, 1985. 48 pp. Ill.

Stryker, Sandy. *The Midnight Ride of Sybil Ludington*. Advocacy Press, 1991. 32 pp. Ill.

MOLLY PITCHER

Stephenson, Augusta. *Molly Pitcher: Young Patriot*. Macmillan Children's Book Group, 1986. 192 pp. Ill. (Childhood of Famous Americans)

POCAHONTAS

Adams, Patricia. *The Story of Pocahontas: Indian Princess*. Dell, 1988. 96 pp. Ill. (Yearling Biographies)

Bulla, Clyde R. *Pocahontas and the Strangers*. Scholastic, 1988. 176 pp. Ill.

Fritz, Jean. *The Double Life of Pocahontas*. Putnam, 1983. 96 pp. Ill.

Holler, Anne. *Pocahontas: Powhatan Ambassador*. Chelsea House, 1993. 112 pp. Ill. (North American Indians of Achievement)

Jassem, Kate. *Pocahontas, Girl of Jamestown*. Troll, 1979. 48 pp. Ill. (Native American Biographies)

Santrey, Laurence. *Pocahontas*. Troll, 1985. 32 pp. Ill. (Famous People Library)

JOHANNA REISS

Reiss, Johanna. *Upstairs Room*. Crowell/Harper Collins, 1972. 196 pp.

DEBORAH SAMPSON

McGovern, Ann. *Secret Soldier, The Story of Deborah Sampson.*
Four Winds, 1987. 62 pp. Ill.

SADAKO SASAKI

Coerr, Eleanor. *Sadako and the Thousand Paper Cranes.* Dell,
1986. 64 pp. Ill.

SAMANTHA SMITH

Galicich, Anne. *Samantha Smith: A Journey for Peace.* Macmillan
Children's Book Group, 1991. 48 pp. Ill. (Taking Part)

ANNIE SULLIVAN

Davidson, Margaret. *Helen Keller's Teacher.* Scholastic, 1989. 160
pp.
Selden, Bernice. *The Story of Annie Sullivan: Helen Keller's
Teacher.* Dell, 1987. 96 pp. Ill. (Yearling Biographies)

RYAN WHITE

White, Ryan, and Ann Marie Cunningham. *Ryan White: My Own
Story.* Dial, 1992. 277 pp.

Intermediate Biographies

HENRY (HANK) AARON (Athlete)

Rennert, Richard. *Henry Aaron.* Chelsea House, 1993. 104 pp.
Ill. (Black Americans of Achievement)
Tackach, James. *Hank Aaron.* Chelsea House, 1992. 64 pp. Ill.
(Baseball Legends)

JIM ABBOTT (Athlete)

Gutman, Bill. *Jim Abbott: Star Pitcher.* Millbrook, 1992. 48 pp.
Ill. (Millbrook Sports World)
Johnson, Rick L. *Jim Abbott: Beating the Odds.* Macmillan
Children's Book Group, 1991. 62 pp. Ill. (Taking Part)
Rolfe, John. *Jim Abbott.* Lerner, 1991. 144 pp. Ill. (Sports
Illustrated for Kids Books)

White, Ellen Emerson. *Jim Abbott: Against All Odds*. Scholastic, 1990. 104 pp. Ill.
* A truly inspirational story about the major league player who has only one arm.

ABIGAIL ADAMS (U.S. First Lady)

Fradin, Dennis B. *Abigail Adams: Advisor to a President*. Enslow, 1989. 48 pp. Ill. (Colonial Profiles)

Osborne, Angela. *Abigail Adams*. Chelsea House, 1989. 111 pp. Ill. (American Women of Achievement)
*Adams comes to life in this book through her quotations and descriptions of life during the American Revolutionary period. Many illustrations enhance this work.

Peterson, Helen S. *Abigail Adams: Dear Partner*. Chelsea House, 1991. 80 pp. Ill. (Discovery Biographies)

Sabin, Francene. *Young Abigail Adams*. Troll, 1992. 48 pp. Ill. (Easy Biographies: Women in History)

Wagoner, Jean B. *Abigail Adams: Girl of Colonial Days*. Macmillan Children's Book Group, 1992. 192 pp. Ill. (Childhood of Famous Americans)

Waldrop, Ruth. *Abigail Adams*. Rusk, 1988. 109 pp. Ill. (First Ladies)

Witter, Evelyn. *Abigail Adams*. Mott Media, 1976. 147 pp. Ill. (Sower)

JOHN ADAMS (U.S. President)

Brill, Marlene T. *John Adams: Second President of the United States*. Childrens Press, 1986. 100 pp. Ill. (Encyclopedia of Presidents)

Dwyer, Frank. *John Adams*. Chelsea House, 1989. 112 pp. Ill. (World Leaders Past and Present)
*A detailed volume that describes Adams' life as a public servant during the Revolution and beyond.

Sandak, Cass R. *The John Adamses*. Macmillan Children's Book Group, 1992. 48 pp. Ill. (First Families)

Santrey, Laurence. *John Adams, Brave Patriot*. Troll, 1986. 48 pp. Ill. (Easy Biographies: History)

SAMUEL ADAMS (Colonial American)
  Fritz, Jean. *Why Don't You Get a Horse, Sam Adams?* Putnam,
  1982. 48 pp. Ill.

JANE ADDAMS (Humanitarian)
  Kent, Deborah. *Jane Addams and Hull House.* Childrens Press,
  1992. 32 pp. Ill. (Cornerstones of Freedom)
  Kittredge, Mary. *Jane Addams.* Chelsea House, 1989. 112 pp. Ill.
  (American Women of Achievement)
  Mitchard, Jacquelyn. *Jane Addams: Pioneer in Social Reform and
  Activist for World Peace.* Gareth Stevens, 1991. 64 pp. Ill.
  (People Who Have Helped the World)
  Wheeler, Leslie A. *Jane Addams.* Silver Burdett, 1990. 144 pp.
  Ill. (Pioneers in Change)

LOUISA MAY ALCOTT (Author)
  Burke, Kathleen. *Louisa May Alcott: Author.* Chelsea House, 1988.
  112 pp. Ill. (American Women of Achievement)
  *With much detail, this book describes how Alcott overcame
  family adversity to attain recognition as a writer.
  Greene, Carol. *Louisa May Alcott: Author, Nurse, Suffragette.*
  Childrens Press, 1984. 112 pp. Ill. (People of Distinction)
  McGill, Marci. *The Story of Louisa May Alcott, Determined Writer.*
  Dell, 1988. 92 pp. Ill. (Yearling Biographies)
  *An easy-to-read chronicle of this dedicated writer's difficult and
  unsettled childhood.
  Meigs, Cornelia. *Invincible Louisa: The Story of Louisa May Alcott.*
  Scholastic, 1987. 256 pp. Ill.
  Santrey, Laurence. *Louisa May Alcott, Young Writer.* Troll, 1986.
  48 pp. Ill. (Easy Biographies: Women in History)

RICHARD ALLEN (Religious Leader)

Klots, Steve. *Richard Allen: Religious Leader and Social Activist.*
Chelsea House, 1990. 112 pp. Ill. (Black Americans of Achieve-
ment)
  Youngsters searching for examples of greatness in black history
can look with confidence to Richard Allen, America's first great
African-American leader.

Born into slavery, Allen battled the odds to gain his freedom and help others gain theirs. A man of the cloth, he fought racial discrimination through his ministry in the African Methodist Episcopal (AME) Church.

Allen saw the church as a means to uplift his race. He organized the black community into a political force, initiating the first national convention of black Americans in 1830.

Richard Allen's story is part of the "Black Americans of Achievement" Series, an exceptional collection of biographies that offer the reader a sweeping view of African-American history as well as an opportunity to wonder at the giftedness of the individuals described in their pages.

MUHAMMAD ALI (Athlete)

Denenberg, Barry. *The Story of Muhammad Ali, Heavyweight Champion of the World.* Dell, 1989. 96 pp. Ill. (Yearling Biographies)

Epes, William M. *Muhammad Ali.* Chelsea House, 1993. 80 pp. Ill. (Junior World Biographies)

Lipsyte, Robert. *Free to Be Muhammad Ali.* Harper, 1978. 128 pp.

Rummel, Jack. *Muhammad Ali.* Chelsea House, 1988. 112 pp. Ill. (Black Americans of Achievement)

Sanford, William R. and Carl Green. *Muhammad Ali.* Macmillan Children's Book Group, 1993. 48 pp. Ill. (Sports Immortals)

ROALD AMUNDSEN (Explorer)

Humble, Richard. *The Expeditions of Amundsen.* Watts, 1992. 32 pp. Ill. (Exploration Through the Ages)

HANS CHRISTIAN ANDERSEN (Author)

Greene, Carol. *Hans Christian Anderson: Teller of Tales.* Childrens Press, 1986. 128 pp. Ill. (People of Distinction)

MARIAN ANDERSON (Singer)

Tedards, Anne. *Marian Anderson: Singer.* Chelsea House, 1987. 112 pp. Ill. (American Women of Achievement)

MAYA ANGELOU (Author, Poet)
Shapiro, Miles. *Maya Angelou: Author.* Chelsea House, 1993. 112 pp. Ill. (Black Americans of Achievement)

SUSAN B. ANTHONY (Women's Rights Leader)
Clinton, Susan. *The Story of Susan B. Anthony.* Childrens Press, 1986. 32 pp. Ill. (Cornerstones of Freedom)
Levin, Pam. *Susan B. Anthony.* Chelsea House, 1993. 80 pp. Ill. (Junior World Biographies)
Monsell, Helen A. *Susan B. Anthony: Champion of Women's Rights.* Macmillan Children's Book Group, 1986. 192 pp. Ill. (Childhood of Famous Americans)
Weisberg, Barbara. *Susan B. Anthony: Woman Suffragist.* Chelsea House, 1988. 112 pp. Ill. (American Women of Achievement)

JOHNNY APPLESEED (Pioneer)
Collins, David. *Johnny Appleseed.* Mott Media, 1985. 160 pp. Ill. (Sower)
Le Sueur, Meridel. *Little Brother of the Wilderness, The Story of Johnny Appleseed.* Holy Cow! Press, 1987. 68 pp. Ill.
Sabin, Louis. *Johnny Appleseed.* Troll, 1985. 32 pp. Ill. (Famous Americans Library)
York, Carol B. *Johnny Appleseed.* Troll, 1980. 48 pp. Ill.

LOUIS ARMSTRONG (Musician)

Tanenhaus, Sam. *Louis Armstrong.* Chelsea House, 1989. 128 pp. Ill. (Black Americans of Achievement)
From paragraph one of Louis Armstrong, Tanenhaus plunges us into the midst of the musical world that was Armstrong's life. We witness the metamorphosis of "West End Blues" as the jazz great and his fellow musicians coax, stroke and mold the piece of music into a piece of their collective soul.
The joy and wonder that mark this book's first passage permeate this biography. The author invites us to appreciate the man and his music, to share the atmosphere and passion that color Armstrong's story.

ARTHUR ASHE (Athlete)
Weissburg, Ed. *Arthur Ashe: Tennis Great*. Chelsea House, 1991. 112 pp. Ill. (Black Americans of Achievement)

ROBERT BADEN-POWELL (Humanitarian)
Courtney, Julia. *Robert Baden-Powell: The Man Who Created the International Scouting Movement that Gives Young People Opportunities to Excel*. Gareth Stevens, 1990. 64 pp. Ill. (People Who Have Helped the World)

BENJAMIN BANNEKER (Scientist)
Conley, Kevin. *Benjamin Banneker: Scientist and Mathematician*. Chelsea House, 1990. 112 pp. Ill. (Black Americans of Achievement)
Ferris, Jeri. *What Are You FiguringNow? A Story About Benjamin Banneker*. Carolrhoda, 1988. 64 pp. Ill. (Creative Minds)
*Through the use of dialogue, the author describes Benjamin Banneker's life as an astronomer, mathematician, and assistant surveyor to Andrew Elliott.

CLARA BARTON (Medical Leader, Humanitarian)
Bains, Rae. *Clara Barton: Angel of the Battlefield*. Troll, 1982. 48 pp. Ill. (Easy Biographies: Women in History)
Boylston, Helen D. *Clara Barton, Founder of the American Red Cross*. Random House, 1983. 182 pp. Ill.
Hamilton, Leni. *Clara Barton*. Chelsea House, 1988. 112 pp. Ill. (American Women of Achievement)
Kent, Zachary. *The Story of Clara Barton*. Childrens Press, 1987. 32 pp. Ill. (Cornerstones of Freedom)
*A detailed account of one of America's most ambitious women, who single-handedly created the American Red Cross.
Rose, Mary C. *Clara Barton: Soldier of Mercy*. Chelsea House, 1991. 80 pp. Ill. (Discovery Biographies)
Sonneborn, Liz. *Clara Barton*. Chelsea House, 1992. 80 pp. Ill. (Junior World Biographies)
Stevenson, Augusta. *Clara Barton: Founder of the American Red Cross*. Macmillan Children's Book Group, 1986. 192 pp. Ill. (Childhood of Famous Americans)

JIM BECKWOURTH (Frontiersman)

Blassingame, Wyatt. *Jim Beckwourth: Black Trapper and Indian Chief.* Chelsea House, 1991. 80 pp. Ill. (Discovery Biographies)

Dolan, Sean. *James Beckwourth: Frontiersman.* Chelsea House, 1992. 112 pp. Ill. (Black Americans of Achievement)

Sabin, Louis. *Jim Beckwourth: Adventures of a Mountain Man.* Troll, 1992. 48 pp. Ill. (Easy Biographies: History)

LUDWIG VAN BEETHOVEN (Composer)

Hook, Richard. *Beethoven.* Watts, 1987. 32 pp. Ill. (Great Lives)

Loewen, L. *Beethoven.* Rourke, 1989. 112 pp. Ill. (Profiles in Music)

Sabin, Louis. *Ludwig Van Beethoven: Young Composer.* Troll, 1992. 48 pp. Ill. (Easy Biographies: Arts & Sciences)

Tames, Richard. *Ludwig Van Beethoven.* Watts, 1991. 32 pp. Ill. (Lifetimes)

ALEXANDER GRAHAM BELL (Inventor)

Davidson, Margaret. *The Story of Alexander Graham Bell: Inventor of the Telephone.* Dell, 1989. 92 pp. Ill. (Yearling Biographies)

Dunn, Andrew. *Alexander Graham Bell.* Watts, 1991. 48 pp. Ill. (Pioneers of Science)
  *A concise volume that includes plenty of information on Bell's life, inventions and family.

Lewis, Cynthia C. *Hello, Alexander Graham Bell Speaking.* Macmillan Children's Book Group, 1991. 64 pp. Ill. (Taking Part)

MacKenzie, Catherine. *Alexander Graham Bell: The Man Who Contracted Space.* Ayer, 1991.

Montgomery, Elizabeth Rider. *Alexander Graham Bell: Man of Sound.* Chelsea House, 1992. 80 pp. Ill.

Pelta, Kathy. *Alexander Graham Bell.* Silver Burdett, 1989. 144 pp. Ill. (Pioneers in Change)

Tames, Richard. *Alexander Graham Bell.* Watts, 1990. 32 pp. Ill. (Lifetimes)

BERTA BENZ (Inventor)

Bingham, Mindy. *Berta Benz and the Motorwagen.* Advocacy Press, 1991. 48 pp. Ill.

HENRY BERGH (Humanitarian)

Loeper, John J. *Crusade for Kindness: Henry Bergh and the ASPCA.* Atheneum, 1991. 103 pp. Ill.

MARY McLEOD BETHUNE (Educator)

Anderson, LaVere. *Mary McLeod Bethune.* Chelsea House, 1991. 80 pp. Ill. (Discovery Biographies)

Halasa, Mawlu. *Mary McLeod Bethune: Educator.* Chelsea House, 1989. 112 pp. Ill. (Black Americans of Achievement)

McKissack, Patricia. *Mary McLeod Bethune: A Great American Educator.* Childrens Press, 1985. 111 pp. Ill. (People of Distinction)

McKissack, Patricia and Fredrick. *Mary McLeod Bethune.* Childrens Press, 1992. 32 pp. Ill. (Cornerstones of Freedom)

Meltzer, Milton. *Mary McLeod Bethune: Voice of Black Hope.* Viking, 1987. 64 pp. Ill. (Women of Our Time)

BLACK HAWK (Native American Leader)

Oppenheim, Joanne. *Black Hawk, Frontier Warrior.* Troll, 1979. 48 pp. Ill. (Native American Biographies)

ELIZABETH BLACKWELL (Medical Leader)

Baker, Rachel. *The First Woman Doctor.* Scholastic, 1987. 192 pp. Ill.

Brown, Jordan. *Elizabeth Blackwell: Physician.* Chelsea House, 1989. 112 pp. Ill. (American Women of Achievement)

Latham, Jean L. *Elizabeth Blackwell: Pioneer Woman Doctor.* Chelsea House, 1990. 80 pp. Ill. (Discovery Biographies)

Sabin, Francene. *Elizabeth Blackwell: The First Woman Doctor.* Troll, 1982. 48 pp. Ill. (Easy Biographies: Women in History)

Steelsmith, Shari. *Elizabeth Blackwell.* Parenting Press, 1992. 32 pp. Ill.

GUION BLUFORD (Astronaut)

Haskins, Jim, and Kathleen Benson. *Space Challenger: The Story of Guion Bluford.* Carolrhoda, 1984. 64 pp. Ill. (Trailblazers)

Often, ordinary things can make an extraordinary difference in the life of a potential hero. For Guion Bluford, a stable childhood, educated parents and family support provided him with the solid sense of self that would eventually lead him to become the first African-American astronaut in space.

The authors of *Space Challenger* take us inside the space shuttle that carried Bluford aloft in 1983. We see and hear and experience his view from high above. Black and white and color photos remind us that the sky's the limit for anyone with a dream.

======

NELLIE BLY (Journalist)

Ehrlich, Elizabeth. *Nellie Bly: Journalist*. Chelsea House, 1989. 112 pp. Ill. (American Women of Achievement)

Emerson, Kathy Lynn. *Nellie Bly: Making Headlines*. Macmillan Children's Book Group, 1992. 112 pp. Ill. (People in Focus)

SIMON BOLIVAR (Freedom Fighter)

Gleiter, Jan, and Kathleen Thompson. *Simon Bolivar*. Raintree, 1989. 32 pp. Ill. (Hispanic Stories)

Greene, Carol. *Simon Bolivar: South American Liberator*. Childrens Press, 1989. 112 pp. Ill. (People of Distinction)

Wepman, Dennis. *Simon Bolivar*. Chelsea House, 1985. 112 pp. Ill. (World Leaders Past and Present)

DANIEL BOONE (Frontiersman)

Brandt, Keith. *Daniel Boone: Frontier Adventures*. Troll, 1983. 48 pp. Ill. (Easy Biographies: History)

Chambers, Catherine E. *Daniel Boone and the Wilderness Road*. Troll, 1984. 32 pp. Ill.

Hargrove, Jim. *Daniel Boone: Pioneer Trailblazer*. Childrens Press, 1985. 124 pp. Ill. (People of Distinction)

Retan, Walter. *The Story of Daniel Boone: Wilderness Explorer*. Dell, 1992. 96 pp. Ill. (Yearling Biographies)

Stevenson, Augusta. *Daniel Boone: Young Hunter and Tracker*. Macmillan Children's Book Group, 1986. 192 pp. Ill. (Childhood of Famous Americans)

Wilkie, Katherine E. *Daniel Boone: Taming the Wilds*. Chelsea House, 1990. 80 pp. Ill. (Discovery Biographies)

MARGARET BOURKE-WHITE (Photographer)

Ayer, Eleanor H. *Margaret Bourke-White: Photographing the World*. Macmillan Children's Book Group, 1992. 112 pp. Ill. (People in Focus)

Daffron, Carolyn. *Margaret Bourke-White: Photographer*. Chelsea House, 1988. 112 pp. Ill. (American Women of Achievement) *Liberally illustrated with Bourke-White's own photographs, this volume provides an excellent description of her career.

LOUIS BRAILLE (Inventor)

Rich, Beverly. *Louis Braille: The Inventor of a Way to Read and Write That Has Helped Millions of Blind People Communicate with the World*. Gareth Stevens, 1989. 64 pp. Ill. (People Who Have Helped the World)

JOHN BROWN (Abolitionist)

Collins, James L. *John Brown and the Fight Against Slavery*. Millbrook, 1992. 32 pp. Ill. (Gateway Civil Rights)

PEARL BUCK (Author)

LaFrage, Ann. *Pearl Buck: Author*. Chelsea House, 1988. 112 pp. Ill. (American Women of Achievement)

Mitchell, Barbara. *Between Two Worlds: A Story about Pearl Buck*. Carolrhoda, 1988. 64 pp. Ill. (Creative Minds)

RALPH BUNCHE (Civil Rights Leader)

Jakoubek, Robert. *Ralph Bunche*. Chelsea House, 1993, 112 pp. Ill. (Black Americans of Achievement)

GEORGE BUSH (U.S. President)

Behrens, June. *George Bush: Forty-first President of the United States*. Childrens Press, 1989. 32 pp. Ill.

Buchman, Dian Dincin. *Our 41st President: George Bush*. Scholastic, 1989. 96 pp. Ill.

Kent, Zachary. *George Bush: Forty-first President of the United States*. Childrens Press, 1989. 100 pp. Ill. (Encyclopedia of Presidents)

Sandak, Cass R. *The Bushes*. Macmillan Children's Book Group, 1991. 48 pp. Ill. (First Families)

Spies, Karen. *George Bush: Power of the President*. Macmillan
Childrens Book Group, 1991. 48 pp. Ill.

Sufrin, Mark. *George Bush: The Story of the Forty-first President of
the United States*. Dell, 1989. 96 pp. Ill. (Yearling Biographies)

RACHEL CARSON (Environmentalist)

Foster, Leila M. *The Story of Rachel Carson and the Environmental
Movement*. Childrens Press, 1990. 32 pp. Ill. (Cornerstones of
Freedom)

Goldberg, Jake. *Rachel Carson*. Chelsea House, 1991. 79 pp. Ill.
(Junior World Biographies)

Harlan, Judith. *Rachel Carson: Sounding the Alarm*. Macmillan
Children's Book Group, 1992. 112 pp. Ill. (People in Focus)

Hendricksson, John. *Rachel Carson: The Environmental Movement*.
Millbrook, 1991. 96 pp. Ill.

Jezer, Marty. *Rachel Carson: Biologist and Author*. Chelsea
House, 1988. 112 pp. Ill. (American Women of Achievement)
*With many illustrations, this well-written book presents Carson's
life as an author and environmentalist.

Kudlinski, Kathleen V. *Rachel Carson: Pioneer of Ecology*. Viking,
1988. 56 pp. Ill. (Women of Our Time)
*A well written and inspirational account of this devoted woman's
life as a writer and environmentalist.

Latham, Jean L. *Rachel Carson*. Chelsea House, 1991. 80 pp. Ill.
(Discovery Biographies)

Ransom, Candice F. *Listening to Crickets: A Story about Rachel
Carson*. Carolrhoda, 1993. 60 pp. Ill. (Creative Minds)

Reef, Catherine. *Rachel Carson: The Wonder of Nature*. Childrens
Press, 1992. 72 pp. Ill. (Earth Keepers)

Sabin, Francene. *Rachel Carson: Friend of the Earth*. Troll, 1992.
48 pp. Ill. (Easy Biographies: Women in History)

Wheeler, Leslie A. *Rachel Carson*. Silver Burdett, 1991. 144 pp.
Ill. (Pioneers in Change)

JIMMY CARTER (U.S. President)

Slavin, Ed. *Jimmy Carter: U.S. President*. Chelsea House, 1989.
120 pp. Ill. (World Leaders Past and Present)

Wade, Linda R. *James Carter: Thirty-ninth President of the United States*. Childrens Press, 1989. 100 pp. Ill. (Encyclopedia of Presidents)

GEORGE WASHINGTON CARVER (Scientist)

Adair, Gene. *George Washington Carver*. Chelsea House, 1989. 112 pp. Ill. (Black Americans of Achievement)

Collins, David. *George Washington Carver*. Mott Media, 1981. 131 pp. Ill. (Sower)

Epes, William. *George Washington Carver*. Chelsea House, 1992. 80 pp. Ill.

Epstein, Sam and Beryl. *George Washington Carver*. Dell, 1991. 92 pp. Ill.

Gray, James M. *George Washington Carver*. Silver Burdett, 1990. 144 pp. Ill. (Pioneers in Change)

Means, Florence. *Carvers' George*. Grey Castle, 1991. 160 pp. Ill.

Mitchell, Barbara. *A Pocketful of Goobers: A Story about George Washington Carver*. Carolrhoda, 1986. 64 pp. Ill. (Creative Minds)

Moore, Eva. *Story of George Washington Carver*. Scholastic, 1990. 96 pp. Ill.

Nicholson, Lois P. *George Washington Carver*. Chelsea House, 1993. 80 pp. Ill. (Junior World Biographies)

Rogers, Teresa. *George Washington Carver: Nature's Trailblazer*. Childrens Press, 1992. 72 pp. Ill. (Earth Keepers)

PABLO CASALS (Musician)

Garza, Hedda. *Pablo Casals: Spanish Cellist and Conductor*. Chelsea House, 1993. 112 pp. Ill. (Hispanics of Achievement)

MARY CASSATT (Artist)

Cain, Michael. *Mary Cassatt: Artist*. Chelsea House, 1989. 112 pp. Ill. (American Women of Achievement)

Meyer, Susan E. *Mary Cassatt*. Abrams, 1990. 80 pp. Ill. (First Impressions)

*An excellent depiction of Cassatt's life and her place in art history. Enhanced by the many reproductions of her work.

GEORGE CATLIN (Artist)
Suffrin, Mark. *George Catlin: Painter of the Indian West*.
Macmillan, 1991. 160 pp. Ill.

CESAR CHAVEZ (Labor Leader)
Conord, Bruce. *Cesar Chavez*. Chelsea House, 1992. 80 pp. Ill.
(Junior World Biographies)
Rodriguez, Consuelo. *Cesar Chavez*. Chelsea House, 1991. 112
pp. Ill. (Hispanics of Achievement)

WINSTON CHURCHILL (World Leader)
Driemen, J.E. *Winston Churchill: An Unbreakable Spirit*.
Macmillan Children's Book Group, 1992. 112 pp. Ill. (People
in Focus)
Italia, Bob. *Winston Churchill*. Abdo & Daughters, 1990. 32 pp.
Ill. (World War II Leaders)
Matthews, Rupert. *Winston Churchill*. Watts, 1989. 32 pp. Ill.
(Great Lives)
Rogers, Judith. *Winston Churchill: Prime Minister of England*.
Chelsea House, 1986. 120 pp. Ill. (World Leaders Past and
Present)

BEVERLY CLEARY (Author)
Berg, Julie. *Beverly Cleary*. Abdo & Daughters, 1993. 32 pp. Ill.
(The Young at Heart)

Cleary, Beverly. *A Girl from Yamhill: A Memoir*. Morrow, 1988.
288 pp. Ill.
Beverly Cleary draws us into her own life from sentence one. She
gently combines her experiences of growing up with strikingly
descriptive impressions of her world. Cleary relates the most
mundane information with creativity, sharing moments of joy and
embarrassment, of feeling successful, and of feeling left out.
This popular author of children's books tells the story of her
childhood days in Oregon, her high-school years and her adventures
as a young adult off to college. Throughout, Cleary offers insight
into her growing interest in writing, her eventual vocation.

ROBERTO CLEMENTE (Athlete)

Bjarkman, Peter C. *Roberto Clemente.* Chelsea House, 1991. 64 pp. Ill. (Baseball Legends)

O'Connor, Jim. *The Story of Roberto Clemente: All-Star Hero.* Dell, 1991. 92 pp. Ill. (Yearling Biographies)

Sabin, Louis. *Roberto Clemete, Young Baseball Hero.* Troll, 1992. 48 pp. Ill. (Easy Biographies: Sports Figures)

Walker, Paul R. *Pride of Puerto Rico: The Life of Roberto Clemente.* Harcourt Brace Jovanovich, 1991. 157 pp.

BILL CLINTON (U.S. President)

McMullan, Kate. *The Story of Bill Clinton and Al Gore: Our Nation's Leaders.* Dell, 1992. 96 pp. Ill. (Yearling Biographies)

COCHISE (Native American Leader)

Schwartz, Melissa. *Cochise: Apache Chief.* Chelsea House, 1992. 112 pp. Ill. (North American Indians of Achievement)

"BUFFALO BILL" CODY (Frontiersman)

McCall, Edith. *Hunters Blaze the Trails.* Childrens Press, 1980. 128 pp. Ill.

Stevenson, Augusta. *Buffalo Bill: Frontier Daredevil.* Macmillan Children's Book Group, 1991. 192 pp. Ill. (Childhood of Famous Americans)

CHRISTOPHER COLUMBUS (Explorer)

Adler, David A. *Christopher Columbus: Great Explorer.* Holiday House, 1991. 48 pp. Ill.

Anderson, Joan. *Christopher Columbus: From Vision to Voyage.* Dial, 1991. Ill.

Asimov, Isaac. *Christopher Columbus: Navigator to the New World.* Gareth Stevens, 1991. 64 pp. Ill. (Isaac Asimov's Pioneers of Exploration)

Austin, James. *Christopher Columbus.* Abdo & Daughters, 1990. 32 pp. Ill. (Explorers of the Past and Present)

Bains, Rae. *Christopher Columbus.* Troll, 1985. 32 pp. Ill. (Famous People Library)

Brenner, Barbara. *If You Were There in 1492*. Bradbury, 1991. 106 pp. Ill.

Conrad, Pam. *Pedro's Journal: A Voyage with Christopher Columbus: August 3, 1492-February 14, 1493*. Caroline House: Boyds Mills Press, 1991. 80 pp. Ill.

Dyson, John. *Westward with Columbus: Set Sail on the Voyage That Changed the World*. Scholastic, 1991. 64 pp. Ill.

Fritz, Jean. *The Great Adventure of Christopher Columbus*. Putnam, 1992. 48 pp. Ill.

Fritz, Jean. *Where Do You Think You're Going, Christopher Columbus?* Putnam, 1980. 80 pp. Ill.

Goodnough, David. *Christopher Columbus*. Troll, 1979. 48 pp. Ill. (Adventurers and Heroes)

Haskins, Jim. *Christopher Columbus: Admiral of the Ocean Sea*. Scholastic, 1991. 64 pp. Ill.

Hills, Ken. *The Voyages of Columbus*. Random House, 1991. 32 pp. Ill.

Holland, Margaret. *Christopher Columbus*. Willowisp Press, 1992. 48 pp. Ill. (People Who Shape Our World)

Humble, Richard. *The Voyages of Columbus*. Watts, 1991. 32 pp. Ill. (Exploration Through the Ages)

Italia, Bob. *Christopher Columbus*. Abdo & Daughters, 1990. 32 pp. Ill. (Explorers of the Past and Present)

Kent, Zachary. *Christopher Columbus: Expeditions to the New World*. Childrens Press, 1991. 128 pp. Ill. (The World's Great Explorers)

Las Casas, Bartholomew. *The Log of Christopher Columbus' First Voyage to America In the Year 1492, As Copied Out in Brief by Bartholomew Las Casas*. Shoe String Press, 1989. 84 pp. Ill.

Levinson, Nancy Smiler. *Christopher Columbus: Voyager to the Unknown*. Lodestar, 1990. 128 pp. Ill.

No hero is without fault, and that certainly includes Christopher Columbus. In this easy-to-read biography, the author chronicles Columbus' legendary voyages, and deals frankly with the questionable treatment that Native Americans endured at the hands of Columbus and his men.

Black and white prints and maps offer visual assistance as we follow Columbus' journeys, and a chronology of events is helpful as well. The book also includes an interesting "After Columbus" chapter.

Macht, Norman. *Christopher Columbus*. Chelsea House, 1992. 80 pp. Ill. (Junior World Biographies)

Matthews, Rupert. *The Voyage of Columbus*. Watts, 1989. 32 pp. Ill. (Great Journeys)

Monchieri, Lino. *Christopher Columbus*. Silver Burdett, 1987. 62 pp. Ill.

Morgan, Lee. *Christopher Columbus*. Silver Burdett, 1990. 104 pp. Ill. (What Made Them Great)

Osborne, Mary P. *The Story of Christopher Columbus: Admiral of the Sea*. Dell, 1987. 90 pp. Ill. (Yearling Biographies)
*This presents a concise biography of Columbus and an analysis of his voyages and turbulent life.

Pelta, Kathy. *Discovering Christopher Columbus: How History Was Invented*. Lerner, 1991. 112 pp. Ill.

Rhodes, Bennie. *Christopher Columbus*. Mott Media, 1977. 146 pp. Ill. (Sower)

Roop, Peter and Connie. *I, Columbus: My Journal-1492*. Walker, 1990. 57 pp. Ill.

During the years surrounding the 500th anniversary of Christopher Columbus' voyage to America, scores of books were written about the explorer, his discoveries, and his influence on civilization. They point out his successes; they acknowledge his failures.

But what does Columbus himself have to say?

I, Columbus features excerpts from the explorer's log, kept during his voyages to "the Indies" on behalf of Ferdinand and Isabella. What was important enough to include in this log? Distances traveled. The attitude of his crew. The challenges proffered by the weather and the sea.

And signs of land. During the first several weeks of travel, he often refers to a bird or a floating bit of debris as a sign that the welcome sight of land would soon follow. Was he trying to reassure his restless crew--or himself?

In these journal excerpts, Columbus presents himself as a good leader, an able sailor, and quite benign when dealing with the native inhabitants of islands found. While rather "bare bones" when compared with other detailed biographies of Columbus, it is fascinating reading when one keeps in mind that these are the words of the history maker himself.

Scavone, Daniel C. *Christopher Columbus*. Lucent Books, 1992. 112 pp. (The Importance of ...)

Schlein, Miriam. *I Sailed with Christopher Columbus*. Harper Collins Children's Books, 1991. 192 pp. Ill.

Stein, R. Conrad. *Christopher Columbus*. Childrens Press, 1992. 32 pp. Ill. (Cornerstones of Freedom)

Stone, Elaine M. *Christopher Columbus*. Tyndale, 1991. Ill.

Ventura, Piero. *1492: The Year of the New World*. Putnam, 1992. 94 pp. Ill.

Yolen, Jane. *Encounter*. Harcourt Brace Jovanovich, 1992. 32 pp. Ill.

Yue, Charlotte and David. *Christopher Columbus: How He Did It*. Houghton Mifflin, 1992. 136 pp. Ill.

CAPTAIN JAMES COOK (Explorer)

Harley, Ruth. *Captain James Cook*. Troll, 1979. 48 pp. Ill. (Adventurers and Heroes)

Hook, Jason. *The Voyages of Captain Cook*. Watts, 1990. 32 pp. Ill. (Great Journeys)

Humble, Richard. *The Voyages of Captain Cook*. Watts, 1990. 32 pp. Ill. (Exploration Through the Ages)

Kent, Zachary. *James Cook: Pacific Voyager*. Childrens Press, 1991. 128 pp. Ill. (The World's Great Explorers)

Noonan, Jan. *Captain Cook*. Macmillan Children's Book Group, 1993. 48 pp. Ill. (The Explorers)

BILL COSBY (Entertainer)

Conord, Bruce. *Bill Cosby*. Chelsea House, 1993. 80 pp. Ill. (Junior World Biographies)

Hill, George. *Bill Cosby: Entertainer*. Chelsea House, 1992. 112
pp. Ill. (Black Americans of Achievement)

Woods, Harold and Geraldine. *Bill Cosby: Making America Laugh
and Learn*. Macmillan Children's Book Group, 1989. 64 pp. Ill.
(Taking Part)

JACQUES COUSTEAU (Environmentalist)

Davidson, Margaret. *Jacques Cousteau: A Biography*. Scholastic.
128 pp.

Reef, Catherine. *Jacques Cousteau: Champion of the Sea*.
Childrens Press, 1992. 72 pp. Ill. (Earth Keepers)

Sinnott, Susan. *Jacques-Yves Cousteau: Undersea Adventurer*.
Childrens Press, 1992. 128 pp. Ill. (The World's Great
Explorers)

CRAZY HORSE (Native American Leader)

Wheeler, Jill. *The Story of Crazy Horse*. Abdo & Daughters, 1989.
32 pp. Ill. (Famous Native American Leaders)

DAVY CROCKETT (Frontiersman)

Moseley, Elizabeth. *Davy Crockett*. Chelsea House, 1991. 80 pp.
Ill. (Discovery Biographies)

Parks, Aileen W. *Davy Crockett: Young Rifleman*. Macmillan
Children's Book Group, 1986. 192 pp. Ill. (Childhood of
Famous Americans)

Santrey, Laurence. *Davy Crockett, Young Pioneer*. Troll, 1983. 48
pp. Ill. (Easy Biographies: History)

MARIE CURIE (Scientist)

Birch, Beverly. *Marie Curie: The Polish Scientist Who Discovered
Radium and Its Life-Saving Properties*. Gareth Stevens, 1988. 64
pp. Ill. (People Who Have Helped the World)

Brandt, Keith. *Marie Curie, Brave Scientist*. Troll, 1985. 48 pp.
Ill. (Easy Biographies: Women in History)

Dunn, Andrew. *Marie Curie*. Watts, 1991. 48 pp. Ill. (Pioneers
of Science)

Grady, Sean M. *Marie Curie*. Lucent Books, 1992. 112 pp. (The
Importance of ...)

Greene, Carol. *Marie Curie: Pioneer Physicist*. Childrens Press, 1984. 112 pp. Ill. (People of Distinction)

Keller, Mollie. *Marie Curie*. Watts, 1983. 120 pp.Ill.

Marie Curie had three children. Two were daughters. The third "child" was like none other. Neither fair of face nor full of grace, it intrigued her, motivated her, and ultimately led to her death.

That third child was radium, the element Marie and her husband, Pierre, discovered in 1898. To refer to a scientific entity as an offspring may seem excessive, but Marie Curie's life in the laboratory consumed her as another woman's sons and daughters might dominate hers.

In this biography, author Mollie Keller skillfully describes the highly technical elements of Curie's work in layman's terms, then reaches beyond the laboratory into the heart and soul of this shy, introspective winner of two Nobel Prizes. Keller's book overflows with detail, and she specifically relates the circumstances of Curie's childhood to the choices she later makes in her professional and personal worlds. We are touched by the spartan quality of Curie's life, the strength of her will, and her caring attitude toward her students.

Montgomery, Mary. *Marie Curie*. Silver Burdett, 1990. 104 pp. Ill. (What Made Them Great)

Parker, Steve. *Marie Curie and Radium*. Harper Collins Children's Books, 1993. 32 pp. Ill. (Science Discoveries)

Sabin, Louis. *Marie Curie*. Troll, 1985. 32 pp. Ill. (Famous People Library)

Steinke, Ann. *Marie Curie*. Barron's 1989. 144 pp. Ill. (Solutions: Biographies of Great Scientists)

Tames, Richard. *Marie Curie*. Watts, 1990. 32 pp. Ill. (Lifetimes)

ROALD DAHL (Author)

Dahl, Roald. *Boy: Tales of Childhood*. Farrar, 1984. 160 pp. Ill.

Roald Dahl has not written an autobiography. He has given us the key to his diary and marked the good parts for us.

Ever hide a dead mouse in a jar of candy? He did. Ever hear that if you swallow toothbrush bristles, they make your appendix rot? It's gospel truth, or so says an older and wiser(?) member of Roald's family.

Boy is full of gems like these, as well as talk of boarding school, holidays in Norway and Dahl's first ride in a motor car. The book is a fascinating romp through a field of events, large and small, some funny, some painful, but as the author insists, all true.

THE DALAI LAMA (World Leader)

Gibb, Christopher. *The Dalai Lama: The Exiled Leader of the People of Tibet and Tireless Worker for World Peace.* Gareth Stevens, 1990. 64 pp. Ill. (People Who Have Helped the World)

FATHER DAMIEN (Humanitarian)

Brown, Pam. *Father Damien: The Man Who Lived and Died for the Victims of Leprosy.* Gareth Stevens, 1988. 64 pp. Ill. (People Who Have Helped the World)

CHARLES DARWIN (Scientist)

Nardo, Don. *Charles Darwin.* Chelsea House, 1993. 112 pp. Ill. (Library of Biography)

Parker, Steve. *Charles Darwin and Evolution.* Harper Collins Childrens Books, 1992. 32 pp. Ill. (Science Discoveries)

Skelton, Renee. *Charles Darwin.* Barron's, 1989. 144 pp. Ill. (Solutions: Biographies of Great Scientists)

LEONARDO DA VINCI (Inventor, Artist)

Lafferty, Peter. *Leonardo Da Vinci.* Watts, 1990. 48 pp. Ill. (Pioneers of Science)

Marshall, Norman V. *Leonardo Da Vinci.* Silver Burdett, 1990. 104 pp. Ill. (What Made Them Great)

McLanathan, Richard. *Leonardo Da Vinci.* Abrams, 1990. 72 pp. Ill. (First Impressions)

JOHN DEERE (Inventor)

Collins, David R. *Pioneer Plowmaker: A Story about John Deere*.
Carolrhoda, 1990. 64 pp. Ill. (Creative Minds)
*A thorough description of a hardworking man and the conditions
in which he worked. Illustrations add much to the text.

CHARLES DICKENS (Author)

Collins, David R. *Tales for Hard Times: A Story about Charles
Dickens*. Carolrhoda, 1990. 64 pp. Ill. (Creative Minds)
Hunter, Nigel. *Charles Dickens*. Watts, 1989. 32 pp. Ill. (Great
Lives)

EMILY DICKINSON (Poet)

Barth, Edna. *I'm Nobody! Who Are You? The Story of Emily
Dickinson*. Houghton Mifflin, 1979. 128 pp. Ill.
Olsen, Victoria. *Emily Dickinson*. Chelsea House, 1990. 112 pp.
Ill. (American Women of Achievement)
*An excellent volume that introduces the reader to both Dickins-
on's poetry and her personal life.

WALT DISNEY (Artist, Inventor)

Ford, Barbara. *Walt Disney: A Biography*. Walker, 1989. 160 pp.
Ill.
*A good portrait of the man behind the empire, from his
childhood days through his struggle to fulfill his dreams.
Selden, Bernice. *The Story of Walt Disney: The Maker of Magical
Worlds*. Dell, 1989. 96 pp. Ill. (Yearling Biographies)

DOROTHEA L. DIX (Humanitarian)

Malone, Mary. *Dorothea L. Dix: Hospital Founder*. Chelsea
House, 1991. 80 pp. Ill. (Discovery Biographies)

PLACIDO DOMINGO (Singer)

Stefoff, Rebecca. *Placido Domingo: Spanish Singer*. Chelsea
House, 1992. 112 pp. Ill. (Hispanics of Achievement)

FREDERICK DOUGLASS (Abolitionist)

Banta, Melissa. *Frederick Douglass*. Chelsea House, 1993. 80 pp.
Ill. (Junior World Biographies)

Davidson, Margaret. *Frederick Douglass Fights for Freedom.*
Scholastic, 1990. 80 pp. Ill.

McKissack, Patricia and Fredrick. *Frederick Douglass: The Black
Lion.* Childrens Press, 1987. 136 pp. Ill. (People of Distinction)
*A detailed look at one of America's first leaders in the black
movement, from his birth as a slave to his outstanding accomplishments.

Paterson, Lillie. *Frederick Douglass.* Chelsea House, 1991. 80 pp.
Ill. (Discovery Biographies)

Russell, Sharman. *Frederick Douglass: Abolitionist Editor.* Chelsea
House, 1988. 112 pp. Ill. (Black Americans of Achievement)

Santrey, Laurence. *Young Frederick Douglass: Fight for Freedom.*
Troll, 1983. 48 pp. Ill. (Easy Biographies: History)

Weiner, Eric. *The Story of Frederick Douglass: Voice of Freedom.*
Dell, 1992. 96 pp. Ill. (Yearling Biographies)

W.E.B. DU BOIS (Civil Rights Leader)

Cryan-Hicks, Kathryn T. *W.E.B. Du Bois: Crusader for Peace.*
Discovery Enterprises, Ltd., 1991. 48 pp. Ill.

Stafford, Mark. *W.E.B. Du Bois: Scholar and Activist.* Chelsea
House, 1990. 112 pp. Ill. (Black Americans of Achievement)

PAUL LAURENCE DUNBAR (Poet)

Gentry, Tony. *Paul Laurence Dunbar: Poet.* Chelsea House, 1988.
112 pp. Ill. (Black Americans of Achievement)
*Using many photographs, this work describes Dunbar's struggle
to succeed as a black poet in the late nineteenth century.

McKissack, Patricia. *Paul Laurence Dunbar: A Poet to Remember.*
Childrens Press, 1984. 112 pp. Ill. (People of Distinction)

LOIS DUNCAN (Author)

Duncan, Lois. *Chapters: My Growth as a Writer.* Little, Brown,
1983. 263 pp.

Welcome to the world of the writer. She puts thousands of words
on paper, sometimes for herself, sometimes hoping others will read
them. She yearns for acceptance of her work and cringes when
criticism, however constructive, comes her way. And she learns.
And tries. Because this is what she was meant to do.

Lois Duncan shares her step-by-step journey as a writer with candor and good nature. First published in her teens, Duncan shares many of her stories alongside the life experiences that inspired her to write them.

This is a wonderful, honest introduction to the writing life, particularly for those who hope to enter that life someday.

AMELIA EARHART (Aviator)

Blau, Melinda. *Whatever Happened to Amelia Earhart?* Raintree, 1983. 48 pp. Ill.

Brown, Fern. G. *Amelia Earhart Takes Off.* Whitman, 1985. 64 pp. Ill.

*By covering all of the important events in her life, this highly readable account provides a good description of Amelia Earhart.

Chadwick, Roxane. *Amelia Earhart: Aviation Pioneer.* Lerner, 1987. 56 pp. Ill. (Achievers)

Kerby, Mona. *Amelia Earhart: Courage in the Sky.* Viking, 1990. 57 pp. Ill. (Women of Our Time)

Larsen, Anita. *Amelia Earhart: Missing, Declared Dead.* Macmillan Children's Book Group, 1992. 48 pp. Ill.

Lauber, Patricia. *Lost Star: The Story of Amelia Earhart.* Scholastic, 1990. 112 pp. Ill.

Amelia Earhart was one gutsy lady!

Earhart's spirit of adventure shines through in this up-close and personal story of her life. The author includes a wealth of entertaining stories from Amelia's childhood, revealing much about her family and her parents' tendency to turn everything into a wonderful, learning experience.

We really get to know the enthusiastic young woman who simply loved to fly. The book recounts in detail her fateful flight around the equator in 1937, when she and her navigator disappeared somewhere in the Pacific. Fascinating speculations regarding her whereabouts heighten the mystique surrounding this courageous pioneer of aviation.

Parlin, John. *Amelia Earhart: Pioneer in the Sky.* Chelsea House, 1992. 80 pp. Ill. (Discovery Biographies)

Randolph, Blythe. *Amelia Earhart.* Watts, 1987. 128 pp. Ill.

Sabin, Francene. *Amelia Earhart: Adventure in the Sky.* Troll, 1983. 48 pp. Ill. (Easy Biographies: Women in History)

Shore, Nancy. *Amelia Earhart: Aviator.* Chelsea House, 1987. 112 pp. Ill. (American Women of Achievement)
*Through the use of many photographs, this volume presents an overview of Earhart's life and concentrates on her record-setting flights.

Tames, Richard. *Amelia Earhart.* Watts, 1990. 32 pp. Ill. (Lifetimes)

GEORGE EASTMAN (Inventor)

Holmes, Burnham. *George Eastman.* Silver Burdett, 1992. 144 pp. Ill. (Pioneers in Change)

Mitchell, Barbara. *Click!: A Story about George Eastman.* Carolrhoda, 1986. 64 pp. Ill. (Creative Minds)

THOMAS ALVA EDISON (Inventor)

Buranelli, Vincent. *Thomas Alva Edison.* Silver Burdett, 1989. 142 pp. Ill. (Pioneers in Change)
*A comprehensive portrait of this very inventive man, this well-organized book conveys the sense of the time in which Edison lived as well as his many contributions.

Greene, Carol. *Thomas Alva Edison: Bringer of Light.* Childrens Press, 1985. 128 pp. Ill. (People of Distinction)

Eagan, Louise. *Thomas A. Edison.* Barron's, 1989. 144 pp. Ill. (Solutions: Biographies of Great Scientists)

Lowitz, Sadyebeth and Anson. *Tom Edison Finds Out.* Dell, 1979.

Mitchell, Barbara. *The Wizard of Sound: A Story about Thomas Edison.* Carolrhoda, 1991. 60 pp. Ill. (Creative Minds)

Morgan, Nina. *Thomas Edison.* Watts, 1991. 48 pp. Ill. (Pioneers of Science)

Parker, Steve. *Thomas Edison and Electricity.* Harper Collins Children's Books, 1993. 32 pp. Ill. (Science Discoveries)

Sabin, Louis. *Thomas Alva Edison: Young Inventor.* Troll, 1983. 48 pp. Ill. (Easy Biographies: Arts & Sciences)

Tames, Richard. *Thomas Edison.* Watts, 1990. 32 pp. Ill. (Lifetimes)

ALBERT EINSTEIN (Scientist)

Cwiklik, Robert. *Albert Einstein.* Barron's, 1989. 144 pp. Ill. (Solutions: Biographies of Great Scientists)

Hammontree, Marie. *Albert Einstein: Young Thinker.* Macmillan Children's Book Group, 1986. 192 pp. Ill. (Childhood of Famous Americans)

Hunter, Nigel. *Einstein.* Watts, 1987. 32 pp. Ill. (Great Lives) *This brief, easy-to-read chronology is well-illustrated with photographs. Fascinating details of Einstein as a person breathe life into the book.

Ireland, Karin. *Albert Einstein.* Silver Burdett, 1989. 116 pp. Ill. (Pioneers in Change)

Lafferty, Peter. *Albert Einstein.* Watts, 1992. 48 pp. Ill. (Pioneers of Science)

Redpath, Ann, editor. *Albert Einstein.* Creative Education, 1985. 32 pp. Ill. (Living Philosophies)

Reef, Catherine. *Albert Einstein, Scientist of the 20th Century.* Macmillan Children's Book Group, 1991. 64 pp. Ill. (Taking Part)

Santrey, Laurence. *Young Albert Einstein.* Troll, 1989. 48 pp. Ill. (Easy Biographies: Arts & Sciences)

Smith, Kathie B. *Albert Einstein.* Messner, 1989. 24 pp. Ill. (Great Americans)

DWIGHT DAVID EISENHOWER (U.S. President)

Carpenter, Allan. *Dwight David Eisenhower...The Warring Peacemaker.* Rourke, 1987. 112 pp. Ill.

Deitch, Kenneth M. and JoAnne B. Weisman. *Dwight D. Eisenhower: Man of Many Hats.* Discovery Enterprises, 1990. 48 pp. Ill.

Hargrove, Jim. *Dwight D. Eisenhower: Thirty-fourth President of the United States.* Childrens Press, 1987. 100 pp. Ill. (Encyclopedia of Presidents)
*This well-illustrated book presents a balanced portrait of Ike, revealing both his strengths and weaknesses as a leader.

Hudson, Wilma J. *Dwight D. Eisenhower: Young Military Leader.* Macmillan Children's Book Group, 1992. 192 pp. Ill. (Childhood of Famous Americans)

Sandberg, Peter. *Dwight D. Eisenhower.* Chelsea House, 1986. 112 pp. Ill. (World Leaders Past and Present)

DUKE ELLINGTON (Musician)

Frankl, Ron. *Duke Ellington: Band Leader and Composer.* Chelsea House, 1988. 112 pp. Ill. (Black Americans of Achievement)

DAVID GLASGOW FARRAGUT (Military Leader)

Chrisman, Abbott. *David Farragut.* Raintree, 1989. 32 pp. Ill. (Hispanic Stories)

Foster, Leila M. *David Glasgow Farragut: Courageous Naval Officer.* Childrens Press, 1991. 152 pp. Ill. (People of Distinction)

Latham, Jean L. *David Glasgow Farragut: Our First Admiral.* Chelsea House, 1991. 80 pp. Ill. (Discovery Biographies)

HENRY FORD (Inventor)

Aird, Hazel, and Catherine Ruddiman. *Henry Ford: Young Man with Ideas.* Macmillan Children's Book Group, 1986. 192 pp. Ill. (Childhood of Famous Americans)

Kent, Zachary. *The Story of Henry Ford and the Automobile.* Childrens Press, 1990. 32 pp. Ill. (Cornerstones of Freedom)

Killingray, David. *Henry Ford.* Greenhaven, 1980. 32 pp. Ill.

Mitchell, Barbara. *We'll Race You, Henry: A Story about Henry Ford.* Carolrhoda, 1986. 64 pp. Ill. (Creative Minds)

BENJAMIN FRANKLIN (Inventor, Statesman)

Adler, David A. *Benjamin Franklin: Printer, Inventor, Statesman.* Holiday House, 1992. 48 pp. Ill.

Davidson, Margaret. *The Story of Benjamin Franklin: Amazing American.* Dell, 1988. 60 pp. Ill. (Yearling Biographies)

Donovan, Frank R. *Many Worlds of Benjamin Franklin.* Troll, 1963. 160 pp. Ill. (American Heritage Jr. Library)

Fritz, Jean. *What's the Big Idea, Ben Franklin?* Putnam, 1982. 46 pp. Ill.
*This lively account is a delightful introduction to the "man of many talents." The text draws the young reader into the ways Franklin helped to shape the new nation.

Graves, Charles. *Benjamin Franklin: Man of Ideas.* Chelsea House, 1992. 80 pp. Ill. (Discovery Biographies)

Looby, Christopher. *Benjamin Franklin.* Chelsea House, 1990. 112 pp. Ill. (World Leaders Past and Present)
*Detailed and well-illustrated, this biography presents Franklin, the man of many talents and achievements as a human being, the man with weaknesses and contemporary critics. It is a balanced, documented portrayal.

Osborne, Mary Pope. *The Many Lives of Benjamin Franklin.* Dial, 1990. 130 pp. Ill.

This easy to read volume highlights the inventiveness, foresight, and sheer energy of one of America's most well-known founding fathers. Franklin's extraordinary life story overflows with accounts of accomplishment. Through countless anecdotes, Osborne offers the reader a richly detailed description of Ben's life and times, from his boyhood in Boston through his days as a printer, inventor, statesman and scientist. While Franklin's brilliance is truly awe-inspiring, he seems approachable rather than formidable. We find ourselves sharing his curiosity, his concern for the world around him, and his passion for improving that world.

Potter, Robert. *Benjamin Franklin.* Silver Burdett, 1992. 144 pp. Ill. (Pioneers in Change)

Santrey, Laurence. *Young Ben Franklin.* Troll, 1982. 48 pp. Ill. (Easy Biographies: History)

Stevenson, Augusta. *Benjamin Franklin: Young Printer.* Macmillan Children's Book Group, 1986. 192 pp. Ill. (Childhood of Famous Americans)

Stewart, Gail B. *Benjamin Franklin.* Lucent Books, 1992. 112 pp. Ill. (The Importance of ...)

BETTY FRIEDAN (Women's Rights Leader)

Blau, Justine. *Betty Friedan: Feminist*. Chelsea House, 1991. 112 pp. Ill. (American Women of Achievement)

Meltzer, Milton. *Betty Friedan: A Voice for Women's Rights*. Viking, 1985. 57 pp. Ill. (Women of Our Time)

Taylor-Boyd, Susan. *Betty Friedan: Voice for Women's Rights, Advocate of Human Rights*. Gareth Stevens, 1990. 64 pp. Ill. (People Who Have Helped the World)

ROBERT FROST (Poet)

Bober, Natalie S. *A Restless Spirit: The Story of Robert Frost*. Atheneum, 1991. 224 pp.

Robert Frost's poetry grew from the pain and pleasure he knew in life--that is the truth that guides Bober's presentation of this poet's biography. She entitles each chapter with a line from one of his poems, and sensitively intertwines the details of his sometimes unhappy life with the verses that expressed his spirit and individualism. This updated edition of a book originally published in 1986 also includes the full text of the appropriate poem at the beginning of each chapter. Additional photographs add visual interest as well.

A list of important dates and a guide to Frost's poetry complete this comprehensive, beautifully presented tribute to the poet laureate.

R. BUCKMINSTER FULLER (Architect)

Aaseng, Nathan. *More with Less: The Future World of Buckminster Fuller*. Lerner, 1986. 80 pp. Ill.

Potter, Robert. *R. Buckminster Fuller*. Silver Burdett, 1990. 144 pp. Ill. (Pioneers in Change)

ROBERT FULTON (Inventor)

Henry, Joanne L. *Robert Fulton: Steamboat Builder*. Chelsea House, 1990. 80 pp. Ill. (Discovery Biographies)

Henry, Marguerite. *Robert Fulton: Boy Craftsman*. Miletti Publishers, 1987. 200 pp. Ill.

GALILEO GALILEI (Scientist)

Fisher, Leonard E. *Galileo*. Macmillan Children's Book Group, 1992. 32 pp. Ill.
*This picture-book biography describes the many talents of this mathematician/astronomer/physicist.

Hitzeroth, Deborah. *Galileo Galilei*. Lucent Books, 1992. 112 pp. (The Importance of ...)

McTavish, Douglas. *Galileo*. Watts, 1991. 48 pp. Ill. (Pioneers of Science)

Parker, Steve. *Galileo and the Universe*. Harper Collins Children's Books, 1992. 32 pp. Ill. (Science Discoveries)

MAHATMA GANDHI (World Leader)

Bains, Rae. *Gandhi: Peaceful Warrior*. Troll, 1990. 48 pp. Ill. (Easy Biographies: Arts & Sciences)

Bush, Catherine. *Mohandas K. Gandhi*. Chelsea House, 1985. 122 pp. Ill. (World Leaders Past and Present)

Hunter, Nigel. *Gandhi*. Watts, 1987. 32 pp. Ill. (Great Lives)

Lazo, Caroline. *Mahatma Gandhi*. Macmillan Children's Book Group, 1993. 64 pp. Ill. (Peacemakers)

Nicholson, Michael. *Mahatma Gandhi: The Man Who Freed India and Led the World to Nonviolent Change*. Gareth Stevens, 1988. 64 pp. Ill. (People Who Have Helped the World)

Redpath, Ann, editor. *Mahatma Gandhi*. Creative Education, 1985. 32 pp. Ill. (Living Philosophies)

Shankar, R. *The Story of Gandhi*. Auromere, 1979. Ill.

LOU GEHRIG (Athlete)

Brandt, Keith. *Lou Gehrig, Pride of the Yankees*. Troll, 1986. 48 pp. Ill. (Easy Biographies: Sports Figures)

Macht, Norman. *Lou Gehrig*. Chelsea House, 1993. 64 pp. Ill. (Baseball Legends)

Van Riper, Jr., Guernsey. *Lou Gehrig: One of Baseball's Greatest*. Macmillan Children's Book Group, 1986. 192 pp. Ill. (Childhood of Famous Americans)

GERONIMO (Native American Leader)

Jeffrey, David. *Geronimo*. Raintree, 1990. 32 pp. Ill. (American Indian Stories)

Kent, Zachary. *The Story of Geronimo*. Childrens Press, 1989. 32 pp. Ill. (Cornerstones of Freedom)

Schwartz, Melissa. *Geronimo: Apache Warrior*. Chelsea House, 1992. 128 pp. Ill. (North American Indians of Achievement)

Wheeler, Jill. *The Story of Geronimo*. Abdo & Daughters, 1989. 32 pp. Ill. (Famous Native American Leaders)

GEORGE W. GOETHALS (Engineer)

Latham, Jean L. *George W. Goethals: Panama Canal Engineer*. Chelsea House, 1991. 80 pp. Ill. (Discovery Biographies)

EMMA GOLDMAN (Political Activist)

Waldstreicher, David. *Emma Goldman: Political Activist*. Chelsea House, 1990. 112 pp. Ill. (American Women of Achievement) *A succinct biography of this early 20th century female political activist, who battled for people's rights and for the oppressed.

JANE GOODALL (Scientist)

Fromer, Julie. *Jane Goodall: Living with the Chimps*. Childrens Press, 1992. 72 pp. Ill. (Earth Keepers)

MIKHAIL GORBACHEV (World Leader)

Butson, Thomas. *Mikhail Gorbachev: Soviet Premier*. Chelsea House, 1986. 120 pp. Ill. (World Leaders Past and Present)

Olesky, Walter. *Mikhail Gorbachev: A Leader for Soviet Change*. Childrens Press, 1989. 128 pp. Ill. (People of Distinction)

Selfridge, John. *Mikhail Gorbachev*. Chelsea House, 1991. 72 pp. Ill. (Junior World Biographies)

Sproule, Anna. *Mikhail Gorbachev: Revolutionary for Democracy*. Gareth Stevens, 1991. 64 pp. Ill. (People Who Have Helped the World)

AL GORE (Government Official)

McMullan, Kate. *The Story of Bill Clinton and Al Gore: Our Nation's Leaders*. Dell, 1992. 96 pp. Ill. (Yearling Biographies)

ULYSSES S. GRANT (U.S. President)

O'Brian, Stephen. *Ulysses S. Grant*. Chelsea House, 1991. 112 pp. Ill. (World Leaders Past and Present)

*The primary focus of this book is Grant's command during the
Civil War, but his failures as president are not whitewashed.

JOHN HANCOCK (Colonial American)

Fradin, Dennis. *John Hancock: First Signer of the Declaration of
Independence.* Enslow, 1989. 48 pp. Ill. (Colonial Profiles)

Fritz, Jean. *Will You Sign Here, John Hancock?* Putnam, 1982.
48 pp. Ill.

PATRICK HENRY (Colonial American)

Fradin, Dennis. *Patrick Henry: "Give Me Liberty or Give Me Death."*
Enslow, 1990. 48 pp. Ill. (Colonial Profiles)

Fritz, Jean. *Where Was Patrick Henry on the 29th of May?* Putnam,
1982. 48 pp. Ill.

Reische, Diana. *Patrick Henry.* Watts, 1987. 92 pp. Ill.

Sabin, Louis. *Patrick Henry: Voice of the American Revolution.*
Troll, 1982. 48 pp. Ill. (Easy Biographies: History)

PRINCE HENRY THE NAVIGATOR (Explorer)

Fisher, Leonard Everett. *Prince Henry the Navigator.* Macmillan,
1990. 32 pp. Ill.

Here was a lover of exploration who did not participate in
adventures himself. Instead, he made them possible.

Prince Henry established the first school of navigation in the 15th
century, where important navigational tools were improved and a
faster sailing ship was developed. With lively prose and superb
illustrations, this biography describes the ground-breaking work
done at Prince Henry's school, work that would make great future
discoveries achievable.

JIM HENSON (Entertainer)

Aaseng, Nathan. *Jim Henson: Muppet Master.* Lerner, 1988. 40
pp. Ill.

St. Pierre, Stephanie. *The Story of Jim Henson: Creator of the
Muppets.* Dell, 1991. 96 pp. Ill. (Yearling Biographies)

Woods, Geraldine. *Jim Henson: From Puppets to Muppets.* Macmillan Children's Book Group, 1991. 64 pp. Ill. (Taking Part)

MATTHEW HENSON (Explorer)

Dolan, Sean. *Matthew Henson.* Chelsea House, 1992. 72 pp. Ill. (Junior World Biographies)

Ferris, Jeri. *Arctic Explorer: The Story of Matthew Henson.* Carolrhoda, 1989. 80 pp. Ill. (Trailblazers)

When Robert Peary planted the American flag at the North Pole, Matthew Henson was part of the team who helped him get there. Henson organized supplies, communicated with Eskimos and played a key role in the success of Peary's expedition.

Henson's accomplishments are amazing for any man; they are astonishing for an African-American in 1909.

Ferris has written a biography that acknowledges the issue of color and the motivation it provided for Henson to succeed. Yet most of this book is about adventure. She so vividly details the hardships these explorers encountered that we are amazed that they continued at all. Arctic Explorer is full of irony; Peary refers to the indispensable Henson as a "colored boy," though "the equal of others in the party."

Black and white photos and maps give us solid visual hooks on which to hang our imaginations as we read this inspiring, exciting tale.

Gilman, Michael. *Matthew Henson: Explorer.* Chelsea House, 1988. 110 pp. Ill. (Black Americans of Achievement)

Here is a life story about which movies and miniseries are made.

Henson, a black man born 16 months after the end of the Civil War, managed to become a skilled sailor, a world traveler and a history-making explorer. In 1909, Henson accompanied Robert Peary on the first expedition ever to reach the North Pole.

Michael Gilman packs a stack of information into this well-written biography, but the facts are never overwhelming. Rather, the details help us appreciate the scope of Henson's accomplishments. We

come to realize that life as an explorer offered this gifted man
opportunities that would have been denied him had he stayed in the
U.S. Despite his extraordinary life, however, Henson was not
untouched by racism, and Gilman effectively covers the hero's
struggles.
  An inspiring introduction by Coretta Scott King sets the tone for
this tale of ambition and dignity.

KATHARINE HEPBURN (Entertainer)
Latham, Caroline. *Katharine Hepburn*. Chelsea House, 1988. 112
  pp. Ill. (American Women of Achievement)

HIAWATHA (Native American Leader)
Bonvillain, Nancy. *Hiawatha: Founder of the Iroquois Confederacy*.
  Chelsea House, 1992. 112 pp. Ill. (North American Indians of
  Achievement)
Wheeler, Jill. *The Story of Hiawatha*. Abdo & Daughters, 1989.
  32 pp. Ill. (Famous Native American Leaders)

HERBERT HOOVER (U.S. President)
Clinton, Susan. *Herbert Hoover: Thirty-First President of the United
  States*. Childrens Press, 1988. 100 pp. Ill. (Encyclopedia of
  Presidents)
Hilton, Suzanne. *The World of Young Herbert Hoover*. Walker,
  1987. 103 pp. Ill.
  *A well-written biography that gives the reader insight into
  Hoover's personality during his childhood and through his college
  days at Stanford.

HARRY HOUDINI (Entertainer)
Borland, Kathryn K., and Helen R. Speicher. *Harry Houdini:
  Young Magician*. Macmillan Children's Book Group, 1991. 192
  pp. Ill. (Childhood of Famous Americans)
Kraske, Robert. *Harry Houdini: Master of Magic*. Scholastic, 1991.
  72 pp. Ill.
Levy, Elizabeth. *Running Out of Magic with Houdini*. Knopf,
  1981. 128 pp. Ill.

Sabin, Louis. *The Great Houdini, Daring Escape Artist*. Troll, 1990. 48 pp. Ill. (Easy Biographies: Arts & Sciences)

SAM HOUSTON (Statesman)
Fritz, Jean. *Make Way for Sam Houston*. Putnam, 1986. 109 pp. Ill.

Latham, Jean L. *Sam Houston: Hero of Texas*. Chelsea House, 1991. 80 pp. Ill. (Discovery Biographies)

HENRY HUDSON (Explorer)
Asimov, Isaac. *Henry Hudson: Arctic Explorer and North American Adventurer*. Gareth Stevens, 1991. 48 pp. Ill. (Isaac Asimov's Pioneers of Exploration)

Harley, Ruth. *Henry Hudson*. Troll, 1979. 48 pp. Ill. (Adventurers and Heroes)

Syme, Ronald. *Henry Hudson*. Cavendish, Marshall Corp., 1991. 152 pp. Ill.

Weiner, Eric. *The Story of Henry Hudson: Master Explorer*. Dell, 1991. 96 pp. Ill. (Yearling Biographies)

LANGSTON HUGHES (Poet)
Rummel, Jack. *Langston Hughes: Poet*. Chelsea House, 1988. 112 pp. Ill. (Black Americans of Achievement)

ZORA NEALE HURSTON (Author)
Cahart, Roz. *Zora Neale Hurston*. Chelsea House, 1993. 80 pp. Ill. (Junior World Biographies)

Porter, A.P. *Jump at de Sun: The Story of Zora Neale Hurston*. Carolrhoda, 1993. 88 pp. Ill. (Trailblazers)

Witcover, Paul. *Zora Neale Hurston: Author*. Chelsea House, 1991. 112 pp. Ill. (Black Americans of Achievement)

ANDREW JACKSON (U.S. President)
Gutman, William. *Andrew Jackson and the New Populism*. Childrens Press, 1988. 144 pp. Ill. (Profiles of Great Americans for Young People: Henry Steele Commager's Americans)

Hilton, Suzanne. *The World of Young Andrew Jackson*. Walker, 1988. 118 pp. Ill.

Osinski, Alice. *Andrew Jackson: Seventh President of the United States*. Childrens Press, 1987. 98 pp. Ill. (Encyclopedia of Presidents)

Parlin, John. *Andrew Jackson*. Chelsea House, 1991. 80 pp. Ill. (Discovery Biographies)

Sabin, Louis. *Andrew Jackson, Frontier Patriot*. Troll, 1986. 48 pp. Ill. (Easy Biographies: History)

Sandak, Cass R. *The Jacksons*. Macmillan Children's Book Group, 1992. 48 pp. Ill. (First Families)

Viola, Herman. *Andrew Jackson*. Chelsea House, 1986. 112 pp. Ill. (World Leaders Past and Present)

JESSE JACKSON (Civil Rights Leader)

Celsi, Teresa. *Jesse Jackson and Political Power*. Millbrook, 1992. 32 pp. Ill. (Gateway Civil Rights)

Chaplik, Dorothy. *Jesse Jackson: Up with Hope*. Macmillan Children's Book Group, 1992. 112 pp. Ill. (People in Focus)

Jakoubek, Robert. *Jesse Jackson: Civil Rights Leader and Politician*. Chelsea House, 1991. 112 pp. Ill. (Black Americans of Achievement)

McKissack, Patricia. *Jesse Jackson: A Biography*. Scholastic, 1990. 112 pp. Ill.

Some people love him. Some can't stand him. Patricia McKissack tells us who he is.

Her work follows Jackson through his youth, his early days in the civil rights movement, and his involvement in two Presidential elections. While she does not disguise her admiration for his ability to make such a difference in the American mainstream, she also acknowledges some black leaders' aversion to Jackson's style. McKissack's extensive coverage of Jackson's bids for the Presidency in 1984 and 1988 give the reader an appreciation for the development of his political sophistication.

This biography provides a good beginning for the young reader who plans to follow the future activities of this "consistent voice against racism and racial discrimination."

MAHALIA JACKSON (Singer)

Witter, Evelyn. *Mahalia Jackson*. Mott Media, 1985. 128 pp. Ill. (Sower)

Wolfe, Charles. *Mahalia Jackson: Born to Sing Gospel Music*. Chelsea House, 1990. 112 pp. Ill. (American Women of Achievement)

STONEWALL JACKSON (Military Leader)

Fritz, Jean. *Stonewall*. Putnam, 1979. 48 pp. Ill.

Ludwig, Charles. *Stonewall Jackson*. Mott Media, 1989. 177 pp. Ill. (Sower)

THOMAS JEFFERSON (U.S. President)

Bruns, Roger. *Thomas Jefferson*. Chelsea House, 1986. 112 pp. Ill. (World Leaders Past and Present)

Colver, Anne. *Thomas Jefferson: Author of Independence*. Chelsea House, 1992. 80 pp. Ill. (Discovery Biographies)

Crisman, Ruth. *Thomas Jefferson: The Man With a Vision*. Scholastic, 1993. 128 pp. Ill.

Hargrove, Jim. *Thomas Jefferson: Third President of the United States*. Childrens Press, 1986. 100 pp. Ill. (Encyclopedia of Presidents)

*Well-illustrated and concise, this biography provides an excellent overview of Thomas Jefferson.

Hilton, Suzanne. *The World of Young Thomas Jefferson*. Walker, 1986. 96 pp. Ill.

Milton, Joyce. *The Story of Thomas Jefferson*. Dell, 1990. 96 pp. Ill.

*A well-written biography that brings Jefferson to life for the reader because of its use of fascinating personal information.

Milton, Joyce and Tom LaPadula. *The Story of Thomas Jefferson, Prophet of Liberty*. Dell, 1989. 96 pp. Ill. (Yearling Biographies)

Monsell, Helen A. *Thomas Jefferson: The Third President of the United States*. Macmillan Children's Book Group, 1989. 192 pp. Ill. (Childhood of Famous Americans)

Moscow, Henry. *Thomas Jefferson and His World*. Troll, 1960. 160 pp. Ill. (American Heritage Jr. Library)

Nardo, Don. *Thomas Jefferson*. Lucent Books, 1993. 112 pp.
(The Importance of ...)

Patterson, Charles. *Thomas Jefferson*. Watts, 1987. 96 pp. Ill.
*An excellent portrayal of one of America's early leaders,
presenting Jefferson in all his roles: politician, statesman, scientist,
philosopher and architect.

Reef, Catherine. *Monticello*. Macmillan Children's Book Group,
1991. 64 pp. Ill.

Richards, Norman. *The Story of Monticello*. Childrens Press, 1970.
32 pp. Ill.

Sabin, Francene. *Young Thomas Jefferson*. Troll, 1985. 48 pp. Ill.
(Easy Biographies: History)

Sandak, Cass R. *The Jeffersons*. Macmillan Children's Book
Group, 1992. 48 pp. Ill. (First Families)

Santrey, Laurence. *Thomas Jefferson*. Troll, 1985. 32 pp. Ill.
(Famous Americans Library)

Shorto, Russell. *Thomas Jefferson and the American Ideal*.
Childrens Press, 1988. 144 pp. Ill. (Profiles of Great Americans
for Young People: Henry Steele Commager's Americans)

Smith, Kathie B. *Thomas Jefferson*. Messner, 1989. 24 pp. Ill.
(Great Americans)

JOAN OF ARC (Saint, Military Leader)

Banfield, Susan. *Joan of Arc*. Chelsea House, 1988. 112 pp. Ill.
(World Leaders Past and Present)

Christopher, Tracy. *Joan of Arc*. Chelsea House, 1993. 80 pp. Ill.
(Junior World Biographies)

Smith, Dorothy. *Saint Joan: The Girl in Armour*. Paulist, 1990. Ill.

Williams, Brian. *Joan of Arc*. Cavendish, Marshall Corp., 1989.
32 pp. Ill.

EARVIN (MAGIC) JOHNSON (Athlete)

Dolan, Sean. *Magic Johnson: Basketball Great*. Chelsea House,
1993. 112 pp. Ill. (Black Americans of Achievement)

Greenberg, Keith E. *Magic Johnson: Champion with a Cause*.
Lerner, 1992. 64 pp. Ill. (Sports Achievers)

Gutman, Bill. *Magic Johnson: Hero On and Off the Court*.
Millbrook, 1992. 48 pp. Ill. (Millbrook Sports World)

Levin, Richard. *Magic Johnson: Court Magician.* Childrens Press, 1981. 48 pp. Ill. (Sports Stars)

Morgan, Bill. *The Magic: Earvin Johnson.* Scholastic, 1993. 128 pp. Ill.

JOHN PAUL JONES (Military Leader)

Brandt, Keith. *John Paul Jones: Hero of the Seas.* Troll, 1983. 48 pp. Ill. (Easy Biographies: History)

Graff, Stewart. *John Paul Jones: Sailor Hero.* Chelsea House, 1992. 80 pp. Ill. (Discovery Biographies)

Worcester, Donald. *John Paul Jones.* Houghton Mifflin, 1961.

CHIEF JOSEPH (Native American Leader)

Chief Joseph's Own Story As Told by Chief Joseph in 1879. Council for Indian Education, 1972.

Fox, Mary V. *Chief Joseph of the Nez Perce Indians: Champion of Liberty.* Childrens Press, 1992. 152 pp. Ill. (People of Distinction)

Jassem, Kate. *Chief Joseph, Leader of Destiny.* Troll, 1979. 48 pp. Ill. (Native American Biographies)

Trateer, Clifford. *Chief Joseph: Nez Perce Leader.* Chelsea House, 1993. 112 pp. Ill. (North American Indians of Achievement)

Warburton, Lois. *Chief Joseph.* Lucent Books, 1992. 112 pp. (The Importance of ...)

BENITO JUAREZ (Freedom Fighter)

Bains, Rae. *Benito Juarez, Hero of Modern Mexico.* Troll, 1992. 48 pp. Ill. (Easy Biographies: History)

HELEN KELLER (Humanitarian)

Graff, Stewart and Polly. *Helen Keller: Toward the Light.* Chelsea House, 1992. 80 pp. Ill. (Discovery Biographies)

Hickok, Lorena. *The Story of Helen Keller.* Scholastic, 1988. 160 pp. Ill.

Hunter, Nigel. *Helen Keller.* Watts, 1986. 32 pp. Ill.

Keller, Helen. *Helen Keller: The Story of My Life.* Troll, 1993. 152 pp.

Keller, Helen. *The Story of My Life.* Scholastic, 1991. 160 pp.

Kudlinski, Kathleen V. *Helen Keller: A Light for the Blind*. Viking Children's Books, 1989. 64 pp. Ill. (Women of Our Time)

In her reflections on the writing of this book, Kathleen Kudlinski admits that she could only write it after she acknowledged that Helen Keller's mind was not necessarily different from her own simply because her senses were. She heeded Helen's plea that "we forget she is deaf and blind and think of her as an ordinary woman."

The author does a fine job of portraying Keller and her teacher, Annie Sullivan, not as saints but as challenged women who worked hard and did well. We meet the human beings behind the "Miracle Worker" legend and follow them through triumphs and trials.

Did you know that Keller and Sullivan once performed on a vaudeville stage when finances were low? Anecdotes like this are many in *Helen Keller*, a fascinating, thought-provoking book about someone we may think we know.

Peare, Catherine O. *The Helen Keller Story*. Harper Collins Children's Books, 1990. 192 pp.

Sabin, Francene. *Courage of Helen Keller*. Troll, 1982. 48 pp. Ill. (Easy Biographies: Women in History)

Santrey, Laurence. *Helen Keller*. Troll, 1985. 32 pp. Ill. (Famous People Library)

Tames, Richard. *Helen Keller*. Watts, 1989. 32 pp. Ill. (Lifetimes)

Wepman, Dennis. *Helen Keller*. Chelsea House, 1987. 112 pp. Ill. (American Women of Achievement)

*Numerous photographs make this competent biography of Keller an excellent source of information.

Wilkie, Katherine E. *Helen Keller: From Tragedy to Triumph*. Macmillan Children's Book Group, 1986. 192 pp. Ill. (Childhood of Famous Americans)

JOHN F. KENNEDY (U.S. President)

Denenberg, Barry. *John Fitzgerald Kennedy: America's 35th President*. Scholastic, 1988. 128 pp. Ill.

Frisbee, Lucy P. *John Fitzgerald Kennedy: America's Youngest President*. Macmillan Children's Book Group, 1986. 192 pp. Ill. (Childhood of Famous Americans)

Frolick, S.J. *Once There Was a President*. Black Star, 1980. 46 pp.

Graves, Charles P. *John F. Kennedy*. Dell, 1981. 80 pp. Ill.

Graves, Charles P. *John F. Kennedy: New Frontiersman*. Chelsea House, 1992. 80 pp. Ill. (Discovery Biographies)

Hamilton, Sue. *The Assassination of a President: John F. Kennedy*. Abdo & Daughters, 1990. 32 pp. Ill.

Kent, Zachary. *John F. Kennedy: Thirty-fifth President of the United States*. Childrens Press, 1987. 100 pp. Ill. (Encyclopedia of Presidents)

Langley, Andrew. *John F. Kennedy*. Watts, 1986. 32 pp. Ill.

Levine, I.E. *John F. Kennedy: Young Man in the White House*. Grey Castle, 1991. 176 pp. Ill.

Randall, Marta. *John F. Kennedy*. Chelsea House, 1988. 112 pp. Ill. (World Leaders Past and Present)

Sandak, Cass R. *The Kennedys*. Macmillan Children's Book Group, 1992. 48 pp. Ill. (First Families)

Smith, Kathie B. *John F. Kennedy*. Messner, 1987. 24 pp. Ill. (Great Americans)

Stein, R. Conrad. *The Assassination of John F. Kennedy*. Childrens Press, 1992. 32 pp. Ill. (Cornerstones of Freedom)

SISTER ELIZABETH KENNY (Medical Leader)

Crofford, Emily. *Healing Warrior: A Story about Sister Elizabeth Kenny*. Carolrhoda, 1989. 64 pp. Ill. (Creative Minds)

Sister Kenny was a self-taught nurse who grew up in the Australian bushlands. On the surface, she was hardly a likely candidate for greatness.

Yet, Sister Kenny developed a treatment for polio that did what accepted treatments at the time failed to do: it made twisted limbs function again.

Healing Warrior is written in a straightforward style that reflects the directness of Sister Kenny. The heroine's actions speak for themselves, as Crofford describes Sr. Kenny's struggle for credibility among medical professionals, and her discovery of opportunities in America. Crofford's sources are primary: interviews with Sr.

Kenny's friends, patients and co-workers; unpublished letters to and from Sr. Kenny, as well as her handwritten memoirs.

FRANCIS SCOTT KEY (Colonial American)
Collins, David. *Francis Scott Key*. Mott Media, 1982. 113 pp. Ill. (Sower)
Patterson, Lillie. *Francis Scott Key*. Chelsea House, 1991. 80 pp. Ill. (Discovery Biographies)

CORETTA SCOTT KING (Civil Rights Leader)
Wheeler, Jill. *Coretta Scott King*. Abdo & Daughters, 1992. 32 pp. Ill. (Leading Ladies)

MARTIN LUTHER KING, JR. (Civil Rights Leader)
Bains, Rae. *Martin Luther King*. Troll, 1984. 32 pp. Ill. (Famous Americans Library)
Clayton, Ed. *Martin Luther King: The Peaceful Warrior*. Pocket Books, 1986. 128 pp. Ill.
Davidson, Margaret. *I Have a Dream: The Story of Martin Luther King*. Scholastic, 1991.
Fox, Mary V. *About Martin Luther King Day*. Enslow, 1989. 64 pp. Ill.
Hakim, Rita. *Martin Luther King, Jr., and the March Toward Freedom*. Millbrook, 1992. 32 pp. Ill. (Gateway Civil Rights)
Hamilton, Sue. *The Killing of a Leader: Dr. Martin Luther King*. Abdo & Daughters, 1989. 32 pp. Ill.
Harris, Jacqueline. *Martin Luther King, Jr.* Watts, 1983. 128 pp. Ill.
Haskins, Jim. *The Day Martin Luther King, Jr. Was Shot: A Photo History of the Civil Rights Movement*. Scholastic, 1993. 96 pp. Ill.
Haskins, Jim. *I Have a Dream: The Life and Words of Martin Luther King, Jr.* Millbrook, 1992. 112 pp. Ill.
Holland, Margaret. *Martin Luther King*. Willowisp Press, 1990. 48 pp. Ill. (People Who Shape Our World)

Hunter, Nigel. *Martin Luther King, Jr.* Watts, 1985. 32 pp. Ill. (Great Lives)
*A comprehensive look at the Civil Rights leader's life.

Jakoubik, Robert. *Martin Luther King, Jr.: Civil Rights Leader.* Chelsea House, 1990. 112 pp. (Black Americans of Achievement)
This is a magnificent book. An introduction by Coretta Scott King sets the tone for this inspiring story of an inspiring individual.

We are touched by Dr. King the person, impressed by the immense responsibilities he chose to undertake, and stirred by his strong words as he offers hope to his people.

The book includes a great deal of information about Dr. King's childhood as well as conversations with many people who knew him through the years.

King's strategy of non-violence, borrowed from the philosophy of Mahatma Gandhi, is prominently and proudly featured.

Lambert, Kathy. *Martin Luther King, Jr.* Chelsea House, 1993. 80 pp. Ill. (Junior World Biographies)

Levine, Ellen. *If You Lived at the Time of Martin Luther King.* Scholastic, 1990. 72 pp. Ill.

McKissack, Patricia. *Martin Luther King, Jr.: A Man to Remember.* Childrens Press, 1984. 128 pp. Ill. (People of Distinction)

Millender, Dharathula H. *Martin Luther King, Jr.: Young Man with a Dream.* Macmillan Children's Book Group, 1986. 192 pp. Ill. (Childhood of Famous Americans)

Milton, Joyce. *Marching to Freedom: The Story of Martin Luther King, Jr.* Dell, 1987. 92 pp. Ill. (Yearling Biographies)
*A concise portrait of King's life and work, written in a lively style.

Peck, Ira. *The Life and Words of Martin Luther King, Jr.* Scholastic, 1986. 96 pp. Ill.

Schloredt, Valerie. *Martin Luther King, Jr.: America's Great Nonviolent Leader in the Struggle for Human Rights.* Gareth Stevens, 1988. 68 pp. Ill. (People Who Have Helped the World)
*This volume provides an exhaustive account of King's contributions to the civil rights movement.

Schmidt, Fran and Alice Friedman. *Fighting Fair: Dr. Martin Luther King for Kids.* Grace Contrino Abrams Peace Education Foundation, 1990. 69 pp. Ill.

Shuker, Nancy F. *Martin Luther King, Jr.* Chelsea House, 1985. 112 pp. Ill. (World Leaders Past and Present)

Smith, Kathie B. *Martin Luther King, Jr.* Messner, 1987. 24 pp. Ill. (Great Americans)

MARQUIS de LAFAYETTE (Freedom Fighter)

Brandt, Keith. *Lafayette, Hero of Two Nations.* Troll, 1990. 48 pp. Ill. (Easy Biographies: History)

ROBERT E. LEE (Military Leader)

Bains, Rae. *Robert E. Lee, Brave Leader.* Troll, 1986. 48 pp. Ill. (Easy Biographies: History)

Brandt, Keith. *Robert E. Lee.* Troll, 1985. 32 pp. Ill. (Famous Americans Library)

Brown, Warren. *Robert E. Lee.* Chelsea House, 1992. 112 pp. Ill. (World Leaders Past and Present)

Graves, Charles P. *Robert E. Lee.* Chelsea House, 1991. 80 pp. Ill. (Discovery Biographies)

Monsell, Helen A. *Robert E. Lee: Young Confederate.* Macmillan Children's Book Group, 1986. 192 pp. Ill. (Childhood of Famous Americans)

Morrison, Ellen E. *Gentle Man of Destiny: A Portrait of Robert E. Lee.* Morielle Press, 1984. 16 pp. Ill.

Roddy, Lee. *Robert E. Lee.* Mott Media, 1977. 169 pp. Ill. (Sower)

MERIWETHER LEWIS AND WILLIAM CLARK (Explorers)

Andrist, Ralph K. *To the Pacific with Lewis and Clark.* Troll, 1967. 160 pp. Ill. (American Heritage Jr. Library)

Blumberg, Rhoda. *The Incredible Journey of Lewis and Clark.* Lothrop, Lee and Shepard, 1987. 128 pp. Ill.

Fitz-gerald, Christine A. *Meriwether Lewis and William Clark: The Northwest Expedition.* Childrens Press, 1991. 128 pp. Ill. (The World's Great Explorers)

Noonan, Jon. *Lewis and Clark.* Macmillan Children's Book Group, 1993. 48 pp. Ill. (The Explorers)

Peterson, David, and Mark Coburn. *Meriwether Lewis and William Clark: Soldiers, Explorers, and Partners in History.* Childrens Press, 1988. 120 pp. Ill. (People of Distinction)

Sabin, Francene. *Lewis and Clark.* Troll, 1985. 32 pp. Ill. (Famous People Library)

Stefoff, Rebecca. *Lewis & Clark.* Chelsea House, 1992. 80 pp. Ill. (Junior World Biographies)

Stein, R.C. *The Story of the Lewis and Clark Expedition.* Childrens Press, 1978. 32 pp. Ill. (Cornerstones of Freedom)

ABRAHAM LINCOLN (U.S. President)

Bains, Rae. *Abraham Lincoln.* Troll, 1985. 32 pp. Ill. (Famous Americans Library)

Brandt, Keith. *Abe Lincoln: The Young Years.* Troll, 1982. 48 pp. Ill. (Easy Biographies: History)

Bruns, Roger. *Abraham Lincoln.* Chelsea House, 1986. 112 pp. Ill. (World Leaders Past and Present)

Collins, David R. *Abraham Lincoln.* Mott Media, 1976. 150 pp. Ill. (Sower)

Colver, Anne. *Abraham Lincoln.* Dell, 1981. 76 pp. Ill.

Colver, Anne. *Abraham Lincoln: For the People.* Chelsea House, 1992. 80 pp. Ill. (Discovery Biographies)

Hamilton, Sue. *The Assassination of Abraham Lincoln.* Abdo & Daughters, 1990. 32 pp. Ill.

Hargrove, Jim. *Abraham Lincoln: Sixteenth President of the United States.* Childrens Press, 1988. 100 pp. Ill. (Encyclopedia of Presidents)

Holland, Margaret. *Abraham Lincoln.* Willowisp Press, 1991. 48 pp. Ill. (People Who Shape Our World)

Jacobs, William J. *Lincoln.* Macmillan Childrens Book Group, 1991. 42 pp. Ill.
*This well-written book focuses on the personality of Lincoln, and how it made him a great leader.

Kent, Zachary. *The Story of the Election of Abraham Lincoln.* Childrens Press, 1986. 32 pp. Ill. (Cornerstones of Freedom)

Kent, Zachary. *The Story of Ford's Theater and the Death of Lincoln.* Childrens Press, 1987. 32 pp. Ill.

McNeer, May. *America's Abraham Lincoln.* Grey Castle, 1991. 128 pp. Ill.

Metzger, Larry. *Abraham Lincoln*. Watts, 1987. 93 pp. Ill.

Morgan, Lee, and Piero Cattaneo. *Abraham Lincoln*. Silver Burdett, 1990. 104 pp. Ill. (What Made Them Great)

Sandak, Cass R. *The Lincolns*. Macmillan Children's Book Group, 1992. 48 pp. Ill. (First Families)

Shorto, Russell. *Abraham Lincoln and the End of Slavery*. Millbrook, 1992. 32 pp. Ill. (Gateway Civil Rights)

Smith, Kathie B. *Abraham Lincoln*. Messner, 1987. 24 pp. Ill. (Great Americans)

Sproule, Anna. *Abraham Lincoln: Leader of a Nation in Crisis*. Gareth Stevens, 1992. 68 pp. Ill. (People Who Have Helped the World)

Stevenson, Augusta. *Abraham Lincoln: The Great Emancipator*. Macmillan Children's Book Group, 1986. 192 pp. Ill. (Childhood of Famous Americans)

Weinberg, Larry. *The Story of Abraham Lincoln: President for the People*. Dell, 1991. 96 pp. Ill. (Yearling Biographies)

CHARLES LINDBERGH (Aviator)

Collins, David R. *Charles Lindbergh: Hero Pilot*. Chelsea House, 1990. 80 pp. Ill. (Discovery Biographies)

JEAN LITTLE (Author)

Little, Jean. *Little by Little: A Writer's Education*. Viking, 1988. 240 pp. Ill.

Writer Jean Little calls her autobiography "a tale compounded of truth and imagination." It's a style that serves her well. She presents an engaging combination of emotions and facts that lead us through her youth, her college years and her work as a teacher and author. We witness Little's early encounter with the knowledge that she had "bad eyes." When her impaired vision throws obstacles in her way we become, at times, more frustrated than she does.

JACK LONDON (Author)

Bains, Rae. *Jack London, A Life of Adventure*. Troll, 1992. 48 pp. Ill. (Easy Biographies: Arts and Sciences)

Schroeder, Alan. *Jack London.* Chelsea House, 1992. 128 pp. Ill. (Library of Biography)

JULIETTE LOW (Humanitarian)

Kudlinski, Kathleen V. *Juliette Gordon Low: America's First Girl Scout.* Puffin, 1989. 64 pp. Ill.

DOUGLAS MacARTHUR (Military Leader)

Finkelstein, Norman H. *Douglas MacArthur: The Emperor General.* Macmillan Children's Book Group, 1992. 112 pp. Ill. (People in Focus)

Skipper, G.C. *MacArthur and the Philippines.* Childrens Press, 1982. 48 pp. Ill.

DOLLEY MADISON (U.S. First Lady)

Davidson, Mary R. *Dolley Madison.* Chelsea House, 1992. 80 pp. Ill. (Discovery Biographies)

Waldrop, Ruth. *Dolley Madison.* Rusk, 1990. 112 pp. Ill. (First Ladies)

JAMES MADISON (U.S. President)

Clinton, Susan. *James Madison: Fourth President of the United States.* Childrens Press, 1986. 98 pp. Ill. (Encyclopedia of Presidents)

*This well-illustrated and detailed account of Madison will bring him alive to the reader.

Kelly, Regina Z. *James Madison: Statesman and President.* Grey Castle, 1991. 144 pp. Ill.

Leavell, Perry. *James Madison.* Chelsea House, 1988. 112 pp. Ill. (World Leaders Past and Present)

Sandak, Cass R. *The Madisons.* Macmillan Children's Book Group, 1992. 48 pp. Ill. (First Families)

MALCOLM X (Civil Rights Leader)

Adoff, Arnold. *Malcolm X.* Harper Collins Childrens Books, 1993. 48 pp. Ill.

Collins, David. *Malcolm X: Black Rage.* Macmillan Children's Book Group, 1992. 112 pp. Ill. (People in Focus)

Cwiklik, Robert. *Malcolm X and Black Pride*. Millbrook, 1992. 32 pp. Ill. (Gateway Civil Rights)

Rummel, Jack. *Malcolm X: Militant Black Leader*. Chelsea House, 1989. 112 pp. Ill. (Black Americans of Achievement)

NELSON MANDELA (Political Activist/Leader)

Denenberg, Barry. *Nelson Mandela: "No Easy Walk to Freedom."* Scholastic, 1990. 176 pp.

Feinberg, Brian. *Nelson Mandela*. Chelsea House, 1992. 76 pp. Ill. (Junior World Biographies)

Hargrove, Jim. *Nelson Mandela: South Africa's Silent Voice of Protest*. Childrens Press, 1989. 125 pp. Ill. (People of Distinction)

Hughes, Libby. *Nelson Mandela: Voice of Freedom*. Macmillan Children's Book Group, 1992. 112 pp. Ill. (People in Focus)

Pogrund, Benjamin. *Nelson Mandela: Strength and Spirit of a Free South Africa*. Gareth Stevens, 1992. 64 pp. Ill. (People Who Have Helped the World)

Tames, Richard. *Nelson Mandela*. Watts, 1991. 32 pp. Ill. (Lifetimes)

Vail, John. *Nelson and Winnie Mandela*. Chelsea House, 1989. 112 pp. Ill. (World Leaders Past and Present)

WINNIE MANDELA (Political Activist)

Meltzer, Milton. *Winnie Mandela: The Soul of South Africa*. Viking, 1986. 64 pp. Ill. (Women of Our Time)

MICKEY MANTLE (Athlete)

Gallagher, Mark. *Mickey Mantle*. Chelsea House, 1991. 64 pp. Ill. (Baseball Legends)

Wheeler, Lonnie. *The Official Baseball Hall of Fame Story of Mickey Mantle*. Simon & Schuster, 1989. 95 pp. Ill.

THURGOOD MARSHALL (U.S. Supreme Court Justice, Civil Rights Leader)

Aldred, Lisa. *Thurgood Marshall*. Chelsea House, 1990. 112 pp. Ill. (Black Americans of Achievement)

Bains, Rae. *Thurgood Marshall: Fight for Justice*. Troll, 1993. 48 pp. Ill.

Cavan, Seamus. *Thurgood Marshall and Equal Justice*. Millbrook, 1993. 32 pp. Ill. (Gateway Civil Rights)

Prentzes, G.S. *Thurgood Marshall*. Chelsea House, 1993. 80 pp. Ill. (Junior World Biographies)

MAYO BROTHERS (Medical Leaders)

Crofford, Emily. *Frontier Surgeons: A Story about the Mayo Brothers*. Carolrhoda, 1989. 64 pp. Ill. (Creative Minds)
*This book provides the reader with insight into medical practices of the late 19th and early 20th centuries by following the careers of the Mayo Brothers.

WILLIE MAYS (Athlete)

Grabowski, John. *Willie Mays*. Chelsea House, 1990. 64 pp. Ill. (Baseball Legends)

Sabin, Louis. *Willie Mays*. Troll, 1989. 48 pp. Ill. (Easy Biographies: Sports Figures)

MARGARET MEAD (Anthropologist)

Castiglia, Julie. *Margaret Mead*. Silver Burdett, 1989. 144 pp. Ill. (Pioneers in Change)

Saunders, Susan. *Margaret Mead: The World Was Her Family*. Viking, 1988. 64 pp. Ill. (Women of Our Time)

Ziesk, Edra. *Margaret Mead: Anthropologist*. Chelsea House, 1990. 112 pp. Ill. (American Women of Achievement)

GOLDA MEIR (World Leader)

Adler, David A. *Our Golda: The Story of Golda Meir*. Viking, 1984. 64 pp. Ill. (Women of Our Time)

The first group that Golda Meir ever organized was called the American Young Sisters Society. Golda sent out invitations and even rented a room for this meeting.

She was only in the fourth grade!

Our Golda is full of little known events like this, so indicative of the character of Golda Meir. The story moves quickly and provides colorful details of the places that she called home. Adler emphasizes Golda's childhood and youth in Russia and America, the strength she drew from her family and her dedication to the pursuit of peace as Israel's Prime Minister.

McAuley, Karen. *Golda Meir.* Chelsea House, 1985. 112 pp. Ill. (World Leaders Past and Present)

MICHELANGELO (Artist)
Lace, William W. *Michelangelo.* Lucent Books, 1993. 112 pp. (The Importance of ...)
McLanathan, Richard. *Michelangelo.* Abrams, 1993. 92 pp. Ill. (First Impressions)

Ventura, Piero. *Michelangelo's World.* Putnam, 1989. 48 pp. Ill.
The narrator of this story is an old, old man, preparing his tomb and reflecting on a long and full life.

The man is Michelangelo, telling his own life story in this cleverly written biography. Ventura brings the master to life, inviting us into his world with entertaining prose and lively illustrations. We learn of the effects of history on Michelangelo's life and work, and are introduced to the people he worked with and for.

Michelangelo's World includes photos of the artist's principal works as well as a chronology of major events in his life.

JAMES MONROE (U.S. President)
Bains, Rae. *James Monroe, Young Patriot.* Troll, 1986. 48 pp. Ill. (Easy Biographies: History)
Fitz-gerald, Christine M. *James Monroe: Fifth President of the United States.* Childrens Press, 1987. 100 pp. Ill. (Encyclopedia of Presidents)
Sandak, Cass R. *The Monroes.* Macmillan Children's Book Group, 1992. 48 pp. Ill. (First Families)
Wetzel, Charles. *James Monroe.* Chelsea House, 1989. 112 pp. Ill. (World Leaders Past and Present)
*Numerous illustrations highlight this competent biography of Monroe, which focuses on his public life.

MARIA MONTESSORI (Educator)

O'Connor, Barbara. *Mammolina: A Story about Maria Montessori.* Carolrhoda, 1992. 60 pp. Ill. (Creative Minds)

Pollard, Michael. *Maria Montessori: The Italian Doctor Who Revolutionized Education for Young Children.* Gareth Stevens, 1990. 64 pp. Ill. (People Who Have Helped the World)

CARLOS MONTEZUMA (Native American Leader)

Iverson, Peter. *Carlos Montezuma.* Raintree, 1989. 32 pp. Ill. (American Indian Stories)

JULIA MORGAN (Architect)

James, Cary. *Julia Morgan: Architect.* Chelsea House, 1990. 112 pp. Ill. (American Women of Achievement)

GRANDMA MOSES (Artist)

Oneal, Zibby. *Grandma Moses: Painter of Rural America.* Viking, 1986. 64 pp. Ill. (Women of Our Time)

Tompkins, Nancy. *Grandma Moses: Painter.* Chelsea House, 1989. 112 pp. Ill. (American Women of Achievement)

LUCRETIA MOTT (Women's Rights Leader)

Sawyer, Kem K. *Lucretia Mott: Friend of Justice.* Discovery Enterprises, Ltd., 1991. 48 pp. Ill.

WOLFGANG AMADEUS MOZART (Composer)

Blakely, Roger K. *Wolfgang Amadeus Mozart.* Lucent Books, 1993. 112 pp. (The Importance of ...)

Gallaz, Christopher. *Mozart.* Creative Education, 1993. 32 pp. Ill.

Greene, Carol. *Wolfgang Amadeus Mozart: Musician.* Childrens Press, 1987. 152 pp. Ill. (People of Distinction)

Patton, Barbara W. *Introducing Wolfgang Amadeus Mozart.* Soundboard Books, 1991. 48 pp. Ill.

Sabin, Francene. *Mozart, Young Music Genius.* Troll, 1990. 48 pp. Ill. (Easy Biographies: Arts & Sciences)

Tames, Richard. *Wolfgang Amadeus Mozart.* Watts, 1991. 32 pp. Ill. (Lifetimes)

Young, Percy. *Mozart.* Watts, 1988. 32 pp. Ill. (Great Lives)

JOHN MUIR (Environmentalist)

Force, Eden. *John Muir*. Silver Burdett, 1990. 144 pp. Ill. (Pioneers in Change)

Tolan, Sally. *John Muir: Naturalist, Writer, and Guardian of the North American Wilderness*. Gareth Stevens, 1990. 64 pp. Ill. (People Who Have Helped the World)

ISAAC NEWTON (Scientist)

Ipsen, David C. *Isaac Newton: Reluctant Genius*. Enslow, 1985. 96 pp. Ill.

Tiner, John H. *Isaac Newton: The True Story of His Life*. Mott Media, 1975. 144 pp. Ill. (Sower)

FLORENCE NIGHTINGALE (Medical Leader)

Brown, Pam. *Florence Nightingale: The Determined Englishwoman who Founded Modern Nursing & Reformed Military Medicine*. Gareth Stevens, 1989. 64 pp. Ill. (People Who Have Helped the World)

Collins, David. *Florence Nightingale*. Mott Media, 1985. 160 pp. Ill. (Sower)

Colver, Anne. *Florence Nightingale: War Nurse*. Chelsea House, 1992. 80 pp. Ill. (Discovery Biographies)

Shore, Donna. *Florence Nightingale*. Silver Burdett, 1990. 104 pp. Ill. (What Made Them Great)

Siegel, Beatrice. *Faithful Friend: The Story of Florence Nightingale*. Scholastic, 1991. 144 pp. Ill.

Tames, Richard. *Florence Nightingale*. Watts, 1990. 32 pp. Ill. (Lifetimes)

RICHARD NIXON (U.S. President)

Barr, Roger. *Richard Nixon*. Lucent Books, 1992. 112 pp. (The Importance of ...)

Hargrove, Jim. *Richard M. Nixon: The Thirty-Seventh President*. Childrens Press, 1985. 128 pp. Ill. (People of Distinction)

Lillegard, Dee. *Richard Nixon: Thirty-seventh President of the United States*. Childrens Press, 1988. 100 pp. Ill. (Encyclopedia of Presidents)

Ripley, C. Peter. *Richard Nixon*. Chelsea House, 1987. 112 pp. Ill. (World Leaders Past and Present)

Sandak, Cass R. *The Nixons*. Macmillan Children's Book Group, 1992. 48 pp. Ill. (First Families)

ANNIE OAKLEY (Frontierswoman)
Graves, Charles P. *Annie Oakley*. Chelsea House, 1991. 80 pp. Ill. (Discovery Biographies)
Levine, Ellen. *Ready, Aim, Fire! The Real Adventures of Annie Oakley*. Scholastic, 1989. 144 pp. Ill.
Wilson, Ellen. *Annie Oakley*. Macmillan Children's Book Group, 1989. 192 pp. Ill.

SANDRA DAY O'CONNOR (U.S. Supreme Court Justice)
Deegan, Paul, and Bob Italia. *Sandra Day O'Connor*. Abdo & Daughters, 1992. 40 pp. (United States Supreme Court Library)
Gherman, Beverly. *Sandra Day O'Connor: Justice for All*. Viking, 1991. 64 pp. Ill. (Women of Our Time)
Huber, Peter. *Sandra Day O'Connor: Supreme Court Justice*. Chelsea House, 1990. 112 pp. Ill. (American Women of Achievement)
Macht, Norman. *Sandra Day O'Connor*. Chelsea House, 1992. 80 pp. Ill. (Junior World Biographies)
Woods, Harold and Geraldine. *Sandra Day O'Connor: Equal Justice*. Macmillan Children's Book Group, 1992. 112 pp. Ill. (People in Focus)

GEORGIA O'KEEFFE (Artist)
Berry, Michael. *Georgia O'Keeffe: Painter*. Chelsea House, 1988. 112 pp. Ill. (American Women of Achievement)
Gherman, Beverly. *Georgia O'Keeffe: The Wideness and Wonder of Her World*. Atheneum, 1986. 131 pp. Ill.
Peters, Gerald P., editor. *Georgia O'Keeffe*. Peters, 1990. 48 pp. Ill.

Turner, Robyn Montana. *Georgia O'Keeffe: Portraits of Women Artists for Children*. Little, Brown, 1991. 32 pp. Ill.

Sun Prairie, Wisconsin. How appropriate that Georgia O'Keeffe should be born in a place with such a picturesque name.

Robyn Turner opens the door on the life of this gifted painter in a book that tells us how the mind of an artist works. Turner offers a portrait of a woman who painted her feelings, who saw art everywhere, and who created paintings of bones because she thought they were "very lively subjects"!

Side by side with Turner's fascinating prose are full color reproductions of O'Keeffe's work, inspired by nature and her own internal responses to the world around her.

We develop an admiration for Georgia O'Keeffe's genius as well as an urge to find her work in a museum and lose ourselves in its loveliness.

OSCEOLA (Native American Leader)

Clark, Electa. *Osceola: Young Seminole Indian.* Macmillan Children's Book Group, 1989. 192 pp. Ill. (Childhood of Famous Americans)

Oppenheim, Joanne. *Osceola, Seminole Warrior.* Troll, 1979. 48 pp. Ill. (Native American Biographies)

Viola, Herman J. *Osceola.* Raintree, 1992. 32 pp. Ill. (American Indian Stories)

JESSE OWENS (Athlete)

Gentry, Tony. *Jesse Owens: Champion Athlete.* Chelsea House, 1990. 112 pp. Ill. (Black Americans of Achievement)
*A competent biography enhanced by many photos of this magnificent athlete in action.

Green, Carl R., and William Sanford. *Jesse Owens.* Macmillan Children's Book Group, 1992. 48 pp. Ill. (Sports Immortals)

Rennert, Rick. *Jesse Owens.* Chelsea House, 1992. 79 pp. Ill. (Junior World Biographies)

Sabin, Francene. *Jesse Owens, Olympic Hero.* Troll, 1986. 48 pp. Ill. (Easy Biographies: Sports Figures)

SATCHEL PAIGE (Athlete)

Macht, Norm. *Satchel Paige.* Chelsea House, 1991. 64 pp. Ill. (Baseball Legends)

Shirley, David. *Satchel Paige: Baseball Great.* Chelsea House, 1993. 112 pp. Ill. (Black Americans of Achievement)

QUANAH PARKER (Native American Leader)

Wilson, Claire. *Quanah Parker: Comanche Chief.* Chelsea House, 1992. 112 pp. Ill. (North American Indians of Achievement)

ROSA PARKS (Civil Rights Leader)

Brandt, Keith. *Rosa Parks: Fight for Freedom.* Troll, 1993. 48 pp. Ill.

Celsi, Teresa. *Rosa Parks and the Montgomery Bus Boycott.* Millbrook, 1992. 32 pp. Ill. (Gateway Civil Rights)

Jackson, Garnet N. *Rosa Parks: Hero of Our Time.* Modern Curriculum Press, 1992. Ill.

Parks, Rosa, with Jim Haskins. *Rosa Parks: My Story.* Dial, 1992. 192 pp. Ill.

LOUIS PASTEUR (Scientist)

Bains, Rae. *Louis Pasteur.* Troll, 1985. 32 pp. Ill. (Famous People Library)

Birch, Beverly. *Louis Pasteur: The Scientist Who Found the Cause of Infectious Disease and Invented Pasteurization.* Gareth Stevens, 1989. 68 pp. Ill. (People Who Have Helped the World)

Morgan, Nina. *Louis Pasteur.* Watts, 1992. 48 pp. Ill. (Pioneers of Science)

Sabin, Francene. *Louis Pasteur, Young Scientist.* Troll, 1983. 48 pp. Ill. (Easy Biographies: Arts & Sciences)

Tames, Richard. *Louis Pasteur.* Watts, 1990. 32 pp. Ill. (Lifetimes)

Tiner, John H. *Louis Pasteur.* Mott Media, 1990. 176 pp. Ill. (Sower)

ROBERT PEARY (Explorer)

Kent, Zachary. *The Story of Admiral Peary at the North Pole.* Childrens Press, 1988. 32 pp. Ill. (Cornerstones of Freedom)

BILL PEET (Illustrator)

Peet, Bill. *Bill Peet: An Autobiography.* Houghton Mifflin, 1989. 190 pp. Ill.

MATTHEW PERRY (Explorer)

Blumberg, Rhoda. *Commodore Perry in the Land of the Shogun.*
Lothrop, Lee and Shepard, 1985. 128 pp. Ill.
*This fascinating account of Perry's expedition to "open" Japan
is rich in cultural detail.

Kuhn, Ferdinand. *Commodore Perry and the Opening of Japan.*
Random House, 1955. Ill.

KING PHILIP (Native American Leader)

Fradin, Dennis B. *King Philip: Indian Leader.* Enslow, 1990. 48
pp. Ill. (Colonial Profiles)

Roman, Joseph. *King Philip: Wampanoag Rebel.* Chelsea House,
1992. 112 pp. Ill. (North American Indians of Achievement)

PABLO PICASSO (Artist)

Beardsley, John. *Pablo Picasso.* Abrams, 1991. 92 pp. Ill. (First
Impressions)

Giraudy, Daniele, editor. *Pablo Picasso: The Minotaur, An Art
Play Book.* Abrams, 1988. 32 pp. Ill.

SUSAN LAFLESCHE PICOTTE (Native American Leader)

Brown, Marion M. *Susette LaFlesche: Advocate for Native
American Rights.* Childrens Press, 1992. 112 pp. Ill. (People of
Distinction)

Ferris, Jeri. *Native American Doctor: The Story of Susan LaFlesche
Picotte.* Carolrhoda, 1991. 88 pp. Ill.

Susan LaFlesche was the first Native American woman to
graduate from medical school. Ferris ably conveys LaFlesche's
determination and courage as well as her dedication to her people,
the Omaha Indians. We suffer with LaFlesche Picotte as she
endures the hardships of frontier life. We celebrate with her as she
realizes her dream of opening a hospital for her people. We respect
her humility as well as her ability.

It is interesting to note that the early influences that directed the
course of LaFlesche Picotte's life are identical to those which can
affect young people today: family, a special teacher, an inspira-

tional role model (in this case, a female physician), supportive friends, a rich heritage, and LaFlesche's own inner strength.

ALLAN PINKERTON (Detective)

Wormser, Richard. *Allan Pinkerton: America's First Private Eye.* Walker, 1990. 119 pp. Ill.

This is a fast-paced biography that sometimes reads like a Wild West novel. The Dalton Brothers, Frank and Jesse James and other ornery individuals figure prominently in the life story of America's first private eye.

The book is full of paradoxes. For instance, Pinkerton was an ardent abolitionist who firmly believed in the law, but HE broke it to fight slavery. Although his work in private investigation is his primary claim to fame, he would prefer to be remembered for his struggle against slavery.

Wormser's book on Pinkerton is full of interesting details that transport the reader into Pinkerton's fascinating world.

MARCO POLO (Explorer)

Austin, James, and Bob Italia. *Marco Polo.* Abdo & Daughters, 1992. 32 pp. Ill. (Explorers of the Past and Present)

Graves, Charles P. *Marco Polo.* Chelsea House, 1991. 96 pp. Ill. (Junior World Explorers)

Greene, Carol. *Voyager to the Orient.* Childrens Press, 1987. 112 pp. Ill. (People of Distinction)

Humble, Richard. *Travels of Marco Polo.* Watts, 1990. 32 pp. Ill. (Exploration Through the Ages)

Adventuring with Marco Polo means cleansing our minds of twentieth century clutter and transporting our imaginations to a very long time ago. The wonderful color illustrations in this biography help us picture the 13th century world that Marco Polo set out to explore. The great volume of facts may tend to overwhelm the young reader; this might be a good book to read with an adult.

Humble does provide a glossary of important words and names
that help us mentally organize the details of Marco Polo's far-
reaching explorations.

Italia, Bob. *Marco Polo*. Abdo & Daughters, 1990. 32 pp. Ill.
(Explorers of the Past and Present)

Kent, Zachary. *Marco Polo: Traveler to Central and Eastern Asia*.
Childrens Press, 1992. 128 pp. Ill. (The World's Great Explorers)

Noonan, Jon. *Marco Polo*. Macmillan Children's Book Group,
1993. 48 pp. Ill. (The Explorers)

Rosen, Mike. *The Travels of Marco Polo*. Watts, 1989. 32 pp. Ill.
(Great Journeys)

PONTIAC (Native American Leader)

Fleischer, Jane. *Pontiac, Chief of the Ottawas*. Troll, 1979. 84 pp.
Ill. (Native American Biographies)

Wheeler, Jill. *The Story of Pontiac*. Abdo & Daughters, 1989. 23
pp. Ill. (Famous Native American Leaders)

BEATRIX POTTER (Author)

Aldis, Dorothy. *Nothing is Impossible-The Story of Beatrix Potter*.
Peter Smith, 1988. Ill.

Buchan, Elizabeth. *Beatrix Potter*. Warne, Frederick & Co., 1991.
64 pp.

Collins, David R. *The Country Artist: A Story about Beatrix Potter*.
Carolrhoda, 1989. 56 pp. Ill. (Creative Minds)

COLIN POWELL (Military Leader)

Brown, Warren. *Colin Powell: Military Leader*. Chelsea House,
1992. 112 pp. Ill. (Black Americans of Achievement)

Everston, Jonathan. *Colin Powell*. Dell, 1991. 96 pp. Ill.
(Changing Our World Biographies)

Haskins, Jim. *Colin Powell: A Biography*. Scholastic, 1992. 100 pp.
Ill.

Reef, Catherine. *Colin Powell*. Childrens Press, 1992. 80 pp. Ill.
(African-American Soldiers)

RONALD REAGAN (U.S. President)

Kent, Zachary. *Ronald Reagan: Fortieth President of the United States.* Childrens Press, 1989. 100 pp. Ill. (Encyclopedia of Presidents)

Sandak, Cass R. *The Reagans.* Macmillan Children's Book Group, 1993. 48 pp. Ill. (First Families)

Slavia, Ed. *Ronald Reagan.* Chelsea House, 1991. 112 pp. Ill. (World Leaders Past and Present)

PAUL REVERE (Colonial American)

Brandt, Keith. *Paul Revere: Son of Liberty.* Troll, 1982. 48 pp. Ill. (Easy Biographies: History)

Forbes, Esther. *America's Paul Revere.* Houghton Mifflin, 1990. 48 pp. Ill.

Fritz, Jean. *And Then What Happened, Paul Revere?* Putnam, 1973. 48 pp. Ill.

Graves, Charles P. *Paul Revere.* Chelsea House, 1991. 80 pp. Ill. (Discovery Biographies)

Lee, Martin. *Paul Revere.* Watts, 1987. 96 pp. Ill.

Milton, Joyce. *The Story of Paul Revere: Messenger of Liberty.* Dell, 1990. 108 pp. Ill. (Yearling Biographies)

Stevenson, Augusta. *Paul Revere: Boston Patriot.* Macmillan Children's Book Group, 1986. 192 pp. Ill. (Childhood of Famous Americans)

SALLY RIDE (Astronaut)

Blacknall, Carolyn. *Sally Ride: America's First Woman in Space.* Macmillan Children's Book Group, 1984. 78 pp. Ill. (Taking Part)

Ride, Sally, and Susan Okie. *To Space and Back.* Lothrop, Lee and Shepard, 1986. 96 pp. Ill.
*This well-illustrated book provides a captivating account in non-technical language of America's first woman astronaut.

Verheyden-Hilliard, Mary Ellen. *Scientist and Astronaut: Sally Ride.* Equity Institute, 1985. 31 pp. Ill. (American Women in Science)

DIEGO RIVERA (Artist)

Cockcroft, James D. *Diego Rivera*. Chelsea House, 1991. 112 pp. Ill. (Hispanics of Achievement)

Gleiter, Jan, and Kathleen Thompson. *Diego Rivera*. Raintree, 1989. 32 pp. Ill. (Hispanic Stories)

Hargrove, Jim. *Diego Rivera: Mexican Muralist*. Childrens Press, 1990. 128 pp. Ill. (People of Distinction)

Neimark, Anne E. *Diego Rivera, Artist of the People*. Harper Collins Childrens Books, 1992. 128 pp. Ill.

PAUL ROBESON (Singer/Actor)

Ehrlich, Scott. *Paul Robeson: Singer and Actor*. Chelsea House, 1988. 120 pp. Ill. (Black Americans of Achievement)

JACKIE ROBINSON (Athlete)

Alvarez, Mark. *The Official Baseball Hall of Fame Story of Jackie Robinson*. Simon & Schuster, 1989. 96 pp. Ill.

Brandt, Keith. *Jackie Robinson, A Life of Courage*. Troll, 1992. 48 pp. Ill. (Easy Biographies: Sports Figures)

Cohen, Barbara. *Thank You, Jackie Robinson*. Lothrop, Lee & Shepard, 1988. Ill.

Davidson, Margaret. *The Story of Jackie Robinson: Bravest Man in Baseball*. Dell, 1988. 96 pp. Ill. (Yearling Biographies)

Denenberg, Barry. *Stealing Home: The Story of Jackie Robinson*. Scholastic, 1990. 128 pp.

Diamond, Arthur. *Jackie Robinson*. Lucent Books, 1992. 112 pp. (The Importance of ...)

Grabowski, John. *Jackie Robinson*. Chelsea House, 1991. 64 pp. Ill. (Baseball Legends)

Green, Carl R., and William Sanford. *Jackie Robinson*. Macmillan Children's Book Group, 1992. 48 pp. Ill. (Sports Immortals)

O'Conner, Jim. *Jackie Robinson and the Story of All-Black Baseball*. Random House, 1989. 48 pp. Ill.
*This book concerns itself with a brief biography of Robinson and a history of the black baseball leagues.

Sabin, Francene. *Jackie Robinson*. Troll, 1985. 32 pp. Ill. (Famous People Library)

Scott, Richard. *Jackie Robinson: Baseball Great*. Chelsea House, 1987. 112 pp. Ill. (Black Americans of Achievement)

*An excellent portrait of Robinson's struggle and courage as the first black Major Leaguer.

Shorto, Russell. *Jackie Robinson and the Breaking of the Color Barrier*. Millbrook, 1992. 32 pp. Ill. (Gateway Civil Rights)

WILL ROGERS (Entertainer)

Sonneborn, Elizabeth. *Will Rogers: Cherokee Entertainer*. Chelsea House, 1993. 112 pp. Ill. (North American Indians of Achievement)

ELEANOR ROOSEVELT(Humanitarian, Diplomat, U.S.First Lady)

Faber, Doris. *Eleanor Roosevelt: First Lady of the World*. Viking, 1986. 64 pp. Ill. (Women of Our Time)

McAuley, Karen. *Eleanor Roosevelt*. Chelsea House, 1987. 112 pp. Ill. (World Leaders Past and Present)

Sabin, Francene. *Young Eleanor Roosevelt*. Troll, 1989. 48 pp. Ill. (Easy Biographies: Women in History)

Toor, Rachel. *Eleanor Roosevelt: Diplomat and Humanitarian*. Chelsea House, 1989. 112 pp. Ill. (American Women of Achievement)

Weidt, Maryann N. *Stateswoman to the World: A Story about Eleanor Roosevelt*. Carolrhoda, 1990. 64 pp. Ill. (Creative Minds)

Weil, Ann. *Eleanor Roosevelt*. Macmillan Children's Book Group, 1989. 192 pp. Ill. (Childhood of Famous Americans)

Whitney, Sharon. *Eleanor Roosevelt*. Watts, 1983. 113 pp. Ill.

Living side-by-side with such an imposing presence as Franklin Delano Roosevelt was surely no easy task, but it brought out the best in Eleanor. A lesser person would have been swallowed up in F.D.R.'s shadow, but Mrs. Roosevelt used her position as First Lady to embrace the world.

Sharon Whitney offers a very thorough portrait of Eleanor Roosevelt in this biography. She chronicles Eleanor's highs and lows, includes many personal details, and helps the reader appreciate the sensitivity and strength of character of this inspiring woman.

Winner, David. *Eleanor Roosevelt: Defender of Human Rights & Democracy.* Gareth Stevens, 1992. 68 pp. Ill. (People Who Have Helped the World)

FRANKLIN DELANO ROOSEVELT (U.S. President)

Feinberg, Barbara S. *Franklin D. Roosevelt, Gallant President.* Lothrop, Lee and Shepard, 1981. 94 pp. Ill.

Freedman, Russell. *Franklin Delano Roosevelt.* Houghton Mifflin, 1990. 208 pp. Ill.

Franklin Delano Roosevelt was one of those presidents about whom people just have to have an opinion. After reading Russell Freedman's biography of F.D.R., we can decide for ourselves whether he was a fiend or a godsend. Regardless of our opinion, we cannot deny that Roosevelt had an enormous impact on our country's direction.

Full of photos and details, this book follows F.D.R. through his privileged youth, his early days in politics and his eventful career in government. Personal anecdotes reveal a sensitivity to human suffering that would eventually move F.D.R. to make decisions that would change America forever.

Freedman ably conveys the president's trademark exuberance and determination, even during the most trying times in America's history.

A chapter on "Places to Visit" and an F.D.R. photo album complete this well-researched biography.

Hacker, Jeffrey. *Franklin D. Roosevelt.* Cavendish, Marshall, 1991. 176 pp. Ill.

Israel, Fred L. *Franklin Delano Roosevelt.* Chelsea House, 1985. 112 pp. Ill. (World Leaders Past and Present)

Italia, Bob. *Franklin D. Roosevelt.* Abdo & Daughters, 1990. 32 pp. Ill. (World War II Leaders)

Osinski, Alice. *Franklin D. Roosevelt: Thirty-second President of the United States.* Childrens Press, 1987. 100 pp. Ill. (Encyclopedia of Presidents)

Sandak, Cass R. *The Franklin Roosevelts*. Macmillan Children's Book Group, 1992. 48 pp. Ill. (First Families)

Shebar, Sharon. *Franklin D. Roosevelt and the New Deal*. Childrens Press, 1988. 144 pp. Ill. (Profiles of Great Americans for Young People: Henry Steele Commager's Americans)

THEODORE ROOSEVELT (U.S. President)

Beach, James C. *Theodore Roosevelt*. Chelsea House, 1991. 80 pp. Ill. (Discovery Biographies)

Force, Eden. *Theodore Roosevelt*. Watts, 1987. 94 pp. Ill.

Fritz, Jean. *Bully for You, Teddy Roosevelt!*. Putnam, 1991. 128 pp. Ill.

Here's another "bully" offering by noted young people's author Jean Fritz. Fritz employs lively prose worthy of the hero of San Juan hill. She leads us from his early days as a sickly, timid child to his triumphs as a world leader and charismatic public figure.

Even the **notes** Fritz includes at the end of the book are written with creativity.

This is a marvelous addition to Jean Fritz's impressive collection of works.

Kent, Zachary. *Theodore Roosevelt: Twenty-sixth President of the United States*. Childrens Press, 1988. 100 pp. Ill. (Encyclopedia of Presidents)

*An excellent account of Roosevelt's life and career, enhanced by many exciting photographs.

Markham, Lois. *Theodore Roosevelt*. Chelsea House, 1985. 112 pp. Ill. (World Leaders Past and Present)

Parks, Edd W. *Teddy Roosevelt: All-Round Boy*. Macmillan Children's Book Group, 1989. 192 pp. Ill. (Childhood of Famous Americans)

Sabin, Louis. *Teddy Roosevelt, Rough Rider*. Troll, 1986. 48 pp. Ill. (Easy Biographies: History)

Sandak, Cass R. *The Theodore Roosevelts*. Macmillan Children's Book Group, 1991. 48 pp. Ill. (First Families)

Whitelaw, Nancy. *Theodore Roosevelt Takes Charge*. Whitman, 1991. 176 pp.

BETSY ROSS (Colonial American)

Weil, Ann. *Betsy Ross: Designer of Our Flag*. Macmillan Children's Book Group, 1986. 192 pp. Ill. (Childhood of Famous Americans)

WILMA RUDOLPH (Athlete)

Biracree, Tom. *Wilma Rudolph: Champion Athlete*. Chelsea House, 1988. 112 pp. Ill. (American Women of Achievement)

BERTRAND RUSSELL (Philosopher)

Redpath, Ann, editor. *Bertrand Russell*. Creative Education, 1985. 32 pp. Ill. (Living Philosophies)

BILL RUSSELL (Athlete)

Shapiro, Miles. *Bill Russell: Basketball Great*. Chelsea House, 1991. 112 pp. Ill. (Black Americans of Achievement)

BABE RUTH (Athlete)

Bains, Rae. *Babe Ruth*. Troll, 1985. 32 pp. Ill. (Famous People Library)

Brandt, Keith. *Babe Ruth, Home Run Hero*. Troll, 1985. 48 pp. Ill. (Easy Biographies: Sports Figures)

Eisenberg, Lisa. *The Story of Babe Ruth: Baseball's Great Legend*. Dell, 1990. 96 pp. Ill. (Yearling Biographies)

Green, Carl R., and William Sanford. *Babe Ruth*. Macmillan Children's Book Group, 1992. 48 pp. Ill. (Sports Immortals)

Macht, Norm. *Babe Ruth*. Chelsea House, 1991. 64 page. Ill. (Baseball Legends)

Van Riper, Guernsey, Jr. *Babe Ruth: One of Baseball's Greatest*. Macmillan Children's Book Group, 1986. 192 pp. Ill. (Childhood of Famous Americans)

FLORENCE SABIN (Medical Leader)

Kronstadt, Janet. *Florence Sabin: Medical Researcher*. Chelsea House, 1990. 112 pp. Ill. (American Women of Achievement)

*A readable account of this researcher, humanitarian, educator, and doctor.

SACAJAWEA (Native American Leader)

Brown, Marion M. *Sacajawea: Indian Interpreter to Lewis and Clark*. Childrens Press, 1988. 128 pp. Ill. (People of Distinction)

Jassem, Kate. *Sacajawea, Wilderness Guide*. Troll, 1979. 48 pp. Ill. (Native American Biographies)

Rowland, Della. *The Story of Sacajawea: Guide to Lewis and Clark*. Dell, 1989. 96 pp. Ill. (Yearling Biographies)

Seymour, Flora W. *Sacajawea: American Pathfinder*. Macmillan Children's Book Group, 1991. 192 page. Ill. (Childhood of Famous Americans)

ANWAR EL-SADAT(World Leader)

Aufderheide, P. *Anwar Sadat*. Chelsea House, 1985. 112 pp. Ill. (World Leaders Past and Present)

Rosen, Deborah N. *Anwar el-Sadat: A Man of Peace*. Childrens Press, 1986. 128 pp. Ill. (People of Distinction)

JONAS SALK (Medical Leader)

Curson, Marjorie. *Jonas Salk*. Silver Burdett, 1990. 144 pp. Ill. (Pioneers in Change)

Hargrove, James. *The Story of Jonas Salk and the Discovery of the Polio Vaccine*. Childrens Press, 1990. 32 pp. Ill. (Cornerstones of Freedom)

CARL SANDBURG (Author)

Hacker, Jeffrey H. *Carl Sandburg*. Watts, 1984. 128 pp. Ill.

Mitchell, Barbara. *"Good Morning, Mr. President": A Story about Carl Sandburg*. Carolrhoda, 1988. 56 pp. Ill. (Creative Minds)

Sandburg, Carl. *Prairie-Town Boy*. Harcourt Brace Jovanovich, 1990. 208 pp. Ill.

ALBERT SCHWEITZER(Humanitarian)

Bentley, James. *Albert Schweitzer: The Doctor Who Gave Up a Brilliant Career to Serve the People of Africa*. Gareth Stevens, 1989. 64 pp. Ill. (People Who Have Helped the World)

Cranford, Gail. *Albert Schweitzer*. Silver Burdett, 1990. 104 pp. Ill. (What Made Them Great)
Redpath, Ann, editor. *Albert Schweitzer*. Creative Education, 1985. 32 pp. Ill. (Living Philosophies)

SEQUOYAH (Native American Leader)

Klausner, Janet. *Sequoyah's Gift: A Portrait of the Cherokee Leader*. Harper Collins Childrens Books, 1993. 128 pp. Ill.
Oppenheim, Joanne. *Sequoyah, Cherokee Hero*. Troll, 1979. 48 pp. Ill. (Native American Biographies)
Wheeler, Jill. *The Story of Sequoyah*. Abdo & Daughters, 1989. 32 pp. Ill. (Famous Native American Leaders)

FR. JUNIPERO SERRA (Religious Leader)

Dolan, Sean. *Junipero Serra*. Chelsea House, 1991. 112 pp. Ill. (Hispanics of Achievement)
Duque, Sarah. *Sally and Fr. Serra*. Tabor, 1987. 104 pp. Ill.
Gleiter, Jan, and Kathleen Thompson. *Junipero Serra*. Raintree, 1989. 32 pp. Ill. (Hispanic Stories)
White, Florence Meiman. *The Story of Junipero Serra: Brave Adventurer*. Dell, 1987. 96 pp. Ill. (Yearling Biographies)

DR. SEUSS (THEODOR GEISEL) (Author)

Wheeler, Jill. *Dr. Seuss*. Abdo & Daughters, 1992. 32 pp. Ill. (The Young at Heart)

WILLIAM SHAKESPEARE (Author)

Turner, Dorothy. *William Shakespeare*. Watts, 1985. 32 pp. Ill. (Great Lives)

SITTING BULL (Native American Leader)

Bernotas, Bob. *Sitting Bull: Chief of the Sioux*. Chelsea House, 1992. 112 pp. Ill. (North American Indians of Achievement)
Eisenberg, Lisa. *The Story of Sitting Bull: Great Sioux Chief*. Dell, 1991. 96 pp. Ill. (Yearling Biographies)
Fleischer, Jane. *Sitting Bull, Warrior of the Sioux*. Troll, 1979. 48 pp. Ill. (Native American Biographies)
Hook, John. *Sitting Bull and the Plains Indians*. Watts, 1987. 64 pp. Ill.

Smith, Kathy B. *Sitting Bull.* Messner, 1989. 24 pp. Ill. (Great Americans)

Stein, R. Conrad. *The Story of Little Bighorn.* Childrens Press, 1983. 32 pp. Ill.

Viola, Herman J. *Sitting Bull.* Raintree, 1989. 32 pp. Ill. (American Indian Stories)

Wheeler, Jill. *The Story of Sitting Bull.* Abdo & Daughters, 1989. 32 pp. Ill. (Famous Native American Leaders)

SQUANTO (Native American Leader)

Bulla, Clyde R. *Squanto, Friend of the Pilgrims.* Scholastic, 1985. 112 pp. Ill.

Dubowski, Cathy E. *The Story of Squanto, First Friend to the Pilgrims.* Dell, 1990. 96 pp. Ill. (Yearling Biographies)

Jassem, Kate. *Squanto, The Pilgrim Adventure.* Troll, 1979. 48 pp. Ill. (Native American Biographies)

Ziner, Feenie. *Squanto.* Linnet Books, 1988. 158 pp.

HARRIET BEECHER STOWE (Author)

Ash, Maureen. *The Story of Harriet Beecher Stowe.* Childrens Press, 1990. 32 pp. Ill. (Cornerstones of Freedom)

Bland, Celia. *Harriet Beecher Stowe.* Chelsea House, 1993. 80 pp. Ill. (Junior World Biographies)

Jakoubek, Robert. *Harriet Beecher Stowe.* Chelsea House, 1989. 112 pp. Ill. (American Women of Achievement)

IDA M. TARBELL (Journalist)

Paradis, Adrian A. *Ida M. Tarbell: Pioneer Woman Journalist & Biographer.* Childrens Press, 1985. 120 pp. Ill. (People of Distinction)

TECUMSEH (Native American Leader)

Cwiklik, Robert. *Tecumseh: Shawnee Rebel.* Chelsea House, 1993. 112 pp. Ill. (North American Indians of Achievement)

Fleischer, Jane. *Tecumseh, Shawnee War Chief.* Troll, 1979. 48 pp. Ill. (Native American Biographies)

Kent, Zachary. *Tecumseh.* Childrens Press, 1992. 32 pp. Ill. (Cornerstones of Freedom)

Shorto, Russell. *Tecumseh and the Dream of an American Indian Nation.* Silver Burdett, 1989. 136 pp. Ill.

MOTHER TERESA (Humanitarian)

Clucas, Joan. *Mother Teresa.* Chelsea House, 1988. 112 pp. Ill. (World Leaders Past and Present)

Giff, Patricia Reilly. *Mother Teresa: Sister to the Poor.* Viking, 1986. 64 pp. Ill. (Women of Our Time)

Gray, Charlotte. *Mother Teresa: Her Mission to Serve God by Caring for the Poor.* Gareth Stevens, 1989. 64 pp. Ill. (People Who Have Helped the World)

Holland, Margaret. *Mother Teresa.* Willowisp Press, 1992. 48 pp. Ill. (People Who Shape Our World)

Lazo, Caroline. *Mother Teresa.* Macmillan Childrens Book Group, 1993. 64 pp. Ill. (Peacemakers)

Leigh, Vanora. *Mother Teresa.* Watts, 1986. 32 pp. Ill.

Mohan, Claire J. *Mother Teresa's Someday: The Young Life of Mother Teresa of Calcutta.* Young Sparrow Press, 1990. 60 pp. Ill.

Pond, Mildred. *Mother Teresa.* Chelsea House, 1992. 80 pp. Ill. (Junior World Biographies)

Tames, Richard. *Mother Teresa.* Watts, 1990. 32 pp. Ill. (Lifetimes)

Watson, D. Jeanene. *Teresa of Calcutta.* Mott Media, 1984. 172 pp. Ill. (Sower)

Wheeler, Jill. *Mother Teresa.* Abdo & Daughters, 1992. 32 pp. Ill. (Leading Ladies)

MARGARET THATCHER (World Leader)

Faber, Doris. *Margaret Thatcher: Britain's "Iron Lady."* Viking, 1985. 64 pp. Ill.

Intelligence, self-confidence and strength of will can take a woman anywhere, even to Great Britain's No. 10 Downing Street. (England's "White House")

That is what we learn from Margaret Thatcher's story. Doris Faber reveals the strong personality that helped carry this grocer's daughter to Parliament, and eventually to the Prime Minister's office.

Thatcher's success as well as her frustrations are dealt with honestly, including her struggle over the public's view of a "working mother" in government.

Foster, Leila M. *Margaret Thatcher: First Woman Prime Minister of Great Britain.* Childrens Press, 1990. 128 pp. Ill. (People of Distinction)

Garfinkel, Bernard. *Thatcher.* Chelsea House, 1985. 112 pp. Ill. (World Leaders Past and Present)

Hughes, Libby. *Margaret Thatcher: Madam Prime Minister.* Macmillan Children's Book Group, 1992. 112 pp. Ill. (People in Focus)

HENRY DAVID THOREAU (Author)

Burleigh, Robert. *A Man Named Thoreau.* Macmillan Children's Book Group, 1985. 48 pp. Ill.

*This excellent biography brings Thoreau and all his complexities to life through a poetic style.

Reef, Catherine. *Henry David Thoreau: A Neighbor to Nature.* Childrens Press, 1992. 72 pp. Ill. (Earth Keepers)

JIM THORPE (Athlete)

Bernotas, Bob. *Jim Thorpe: Sac and Fox Athlete.* Chelsea House, 1992. 112 pp. Ill. (North American Indians of Achievement)

Green, Carl R., and William R. Sanford. *Jim Thorpe.* Macmillan Children's Book Group, 1992. 48 pp. Ill. (Sports Immortals)

Richards, Gregory. *Jim Thorpe: World's Greatest Athlete.* Childrens Press, 1984. 112 pp. Ill. (People of Distinction)

Rivinus, Edward F. *Jim Thorpe.* Raintree, 1990. 32 pp. Ill. (American Indian Stories)

Santrey, Laurence. *Jim Thorpe, Young Athlete.* Troll, 1983. 48 pp. Ill. (Easy Biographies: Sports Figures)

Van Riper, Guernsey, Jr. *Jim Thorpe: Olympic Champion.* Macmillan Children's Book Group, 1986. 192 pp. Ill. (Childhood of Famous Americans)

LEE TREVINO (Athlete)
Gilbert, Tom. *Lee Trevino: Mexican-American Golfer.* Chelsea House, 1992. 112 pp. Ill. (Hispanics of Achievement)

HARRY S. TRUMAN (U.S. President)
Collins, David R. *Harry S. Truman.* Chelsea House, 1990. 80 pp. Ill. (Discovery Biographies)

Greenberg, Morrie. *Harry Truman: The Buck Stops Here.* Macmillan Children's Book Group, 1992. 112 pp. Ill. (People in Focus)

Hargrove, Jim. *Harry S. Truman: Thirty-third President of the United States.* Childrens Press, 1987. 100 pp. Ill. (Encyclopedia of Presidents)

Hudson, Wilma J. *Harry S. Truman: Missouri Farm Boy.* Macmillan Children's Book Group, 1992. 192 pp. Ill. (Childhood of Famous Americans)

Leavell, Perry. *Harry Truman.* Chelsea House, 1988. 112 pp. Ill. (World Leaders Past and Present)
*A concise, straightforward biography of Truman that is enhanced by many photographs.

O'Neal, Michael. *President Truman and the Atomic Bomb: Opposing Viewpoints.* Greenhaven, 1990. 112 pp. Ill.

Sandak, Cass R. *The Trumans.* Macmillan Children's Book Group, 1992. 48 pp. Ill. (First Families)

SOJOURNER TRUTH (Abolitionist)
Claflin, Edward B. *Sojourner Truth and the Struggle for Freedom.* Childrens Press, 1988. 144 pp. Ill. (Profiles of Great Americans for Young People: Henry Steele Commager's Americans)

Ferris, Jeri. *Walking the Road to Freedom: A Story about Sojourner Truth.* Carolrhoda, 1988. 64 pp. Ill. (Creative Minds)
*This inspirational book provides the reader with an in-depth look at Truth and her work as an abolitionist.

Krass, Peter. *Sojourner Truth: Anti-Slavery Activist.* Chelsea House, 1988. 112 pp. Ill. (Black Americans of Achievement)

Macht, Norman. *Sojourner Truth.* Chelsea House, 1992. 80 pp. Ill. (Junior World Biographies)

McKissack, Patricia and Fredrick. *Sojourner Truth: Ain't I a Woman?* Scholastic, 1992. 144 pp.

Shumante, Jane. *Sojourner Truth and the Voice of Freedom.*
Millbrook, 1992. 32 pp. Ill. (Gateway Civil Rights)

Taylor-Boyd, Susan. *Sojourner Truth: The Courageous Former Slave
Whose Eloquence Helped Promote Human Equality.* Gareth
Stevens, 1990. 64 pp. Ill. (People Who Have Helped the World)

HARRIET TUBMAN (Abolitionist)

Bains, Rae. *Harriet Tubman: The Road to Freedom.* Troll, 1982.
48 pp. Ill. (Easy Biographies: Women in History)

Bisson, Terry. *Harriet Tubman: Anti-Slavery Activist.* Chelsea
House, 1991. 112 pp. Ill. (Black Americans of Achievement)

Burns, Bree. *Harriet Tubman.* Chelsea House, 1992. 80 pp. Ill.
(Junior World Biographies)

Ferris, Jeri. *Go Free or Die: A Story about Harriet Tubman.*
Carolrhoda, 1988. 64 pp. Ill. (Creative Minds)

McGovern, Ann. *"Wanted Dead or Alive": The True Story of Harriet
Tubman.* Scholastic, 1991. 64 pp. Ill.

McMullan, Kate. *The Story of Harriet Tubman: Conductor of the
Underground Railroad.* Dell, 1991. 92 pp. Ill. (Yearling
Biographies)

Sabin, Francene. *Harriet Tubman.* Troll, 1985. 32 pp. Ill.
(Famous Americans Library)

Smith, Kathie B. *Harriet Tubman.* Messner, 1989. 24 pp. Ill.
(Great Americans)

Sterling, Dorothy. *Freedom Train: The Story of Harriet Tubman.*
Scholastic, 1987. 192 pp.

Taylor, M.W. *Harriet Tubman.* Chelsea House, 1990. 112 pp. Ill.
(Black Americans of Achievement)

DESMOND TUTU (Political Activist/Leader)

Winner, David. *Desmond Tutu: The Courageous and Eloquent
Archbishop Struggling Against Apartheid in South Africa.* Gareth
Stevens, 1989. 64 pp. Ill. (People Who Have Helped the World)

MARK TWAIN (Author)

Hargrove, Jim. *Mark Twain: The Story of Samuel Clemens.*
Childrens Press, 1984. 128 pp. Ill. (People of Distinction)

Mason, Miriam E. *Mark Twain: Young Writer.* Macmillan
Children's Book Group, 1991. 192 pp. Ill. (Childhood of
Famous Americans)
Sabin, Louis. *Young Mark Twain.* Troll, 1989. 48 pp. Ill. (Easy
Biographies: Arts & Sciences)

JULES VERNE (Author)

Quackenbush, Robert. *Who Said There's No Man on the Moon? A
Story of Jules Verne.* Prentice, 1985. 32 pp. Ill.
If biographies are meant to transport us through the lives of
famous people, we'd better don our running shoes for this trip. We
are in hot pursuit of Jules Verne, the 19th century author of
adventure and science fiction novels. Quackenbush keeps us moving
through Verne's story, lingering over details just long enough to
impress the reader with Verne's insight and creativity.
We are treated to whimsical cartoons that remind us how much
fun Verne must have had as he chased his imagination under,
around and above the world.
Quackenbush mentions many of the tales in which Verne
predicted space travel, the submarine, and other modern achievements: *20,000 Leagues Under the Sea, Journey to the Center of the
Earth, Five Weeks in a Balloon,* and others.

AMERIGO VESPUCCI (Explorer)
Alper, Ann. *Forgotten Voyager: The Story of Amerigo Vespucci.*
Carolrhoda, 1990. 80 pp. Ill. (Trailblazers)
Jaeger, Gerard. *Vespucci.* Creative Education, 1993. 32 pp. Ill.

LECH WALESA (Political Activist/Leader)
Craig, Mary. *Lech Walesa: The Leader of Solidarity and
Campaigner for Freedom and Human Rights in Poland.* Gareth
Stevens, 1990. 64 pp. Ill. (People Who Have Helped the World)
Kaye, Tony. *Lech Walesa: Polish Labor Leader.* Chelsea House,
1989. 120 pp. Ill. (World Leaders Past and Present)

RAOUL WALLENBERG (Humanitarian)

Nicholson, Michael and David Winner. *Raoul Wallenberg: The Swedish Diplomat Who Saved 100,000 Jews from the Nazi Holocaust before Mysteriously Disappearing*. Gareth Stevens, 1989. 64 pp. Ill. (People Who Have Helped the World)

BOOKER T. WASHINGTON (Educator)

McKissack, Patricia and Fredrick. *The Story of Booker T. Washington*. Childrens Press, 1991. 32 pp. Ill. (Cornerstones of Freedom)

Paterson, Lillie. *Booker T. Washington*. Chelsea House, 1991. 80 pp. Ill. (Discovery Biographies)

Schroeder, Alan. *Booker T. Washington: Educator*. Chelsea House, 1992. 112 pp. Ill. (Black Americans of Achievement)

GEORGE WASHINGTON (U.S. President)

Brandt, Keith. *George Washington*. Troll, 1985. 32 pp. Ill. (Famous Americans Library)

Bruns, Roger. *George Washington*. Chelsea House, 1987. 112 pp. Ill. (World Leaders Past and Present)

Camp, Norma C. *George Washington: Man of Courage and Prayer*. Mott Media, 1977. Ill. (Sower)

Cunliffe, Marcus. *George Washington and the Making of a Nation*. Troll, 1966. 160 pp. Ill. (American Heritage Jr. Library)

Fleming, Alice. *George Washington Wasn't Always Old*. Simon & Schuster, 1991. 71 pp. Ill.

Graff, Stewart. *George Washington: Father of Freedom*. Chelsea House, 1992. 80 pp. Ill. (Discovery Biographies)

Jacobs, W.J. *Washington*. Scribners, 1991. 42 pp. Ill.

Kent, Zachary. *George Washington: First President of the United States*. Childrens Press, 1986. 100 pp. Ill. (Encyclopedia of Presidents)

Krensky, Stephen. *George Washington: The Man Who Would Not Be King*. Scholastic, 1991. 64 pp.

Marshall, James. *George and Martha*. Houghton Mifflin, 1987.

Milton, Joyce. *George Washington: Quiet Hero*. Dell, 1988. 96 pp. Ill. (Yearling Biographies)

Osborne, Mary P. *George Washington: Leader of a New Nation.*
Dial Books for Young Readers, 1991. 96 pp. Ill.
*A well-illustrated and detailed account of the man who helped
start our nation.

Sandak, Cass R. *The Washingtons.* Macmillan Children's Book
Group, 1991. 48 pp. Ill. (First Families)

Santrey, Laurence. *George Washington: Young Leader.* Troll, 1982.
48 pp. Ill. (Easy Biographies: History)

Siegel, Beatrice. *George and Martha Washington at Home in New
York.* Four Winds, 1989. 80 pp. Ill.
*An excellent social history volume that gives Martha Washington
as much exposure as her famous husband. It vividly describes life
in the late 18th century in New York, the nation's first capital.

Smith, Kathie B. *George Washington.* Messner, 1987. 24 pp. Ill.
(Great Americans)

Stevenson, Augusta. *George Washington: Young Leader.* Macmillan
Children's Book Group, 1986. 192 pp. Ill. (Childhood of
Famous Americans)

MARTHA WASHINGTON (U.S. First Lady)

Anderson, LaVere. *Martha Washington: First Lady of the Land.*
Chelsea House, 1991. 80 pp. Ill. (Discovery Biographies)

Wagoner, Jean B. *Martha Washington: America's First First Lady.*
Macmillan Children's Book Group, 1986. 192 pp. Ill.
(Childhood of Famous Americans)

Waldrop, Ruth. *Martha Washington.* Rusk, 1987. 112 pp. Ill.
(First Ladies)

DANIEL WEBSTER (Statesman)

Allen, Robert. *Daniel Webster: Defender of the Union.* Mott
Media, 1989. 159 pp. Ill. (Sower)

NOAH WEBSTER (Author)

Collins, David. *Noah Webster: Master of Words.* Mott Media,
1989. 146 pp. Ill. (Sower)

Ferris, Jeri. *What Do You Mean? A Story about Noah Webster.*
Carolrhoda, 1988. 56 pp. Ill. (Creative Minds)

*This volume provides a fascinating and humorous portrait of a man who devoted his life to writing textbooks and dictionaries. The book is greatly enhanced by the illustrations.

PHILLIS WHEATLEY (Poet)

Richmond, Merle. *Phillis Wheatley: Poet*. Chelsea House, 1988. 112 pp. Ill. (American Women of Achievement)
*An excellent biography that makes use of many illustrations and much primary source material in its presentation of America's first black poet.
Sherrow, Victoria. *Phillis Wheatley*. Chelsea House, 1992. 80 pp. Ill. (Junior World Biographies)

E.B. WHITE (Author)

Collins, David R. *To the Point: A Story about E.B. White*. Carolrhoda, 1989. 56 pp. Ill. (Creative Minds)
Gherman, Beverly. *E.B. White: Some Writer!* Macmillan, 1992. 160 pp. Ill.

NARCISSA WHITMAN (Religious Leader)

Sabin, Louis. *Narcissa Whitman: Brave Pioneer*. Troll, 1982. 48 pp. Ill. (Easy Biographies: Women in History)

ELI WHITNEY (Inventor)

Latham, Jean. *Eli Whitney: Great Inventor*. Chelsea House, 1991. 80 pp. Ill. (Discovery Biographies)

LAURA INGALLS WILDER (Author)

Anderson, William. *Laura Ingalls Wilder*. Harper Collins Children's Books, 1992. 240 pp. Ill.
Giff, Patricia Reilly. *Laura Ingalls Wilder: Growing Up in the Little House*. Viking, 1987. 64 pp. Ill. (Women of Our Time)
Stine, Megan. *The Story of Laura Ingalls Wilder: Pioneer Girl*. Dell, 1992. 96 pp. Ill. (Yearling Biographies)
Wheeler, Jill. *Laura Ingalls Wilder*. Abdo & Daughters, 1992. 32 pp. Ill. (The Young at Heart)
Wilder, Laura Ingalls. *Little House on the Prairie*. Harper Collins Children's Books, 1961. 238 pp.

DANIEL HALE WILLIAMS (Medical Leader)

Patterson, Lillie. *Sure Hands, Strong Heart: The Life of Daniel Hale Williams*. Abingdon, 1982. 160 pp. Ill.

Born into a loving family, Daniel Hale Williams finds his life changed forever when his father passes away. He struggles on, however, and becomes a physician with a social conscience. This accomplished African-American surgeon crusaded for better medical care for black people, counseled and assisted many young black medical students, encouraged black women to enter the field of nursing, and helped found one of the first interracial hospitals in America.

With creativity and enthusiasm, Lillie Patterson shares Williams' story of tough beginnings, of courage and encouragement and of excitement and achievement.

Patterson's use of straightforward dialogue brings even more life to a story full of personal and professional detail.

WOODROW WILSON (U.S. President)

Leavell, Perry. *Woodrow Wilson: U.S. President*. Chelsea House, 1987. 120 pp. Ill. (World Leaders Past and Present)

Osinski, Alice. *Woodrow Wilson: Twenty-eighth President of the United States*. Childrens Press, 1989. 100 pp. Ill. (Encylopedia of Presidents)

SARAH WINNEMUCCA (Native American Leader)

Morrow, Mary Frances. *Sarah Winnemucca*. Raintree, 1989. 32 pp. Ill. (American Indian Stories)

Scordato, Ellen. *Sarah Winnemucca: Northern Paiute Writer and Diplomat*. Chelsea House, 1992. 112 pp. Ill. (North American Indians of Achievement)

FRANK LLOYD WRIGHT (Architect)

McDonough, Yona Z. *Frank Lloyd Wright*. Chelsea House, 1992. 112 pp. Ill. (Library of Biography)

WRIGHT BROTHERS (Inventors)

Haynes, Richard M. *The Wright Brothers*. Silver Burdett, 1992. 144 pp. Ill. (Pioneers in Change)

Hook, Jason. *The Wright Brothers*. Watts, 1989. 32 pp. Ill. (Great Lives)

Kaufman, Mervyn D. *The Wright Brothers: Kings of the Air*. Chelsea House, 1992. 80 pp. Ill. (Discovery Biographies)

Ludwig, Charles. *The Wright Brothers: They Gave Us Wings*. Mott Media, 1985. 192 pp. Ill. (Sower)

Sabin, Louis. *Wilbur and Orville Wright, The Flight to Adventure*. Troll, 1983. 48 pp. Ill. (Easy Biographies: Arts & Sciences)

Sobol, Donald J. *The Wright Brothers at Kitty Hawk*. Scholastic, 1987. 128 pp. Ill.

Stein, R. Conrad. *The Story of the Flight at Kitty Hawk*. Childrens Press, 1981. 32 pp. Ill. (Cornerstones of Freedom)

Stevenson, Augusta. *Wilbur and Orville Wright: Young Fliers*. Macmillan Children's Book Group, 1986. 192 pp. Ill. (Childhood of Famous Americans)

Tames, Richard. *The Wright Brothers*. Watts, 1990. 32 pp. Ill. (Lifetimes)

CHUCK YEAGER (Aviator)

Ayres, Carter M. *Chuck Yeager: Fighter Pilot*. Lerner, 1988. 48 pp. Ill. (Achievers)

Geffney, Timothy R. *Chuck Yeager: First Man to Fly Faster Than Sound*. Childrens Press, 1986. 128 pp. Ill. (People of Distinction)

Levinson, Nancy S. *Chuck Yeager: The Man Who Broke the Sound Barrier*. Walker, 1988. 133 pp.

BABE DIDRIKSON ZAHARIAS (Athlete)

Knudson, R.R. *Babe Didrikson: Athlete of the Century*. Viking, 1985. 64 pp. Ill. (Women of Our Time)

Lynn, Elizabeth. *Babe Didrikson Zaharias: Champion Athlete*. Chelsea House, 1989. 112 pp. Ill. (American Women of Achievement)

Sanford, William R., and Carl Green. *Babe Didrikson Zaharias*. Macmillan Children's Book Group, 1993. 48 pp. Ill. (Sports Immortals)

YOUNG PEOPLE BOOKS

Ordinary People in Extraordinary Situations
Real-life stories of individuals who found themselves in very special circumstances

SARAH AARONSOHN
Cowen, Ida, and Irene Gunther. *Spy for Freedom: The Story of Sarah Aaronsohn*. Lodestar/Dutton, 1985. 156 pp. Ill.

PRESTON BRUCE

Bruce, Preston. *From the Door of the White House*. Lothrop, Lee and Shepard, 1984. 176 pp. Ill.

As the White House doorman, Preston Bruce stood beside history makers, and he is very proud of that. With honesty and discretion, he takes us behind those famous doors into the private lives of some very public people.

Bruce's responsibilities at the White House were many, but his connection with five First Families, beginning with the Eisenhowers, extended beyond his professional role there. Bruce's descriptions of day-to-day life in the Executive Mansion are frank, compassionate, and insightful. He gives us the rare perspective of the ordinary person in an extraordinary situation.

ANTHONY BURNS

Hamilton, Virginia. *Anthony Burns: The Defeat and Triumph of a Fugitive Slave*. Knopf, 1988. 208 pp.

In this intense biography, Hamilton takes us inside Anthony Burns' soul. Yes, the author tells us how the recapture of this fugitive slave affected the world around him, but she also relates the loneliness and fear of Burns, the man. With great detail, she exposes the disdain of those who would return Burns to slavery, as well as the fervor of those who want to rescue him from this fate. Hamilton's focus, however, is Burns himself--his pain as well as the memories that sustain him during his struggle.

Hamilton includes selections from the Fugitive Slave Act of 1850, and a "cast of characters" that helps the reader mentally organize the players as Burns' story unfolds.

MICHAEL FOREMAN

Foreman, Michael. *War Boy: A Country Childhood*. Arcade/Little, Brown, 1990. 92 pp. Ill.

ANNE FRANK

Frank, Anne. *Diary of a Young Girl*. Bantam Doubleday, 1989. 258 pp.

Geis, Miep. *Anne Frank Remembered*. Simon & Schuster, 1987. 220 pp.

CHRISTA McAULIFFE

Billings, Charlene. *Christa McAuliffe: Pioneer Space Teacher*. Enslow, 1986. 64 pp. Ill. (Contemporary Women)

JOSEPH MERRICK

Drimmer, Frederick. *The Elephant Man*. Putnam, 1985. 146 pp. Ill.

Drimmer has written a fictional biography that traces the history of Joseph Merrick, afflicted with a disfiguring disease and called "The Elephant Man." The book is based on all available records, including Merrick's own account of his early life and the archives of the London Hospital where he died.

This is a compelling story of compassion as well as cruelty. The author, himself, is a widely known authority on human oddities. Among the black and white photographs included in this volume are several graphic pictures of Merrick. Young children may require some guidance in understanding the photos.

POCAHONTAS (Native American Leader)
O'Dell, Scott. *The Serpent Never Sleeps: A Novel of Jamestown and Pocahontas*. Fawcett, 1988.

HANNAH SZENES (or SENESH)
Atkinson, Linda. *In Kindling Flame: The Story of Hannah Senesh, 1921-1944*. Beech Tree, 1992. 214 pp. Ill.

Schur, Maxine. *Hannah Szenes: A Song of Light*. Jewish Publication Society, 1986. 112 pp. Ill.

This is a story of darkness and light, of desperation and courage, told with respect and admiration by Maxine Schur.

Born into an upper-middle-class family, Hannah Szenes was a self-confident woman who first tasted anti-Semitism in her native Hungary when she was 13 years old. In 1939, she found a new life in Palestine, then returned to Eastern Europe during World War II to save the lives of Jews. Hannah was captured, tortured, and eventually executed as a spy and a traitor. She was only 23 years old when she died.

The title of this biography is taken from a poem Szenes wrote in 1944; Schur wraps the inspiring story of this remarkable woman around several of her works. This Jewish heroine's ability to make such an enormous mark on history at such a young age just might empower a young reader to make a difference in his or her own world.

JONI EARECKSON TADA
Eareckson, Joni. *Joni*. Zondervan, 1976. 192 pp. Ill.

HILTGUNT ZASSENHAUS
Zassenhaus, Hiltgunt. *Walls: Resisting the Third Reich-One Woman's Story*. Beacon, 1993. 256 pp.

SARA ZYSKIND

Zyskind, Sara. *Stolen Years*. Lerner, 1982. 288 pp.

A striking prologue sets the stage in this biography. The author, Sara Zyskind, is 11 years old, living an ordinary, happy childhood. But her peaceful life will soon be shattered.

The year is 1939 and Sara is Jewish.

Stolen Years takes this devastating period in history and breaks it down, day by day, moment by moment. Zyskind recounts the details of her life in the Polish ghetto at Lodz, her experience at Auschwitz, her freedom from bondage at the war's end, and her eventual return to Israel.

Year by year, Zyskind shares the hardships she endured as well as the incidents of kindness that made life bearable.

Young People Biographies

JIM ABBOTT (Athlete)
Savage, Jeff. *Sports Great Jim Abbott*. Enslow, 1993. 64 pp. Ill. (Sports Great Books)

JOHN ADAMS (U.S. President)
Fredman, Lionel E., and Gerald Kurland. *John Adams: American Revolutionary Leader and President*. SamHar, 1973. 32 pp. (Outstanding Personalities)

Stefoff, Rebecca. *John Adams: Second President of the United States*. Garrett, 1988. 128 pp. Ill. (Presidents of the United States)

JOHN QUINCY ADAMS (U.S. President)
Greenblatt, Miriam. *John Quincy Adams: Sixth President of the United States*. Garrett, 1990. 128 pp. Ill. (Presidents of the United States)

Richards, Leonard L. *The Life and Times of John Quincy Adams*. Oxford, 1986. 256 pp.

SAMUEL ADAMS (Colonial American)
Miller, John C. *Sam Adams: Pioneer in Propaganda.* Stanford University Press, 1936. 437 pp. Ill.

JANE ADDAMS (Humanitarian)
Davis, Allen F. *American Heroine: The Life and Legend of Jane Addams.* Oxford, 1975. 362 pp.
Hovde, Jane. *Jane Addams.* Facts on File, 1989. 144 pp. Ill. (Makers of America)

LOUISA MAY ALCOTT (Author)
Johnston, Norma. *Louisa May: The World and Works of Louisa May Alcott.* Macmillan Children's Book Group, 1991. 224 pp. *An excellent volume depicting Alcott's life from childhood to her early death.

MUHAMMAD ALI (Athlete)
Conklin, Thomas. *Muhammad Ali: The Fight for Respect.* Millbrook Press, 1992. 104 pp. Ill. (New Directions)
Riccella, Christopher. *Muhammad Ali: World Heavyweight Boxing Champion.* Holloway House, 1992. 200 pp. Ill. (Black Americans)

ROALD AMUNDSEN (Explorer)
Brown, Warren. *Roald Amundsen and the Quest for the South Pole.* Chelsea House, 1992. 112 pp. Ill. (World Explorers)
Mason, Theodore K. *Two Against the Ice: Amundsen and Ellsworth.* Putnam, 1982.

MARIAN ANDERSON (Singer)

Patterson, Charles. *Marian Anderson.* Watts, 1988. 128 pp. Ill. (Impact Biographies)
Imagine possessing such a glorious singing voice that people around the world want to hear it. What a glamorous life! Traveling, singing, bowing to standing ovations. Perhaps.
Patterson's biography of Marian Anderson looks beyond the romantic. He gives the reader a realistic view of an artistic career. The stress of travel can take its toll; someone must pay for voice

lessons and plane tickets early in a vocalist's career; audiences do not always appreciate an artist's best efforts. And in Marian Anderson's case, racism further complicated an already complex professional lifestyle.

The contralto, however, always faced life with dignity and class. The support of family and church bolstered her determination to learn and to perform. Her undeniable talent opened important doors for her, and ultimately for many more talented African-Americans.

MAYA ANGELOU (Author, Poet)

Shuker, Nancy. *Maya Angelou.* Silver Burdett, 1990. 128 pp. Ill. (Genius! The Artist and the Process)

SUSAN B. ANTHONY (Women's Rights Leader)

Cooper, Ilene. *Susan B. Anthony.* Watts, 1984. 128 pp. (Impact Biography)

LOUIS ARMSTRONG (Musician)

Collier, James L. *Louis Armstrong: An American Success Story.* Macmillan Children's Book Group, 1985. 176 pp. Ill.

This is one of those rags to riches stories that would be totally unbelievable if it were not totally true.

Born into abject poverty, Louis Armstrong would have had nothing going for him if he had not grown up in a city made for music: New Orleans. Fate and good fortune provided opportunity; Louis supplied the talent, and the rest is jazz history.

Collier writes of the highs and lows of Armstrong's career with the expertise of an authority on jazz and the sensitivity of a "Satchmo" admirer. (Satchmo was Armstrong's well-known nickname.) Reading about this special brand of music and its master makes us want to run to the record museum and find some of Armstrong's work. Collier knew we would feel that way--he lists Armstrong's recordings and offers tips on how to find them.

Tanenhaus, Sam. *Louis Armstrong: Musician.* Holloway House, 1992. 200 pp. Ill. (Black Americans)

LEO BAECK (Humanitarian)

Neimark, Anne E. *One Man's Valor: Leo Baeck and the Holocaust.* Lodestar, 1986. 128 pp. Ill.

One mark of a true hero is his or her willingness to defy a clear and present danger. Leo Baeck knew that helping Jews escape Germany during the Second World War placed him at risk every day, every moment. But this rabbi and scholar's belief in what was right compelled him to put his religion into action.

Neimark tells this story with great respect for Baeck and his fortitude in the face of unspeakable injustice. The reader comes to admire him, to suffer with him, to care for him. This well-researched biography is a moving tribute to *One Man's Valor.*

CLARA BARTON (Medical Leader)

Dubowski, Cathy E. *Clara Barton: Healing the Wounds.* Silver Burdett, 1990. 160 pp. Ill. (The History of the Civil War)

Sloate, Susan. *Clara Barton: Founder of the American Red Cross.* Fawcett Book Group, 1990. 128 pp. (Great Lives Biography)

LUDWIG VAN BEETHOVEN (Composer)

Thompson, Wendy. *Ludwig Van Beethoven.* Viking, 1993. 48 pp. Ill. (Composer's World)

ALEXANDER GRAHAM BELL (Inventor)

Quiri, Patricia R. *Alexander Graham Bell.* Watts, 1991. 64 pp. Ill. (First Books-Biographies)

ELIEZER BEN-YEHUDA (Author)

Drucker, Malka. *Eliezer Ben-Yehuda: The Father of Modern Hebrew.* Lodestar, 1987. 96 pp. Ill.

What would motivate a man to resurrect a language lost for 2,000 years?

At the age of 20, Eliezer Ben-Yehuda decided it was time to revive Hebrew as a common spoken language for Jews around the world. He took on a monumental task; today's Hebrew dictionary contains over 100,000 words.

Traditional Jews opposed Ben-Yehuda's plan, wanting to reserve Hebrew for holy writing. Scientists were unconvinced that an ancient language could express new ideas and technology.

But Eliezer Ben-Yehuda persisted and prevailed. This is the intriguing story of how and why he did it.

LEONARD BERNSTEIN (Composer)
Deitch, Kenneth M. *Leonard Bernstein: America's Maestro*. Discovery Enterprises, Ltd., 1991. 48 pp. Ill.
*This book presents the life of this musical genius using original watercolor illustrations.

MARY McLEOD BETHUNE (Educator)
Poole, Bernice. *Mary McLeod Bethune: Educator and Civic Leader*. Holloway House, 1992. 200 pp. Ill. (Black Americans)
Wolfe, Rinna E. *Mary McLeod Bethune*. Watts, 1992. 64 pp. Ill. (First Books-Biographies)

ELIZABETH BLACKWELL (Medical Leader)
Wilson, Dorothy C. *I Will Be a Doctor! The Story of America's First Woman Physician*. Abingdon, 1983. 160 pp.

DANIEL BOONE (Frontiersman)
Cavan, Seamus. *Daniel Boone and the Opening of the Ohio Country*. Chelsea House, 1991. 111 pp. Ill. (World Explorers)
Lawlor, Laurie. *Daniel Boone*. Whitman, 1988. 160 pp. Ill.
*A detailed account of Boone's life as a frontiersman, this exciting adventure story erases many of the misconceptions associated with this amazing man.

JOHN BROWN (Abolitionist)
Graham, Lorenz. *John Brown: A Cry for Freedom*. Harper Collins Children's Books, 1980. 192 pp. Ill.

Scott, John A. *John Brown of Harpers Ferry*. Facts on File, 1988. 192 pp. Ill. (Makers of America)

PEARL BUCK (Author)

Schoen, Celin V. *Pearl Buck: Famed American Author of Oriental Stories*. SamHar, 1972. 32 pp. (Outstanding Personalities)

GEORGE BUSH (U.S. President)

Stefoff, Rebecca. *George H.W. Bush: Forty-first President of the United States*. Garrett, 1990. 128 pp. Ill. (Presidents of the United States)

Sufrin, Mark. *George Bush, The Story of the Forty-first President of the United States*. Delacourte, 1989. 107 pp. Ill.

Sullivan, George. *George Bush*. Messner, 1989. 128 pp. Ill. (In Focus Biographies)

RACHEL CARSON (Environmentalist)

Harlan, Judith. *Sounding the Alarm: A Biography of Rachel Carson*. Macmillan Children's Book Group, 1989. 128 pp. Ill. (People in Focus)

*A detailed biography that not only deals with Carson's career as a writer, but also captures the spirit with which Carson tried to implement environmental reforms.

Stwertka, Eve. *Rachel Carson*. Watts, 1991. 64 pp. Ill. (First Books-Biographies)

Wadsworth, Ginger. *Rachel Carson: Voice for the Earth*. Lerner, 1992. 128 pp. Ill. (Lerner Biographies)

JIMMY CARTER (U.S. President)

Richman, Daniel A. *James E. Carter: Thirty-ninth President of the United States*. Garrett, 1989. 121 pp. Ill. (Presidents of the United States)

*A well-written examination and analysis of Carter's personal and political life.

Smith, Betsy C. *Jimmy Carter, President*. Walker, 1986. 128 pp. Ill.

*An in-depth look at this most underrated man, this biography is a balanced, anecdotal portrayal of both his personal and political life.

GEORGE WASHINGTON CARVER (Scientist)

Coil, Suzanne M. *George Washington Carver*. Watts, 1990. 64 pp.
Ill. (First Books-Biographies)

Neyland, James. *George Washington Carver: Scientist and Educator*. Holloway House, 1992. 200 pp. Ill. (Black Americans)

CESAR CHAVEZ (Labor Leader)

Goodwin, David. *Cesar Chavez: Hope for the People*. Fawcett
Book Group, 1991. 144 pp. Ill. (Great Lives)

"BUFFALO BILL" CODY (Entertainer)

Buntline, Ned. *Buffalo Bill: His Adventures in the West*. Ayer,
1974. 320 pp. Ill.

Robison, Nancy. *Buffalo Bill*. Watts, 1991. 64 pp. Ill. (First
Books-Biographies)

CHRISTOPHER COLUMBUS (Explorer)

Dodge, Stephen. *Christopher Columbus and the First Voyages to the
New World*. Chelsea House, 1991. 127 pp. Ill. (World Explorers)

Dolan, Sean J. *Christopher Columbus: The Intrepid Mariner*.
Fawcett Book Group, 1989. 128 pp. Ill. (Great Lives)

Dor-Ner, Zui, and William Scheller. *Columbus and the Age of
Discovery*. Morrow, 1991. 372 pp. Ill.

Foreman, Michael, and Richard Seaver. *The Boy Who Sailed with
Columbus*. Little, Brown, 1992. 72 pp. Ill.

Fradin, Dennis. *The Nina, the Pinta & the Santa Maria*. Watts,
1991. 64 pp. Ill.

Litowinsky, Olga. *The High Voyage: The Final Crossing of
Christopher Columbus*. Dell, 1992. 160 pp. Ill.

Meltzer, Milton. *Columbus and the World Around Him*. Watts,
1990. 192 pp. Ill.

This is certainly an apt title for this well-researched biography.
Meltzer presents Columbus in the environment that influenced and
motivated him. The author details the world as it was before
Columbus and describes the explorations that would change
Columbus' world forever.

Meltzer thoroughly and honestly covers the negative impact European explorations had on Native Americans, and also points out how the Indians influenced their conquerors.

Morrison, Samuel E. *Christopher Columbus, Mariner.* New American Library/Dutton, 1983. 192 pp. Ill.

Postgate, Oliver, and Naomi Linnell. *Columbus: The Triumphant Failure.* Watts, 1992. 44 pp. Ill.

Ross, Stewart. *Columbus and the Age of Exploration.* Watts, 1985. 64 pp. Ill.

Sandak, Cass. *Columbus Day.* Macmillan Children's Book Group, 1990. 48 pp. Ill.

Soule, Gardner. *Christopher Columbus on the Green Sea of Darkness.* Grey Castle, 1991. 112 pp. Ill.

West, Delno C., and Jean M. *Christopher Columbus: The Great Adventure and How We Know About It.* Atheneum, 1991. 136 pp. Ill.

CAPTAIN JAMES COOK (Explorer)

Blumberg, Rhoda. *The Remarkable Voyages of Captain Cook.* Macmillan, 1991. 144 pp. Ill.

This is a full and fascinating account of a gifted British explorer's adventures. Thanks to Blumberg's use of Cook's journals in her research, the reader receives an "insider's" view of Cook's voyages to Australia, Hawaii and other areas of the Pacific. Each voyage is charted on a map of the world as we know it today.

We are impressed not only with Cook's skills as a navigator, but with his amazing sensitivity to and acceptance of customs and cultures unfamiliar to him. Blumberg acknowledges, however, that Cook's explorations opened an exotic world to the sometimes tragic interference of those less insightful and less tolerant.

Haney, David. *Captain James Cook and the Explorers of the Pacific.*
Chelsea House, 1992. 112 pp. Ill. (World Explorers)
Sylvester, David W. *Captain Cook and the Pacific.* Longman, 1971.
92 pp. Ill.

BILL COSBY (Entertainer)
Kettlekamp, Larry. *Bill Cosby: Family Funny Man.* Simon &
Schuster, 1987. 128 pp. Ill. (In Focus Biographies)
Rosenberg, Robert. *Bill Cosby: The Changing Black Image.*
Millbrook, 1992. 104 pp. Ill. (New Directions)
Ruth, Marianne. *Bill Cosby: Entertainer and Director.* Holloway
House, 1992. 200 pp. Ill. (Black Americans)

MARIE CURIE (Scientist)
Pflaum, Rosalynd. *Marie Curie and Her Daughter, Irene.* Lerner,
1993. 112 pp. Ill. (Lerner Biographies)

GEORGE ARMSTRONG CUSTER (Military Leader)
Bachrach, Deborah. *Custer's Last Stand: Opposing Viewpoints.*
Greenhaven, 1990. 112 pp. Ill.
Reynolds, Quentin. *Custer's Last Stand.* Random House, 1987.
160 pp. Ill.

CLARENCE DARROW (Lawyer)
Kurland, Gerald. *Clarence Darrow: Attorney for the Damned.*
SamHar, 1972. (Outstanding Personalities)

CHARLES DARWIN (Scientist)
Milner, Richard. *Charles Darwin: The Evolution of a Scientist.*
Facts on File, 1993. 144 pp. Ill. (Makers of Modern Science)

CHARLES DICKENS (Author)
Martin, Christopher. *Charles Dickens.* Rourke, 1990. 112 pp. Ill.
(Life and Works)

EMILY DICKINSON (Poet)
Thayer, Bonita. *Emily Dickinson.* Watts, 1989. 144 pp. Ill.
(Impact Biographies)

WALT DISNEY (Artist, Inventor)

Fisher, Maxine P. *The Walt Disney Story*. Watts, 1988. 96 pp. Ill. (First Books-Biographies)

Kurland, Gerald. *Walt Disney: Master of Animation*. SamHar, 1972. 32 pp. (Outstanding Personalities)

FREDERICK DOUGLASS (Abolitionist)

Davis, Ossie. *Escape to Freedom: A Play About Young Frederick Douglass*. Puffin, 1990.

Miller, Douglas T. *Frederick Douglass and the Fight for Freedom*. Facts on File, 1988. 144 pp. Ill. (Makers of America)
*A good biography of one of America's first civil rights activists and his leading role in the abolitionist movement.

Ruth, Marianne. *Frederick Douglass: Patriot and Activist*. Holloway House, 1992. 200 pp. Ill. (Black Americans)

DAVE DRAVECKY (Athlete)

Dravecky, Dave, and Tim Stafford. *Comeback*. Zondervan, 1990. 252 pp.

CHARLES DREW (Medical Leader)

Talmadge, Katherine. *The Life of Charles Drew*. Twenty-first Century Books, 1992. 84 pp. Ill. (Pioneers in Health and Medicine)

Wolfe, Rinna E. *Charles Richard Drew, M.D.* Watts, 1991. 64 pp. Ill. (First Books-Biographies)

W.E.B. DU BOIS (Civil Rights Leader)

Hamilton, Virginia. *W.E.B. Du Bois: A Biography*. Crowell, 1986. 192 pp. Ill.

McKissack, Patricia and Fredrick. *W.E.B. Du Bois*. Watts, 1990. 128 pp. Ill. (Impact Biographies)

AMELIA EARHART (Aviator)

Leder, Jane. *Amelia Earhart: Opposing Viewpoints*. Greenhaven, 1989. 112 pp. Ill.
*A thorough look at the mysterious disappearance of Earhart.

Morrissey, Muriel E., and Carol L. Osborne. *Amelia, My Courageous Sister: Biography of Amelia Earhart*. Aviation, 1987. 320 pp. Ill.

Sloate, Susan. *Amelia Earhart: Challenging the Skies*. Fawcett Book Group, 1990. 118 pp. (Great Lives Biography)

Zierau, Lillee D. *Amelia Earhart: Leading Lady of the Air Age*. SamHar, 1972. 32 pp. (Outstanding Personalities)

THOMAS ALVA EDISON (Inventor)

Cousins, Margaret. *The Story of Thomas Alva Edison*. Random House, 1981. 160 pp. Ill.

Kurland, Gerald. *Thomas Edison: Father of Electricity and Master Inventor of Our Modern Age*. SamHar, 1972. 32 pp. (Outstanding Personalities)

Lampton, Christopher F. *Thomas Alva Edison*. Watts, 1988. 96 pp. Ill.
*Enhanced by many photos and drawings, this book aptly describes Edison's ability to create many new inventions (1,092 patents in his lifetime).

Mintz, Penny. *Thomas Edison: Inventing the Future*. Fawcett Book Group, 1989. 128 pp. Ill. (Great Lives Biography)

ALBERT EINSTEIN (Scientist)

Dank, Milton. *Albert Einstein*. Watts, 1983. 128 pp. Ill.

DWIGHT DAVID EISENHOWER (U.S. President)

Cannon, Marian. *Dwight David Eisenhower: War Hero & President*. Watts, 1990. 160 pp. Ill. (Impact Biographies)
*A well-thought out biography of one of America's great leaders, revealing his weaknesses as well as his strengths.

Darby, Jean. *Dwight D. Eisenhower: A Man Called Ike*. Lerner, 1989. 112 pp. Ill. (Lerner Biographies)
*This well-illustrated volume provides the reader with an excellent portrait of Eisenhower as a military and political leader, totally dedicated to his country and career.

Ellis, Rafaela. *Dwight D. Eisenhower: Thirty-fourth President of the United States*. Garrett, 1989. 128 pp. Ill. (Presidents of the United States)

*Beginning with the momentous event of D-Day in General Eisenhower's career, the book then traces his life in a well-written documentary format.

Van Steenwyk, Elizabeth. *Dwight David Eisenhower, President.* Walker, 1987. 120 pp. Ill.

DUKE ELLINGTON (Musician)

Brown, Gene. *Duke Ellington.* Silver Burdett, 1990. 128 pp. Ill. (Genius! The Artist and the Process)

Collier, James L. *Duke Ellington.* Macmillan, 1991. 144 pp.

Duke Ellington is the story of a man, his music, and his experience as an African-American striving for success in the 20th century.

As an expert on jazz, author James Collier has more than a casual knowledge of the music of Duke Ellington, and it shows. He references many individual works, and provides insight into the jazz world of the 1920's, '30's and '40's.

Collier also shines a spotlight on the challenges facing blacks during the same period of time. He puts Ellington's accomplishments into context; we come to appreciate the importance of the self-esteem Duke Ellington's family instilled in him during his boyhood.

This is a full and carefully researched biography that may send the reader searching for recordings of Ellington's contributions to jazz.

King, Coretta Scott, editor. *Duke Ellington: Bandleader & Composer.* Knowledge Unlimited. 112 pp. Ill.

Smith, Kent. *Duke Ellington: Jazz Musician.* Holloway House, 1992. 200 pp. Ill. (Black Americans)

GERALD FORD (U.S. President)

Collins, David R. *Gerald R. Ford: Thirty-eighth President of the United States.* Garrett, 1990. 128 pp. Ill. (Presidents of the United States)

Randolph, Sallie. *Gerald R. Ford: President*. Walker, 1987. 120 pp. Ill.
*An excellent biography of a man who had a long and successful political career in Congress, only to be President for just two years. Attention is also given to Ford's wife and her recovery from breast cancer and drug and alcohol addiction.

HENRY FORD (Inventor)
Harris, Jacqueline. *Henry Ford*. Watts, 1984. 128 pp.
Kurland, Gerald. *Henry Ford: Pioneer in the Automotive Industry*. SamHar, 1972. 32 pp. (Outstanding Personalities)

BENJAMIN FRANKLIN (Inventor, Statesman)
Cousins, Margaret. *Ben Franklin of Old Philadelphia*. Random House, 1981. 160 pp. Ill.
Feldman, Eve B. *Benjamin Franklin: Scientist and Inventor*. Watts, 1990. 64 pp. Ill. (First Books-Biographies)
Franklin, Benjamin. *Autobiography of Benjamin Franklin*. Viking, 1986. 320 pp.
Kurland, Gerald. *Benjamin Franklin: America's Universal Man*. SamHar Press, 1972. 32 pp. (Outstanding Personalities)
Meltzer, Milton. *Benjamin Franklin: The New American*. Watts, 1988. 288 pp. Ill. (Milton Meltzer Biographies)
*This comprehensive, well-written book uses many primary sources to convey Franklin's personality, including his strengths and weaknesses. The historical context of his life is clearly presented.

JOHN C. FREMONT (Frontiersman)
Harris, Edward D. *John C. Fremont and the Great Western Reconnaissance*. Chelsea House, 1990. 112 pp. Ill. (World Explorers)
*A fascinating portrait of the exploration of the American West. This book is supplemented with many photos and maps.

GALILEO GALILEI (Scientist)
Rosen, Sidney. *Galileo and the Magic Numbers*. Little, Brown & Co., 1958. Ill.

THOMAS GALLAUDET (Educator)

Neimark, Anne E. *A Deaf Child Listened: Thomas Gallaudet, Pioneer in American Education.* Morrow, 1983. 160 pp.

MAHATMA GANDHI (World Leader)

Cheney, Glenn A. *Mohandas Gandhi.* Watts, 1983. 128 pp. Ill.

Faber, Doris and Harold. *Mahatma Gandhi.* Simon & Schuster, 1986. 128 pp. Ill.

The authors assure us that every word of this biography is authentic, based largely on Gandhi's autobiography and on the writings of people who knew the Mahatma well.

The Fabers' coverage of Gandhi's youth in the British Empire's India is fascinating. We follow his political education in South Africa and his long struggles for an independent India. Yet the authors also reveal Gandhi's inner journey, including his discovery of his own religious nature and his embracing of a spiritual doctrine of non-violence that became known as "Soul Force."

Written with respect and admiration, *Mahatma Gandhi* is a revealing window on an exceptional life.

Fischer, Louis. *Gandhi: His Life & Message for the World.* New American Library/Dutton, 1982. 192 pp.

Rawding, F.W. *Gandhi.* Cambridge University, 1980. 48 pp. Ill.

GERONIMO (Native American Leader)

Shorto, Russell. *Geronimo and the Struggle for Apache Freedom.* Silver Burdett, 1989. 144 pp. Ill. (Alvin Josephy's History of the Native Americans)

JOHN GLENN (Astronaut, Government Official)

Angel, Ann. *John Glenn: Space Pioneer.* Fawcett Book Group, 1989. 128 pp. Ill. (Great Lives Biography)

Cole, Michael D. *John Glenn: Astronaut and Senator.* Enslow, 1993. 104 pp. (People to Know)

SAMUEL GOMPERS (Labor Leader)
Kurland, Gerald. *Samuel Gompers: Founder of the American Labor Movement.* SamHar, 1972. 32 pp. (Outstanding Personalities)

MIKHAIL GORBACHEV (World Leader)
Kort, Michael. *Mikhail Gorbachev.* Watts, 1990. 128 pp. Ill. (Impact Biographies)

Otfinoski, Steven. *Mikhail Gorbachev: The Soviet Innovator.* Fawcett Book Group, 1989. 128 pp. Ill. (Great Lives)

Sullivan, George. *Mikhail Gorbachev.* Messner, 1990. 128 pp. Ill. (In Focus Biographies)

ULYSSES S. GRANT (U.S. President)
Booth, F. Norton. *Great American Generals: Ulysses S. Grant.* Longmeadow, 1992. 80 pp. Ill.

Falkof, Lucille. *Ulysses S. Grant: Eighteenth President of the United States.* Garrett, 1990. 128 pp. Ill. (Presidents of the United States)

Rickarby, Laura Ann. *Ulysses S. Grant and the Strategy of Victory.* Silver Burdett, 1991. 125 pp. Ill. (The History of the Civil War)

ALEXANDER HAMILTON (Colonial American)
Keller, Mollie. *Alexander Hamilton.* Watts, 1986. 72 pp. Ill.
*An excellent biography that brings Hamilton out of obscurity and into his own as a patriot, leader and constitutional supporter.

Kurland, Gerald. *Alexander Hamilton: Architect of American Nationalism.* SamHar, 1972. 32 pp. Ill. (Outstanding Personalities)

ERNEST HEMINGWAY (Author)
Ferrell, Keith. *Ernest Hemingway: The Search for Courage.* Evans, 1984. 192 pp.

Lyttle, Richard B. *Ernest Hemingway: The Life and the Legend.* Macmillan, 1992. 224 pp. Ill.

McDowell, Nicholas. *Ernest Hemingway.* Rourke, 1989. 112 pp. Ill. (Life and Works)
*This well-illustrated volume is a solid portrait of this complex, modern-day author. His major works are analyzed and quoted extensively.

Whelan, Gloria. *The Pathless Woods: A Novel of Ernest Hemingway's Sixteenth Summer in Northern Michigan.* Lippincott, 1982. 192 pp. Ill.

Even the famous among us must pass through the stages of life: helpless infancy, adventure-filled childhood, awkward adolescence. Ernest Hemingway suffered growing pains. *The Pathless Woods* chronicles his 16th summer, when he was torn between his love for his family and his need for independence.

The teenaged "Ernie" Hemingway spent his time camping, fishing, hunting, farming, and enjoying nature. While he accepted responsibilities at home, he longed to be just a kid.

This engaging story involves the legendary Hemingway in a collection of circumstances with which we can identify.

Whelan's sources include stories written by Hemingway, books authored by his family members and others who knew him, and Whelan's own memories of summertime in northern Michigan.

MATTHEW HENSON (Explorer)
Gilman, Michael. *Matthew Henson: Explorer and Adventurer.* Holloway House, 1992. 200 pp. Ill. (Black Americans)

HIAWATHA (Native American Leader)
McClard, Megan, and George Ypsilantis. *Hiawatha and the Iroquois League.* Silver Burdett, 1989. 123 pp. Ill. (Alvin Josephy's History of the Native Americans)

LANGSTON HUGHES (Poet)

Davis, Ossie. *Langston: A Play.* Delacorte, 1983. 146 pp.

Langston Hughes was not born into a life that encouraged the nurturing of creativity. But he had to write. His soul demanded it. And thank goodness he answered the call!

Ossie Davis has written a play about his friend, Langston, a passionate poet whose talents emerged during the Harlem Renaissance of the 1920's. A distinguished playwright, actor and director himself, Davis has written a piece for the stage that presents the facts about Hughes as it captures his courage and motivation to create. Through smooth, easy transitions between past and present, Davis highlights the circumstances that helped shape Hughes' literary efforts. We are fortunate that he shares great portions of Langston Hughes' poetry, masterful works that reveal more about the man than another man's words ever could.

Meltzer, Milton. *Langston Hughes: A Biography*. Harper Collins Children's Books, 1988. 296 pp.

ANDREW JACKSON (U.S. President)

Coit, Margaret L. *Andrew Jackson*. Grey Castle, 1991. 176 pp. Ill.

Remini, Robert V. *The Revolutionary Age of Andrew Jackson*. Harper Collins, 1987. Ill.

Stefoff, Rebecca. *Andrew Jackson: Seventh President of the United States*. Garrett, 1988. 128 pp. Ill. (Presidents of the United States)

Ward, John W. *Andrew Jackson: Symbol for an Age*. Oxford, 1962. 286 pp.

JESSE JACKSON (Civil Rights Leader)

Haskins, James. *I Am Somebody! A Biography of Jesse Jackson*. Enslow, 1992. 112 pp. Ill.

Kosof, Anna. *Jesse Jackson*. Watts, 1987. 112 pp. Ill. (Biographies)
*This biography documents Jackson's life and struggle for human rights. It is based mainly on personal observation and interviews.

Otfinoski, Steve. *Jesse Jackson: A Voice for Change*. Fawcett Book Group, 1989. 128 pp. Ill. (Great Lives)

Stone, Eddie. *Jesse Jackson*. Holloway House, 1988. 256 pp.

Wilkinson, Brenda. *Jesse Jackson: Still Fighting for the Dream*. Silver Burdett, 1990. 128 pp. Ill. (The History of the Civil Rights Movement)

MAHALIA JACKSON (Singer)

Donloe, Darlene. *Mahalia Jackson: Gospel Singer*. Holloway House, 1992. 200 pp. Ill. (Black Americans)

Jackson, Jesse. *Make a Joyful Noise Unto the Lord! The Life of Mahalia Jackson, Queen of Gospel Singers.* Crowell, 1974. 176 pp. Ill.

THOMAS JEFFERSON (U.S. President)

Bober, Natalie. *Thomas Jefferson: Man on a Mountain.* Macmillan Children's Book Group, 1988. 288 pp. Ill.
*This competent biography is an excellent source of information on the life of Jefferson, whose creative genius is vividly captured.

Komroff, Manuel. *Thomas Jefferson.* Grey Castle, 1991. 160 pp. Ill.

Meltzer, Milton. *Thomas Jefferson: The Revolutionary Aristocrat.* Watts, 1991. 256 pp. Ill. (Milton Meltzer Biographies)

If there is a hall of fame for biographers, Milton Meltzer should be a charter member.

In *The Revolutionary Aristocrat*, he follows his own tradition of gathering mountains of material from impeccable sources and blending it all into a comprehensive presentation of a great American's life story. Meltzer explores in depth Jefferson's family background, the paradoxical presence of slavery in his world, his vocations, his avocations, everything. In less skillful hands, the extraordinary detail would prove tedious, but Meltzer works magic. He surrounds us with Jefferson's world and makes us glad to have visited there.

Because he specifies points of interest in each source, even Meltzer's bibliography is interesting to read.

Peterson, Merrill D. *Thomas Jefferson and the New Nation.* Oxford, 1970. 1,104 pp.

Selfridge, John. *Thomas Jefferson: The Philosopher President.* Fawcett Book Group, 1991. 128 pp. Ill. (Great Lives)

Stefoff, Rebecca. *Thomas Jefferson: Third President of the United States.* Garrett, 1988. 128 pp. Ill. (Presidents of the United States)

JOAN OF ARC (Saint, Military Leader)

Brooks, Polly S. *Beyond the Myth: The Story of Joan of Arc.* Harper Collins, 1990. 192 pp. Ill.

Dana, Barbara. *Young Joan.* Harper Collins, 1991. 384 pp.

ANDREW JOHNSON (U.S. President)

Dubowski, Cathy E. *Andrew Johnson: Rebuilding the Union.* Silver Burdett, 1991. 126 pp. Ill. (The History of the Civil War)

Paley, Alan L. *Andrew Johnson: The President Impeached.* SamHar, 1972. 32 pp. (Outstanding Personalities)

Stevens, Rita. *Andrew Johnson: Seventeenth President of the United States.* Garrett, 1989. 128 pp. Ill. (Presidents of the United States)

LADY BIRD JOHNSON (U.S. First Lady)

Flynn, Jean. *Lady: The Story of Claudia Alta (Lady Bird) Johnson.* Eakin Press/Sunbelt Media, Inc., 1992. 114 pp.

LYNDON JOHNSON (U.S. President)

Falkof, Lucille. *Lyndon B. Johnson: Thirty-sixth President of the United States.* Garrett, 1989. 128 pp. Ill. (Presidents of the United States)

Kurland, Gerald. *Lyndon Baines Johnson: President Caught in the Ordeal of Power.* SamHar, 1972. 32 pp. (Outstanding Personalities)

SCOTT JOPLIN (Composer)

Preston, Katherine. *Scott Joplin: Musician and Composer.* Holloway House, 1992. 200 pp. Ill. (Black Americans)

CHIEF JOSEPH (Native American Leader)

Scott, Robert A. *Chief Joseph and the Nez Perces.* Facts on File, 1993. 144 pp. Ill. (Makers of America)

HELEN KELLER (Humanitarian)

Gibson, William. *The Miracle Worker.* Bantam, 1989. 128 pp.

St. George, Judith. *Dear Dr. Bell...Your Friend, Helen Keller.* Beech Tree, 1993. 96 pp. Ill.

JOHN F. KENNEDY (U.S. President)

Anderson, Catherine C. *John F. Kennedy: Young People's President.* Lerner, 1991. 144 pp. Ill. (Lerner Biographies)
*Much attention in this book is given to Kennedy's formative years before he became President.

Anderson, Lois E. *John F. Kennedy.* Longmeadow, 1992. 160 pp. Ill.

Falkof, Lucille. *John F. Kennedy: Thirty-fifth President of the United States.* Garrett, 1988. 128 pp. Ill. (Presidents of the United States)

Hoare, Stephen. *The Assassination of John F. Kennedy.* Trafalgar Square, 1989. 64 pp. Ill.

Martin Lills, Judie. *John F. Kennedy.* Watts, 1988. 384 pp. Ill. (Biographies)
*This detailed biography provides the reader with much information concerning Kennedy's youth, family life and rise to the Presidency. Many photographs enhance the text.

Selfridge, John. *John F. Kennedy: Courage in Crisis.* Fawcett Book Group, 1989. 128 pp. Ill. (Great Lives)

Waggoner, Jeffrey. *The Assassination of President Kennedy: Opposing Viewpoints.* Greenhaven, 1989. 112 pp. Ill.

CORETTA SCOTT KING (Civil Rights Leader)

Henry, Sondra, and Emily Taitz. *Coretta Scott King.* Enslow, 1992. 128 pp. Ill. (Contemporary Women)

Patrick, Diane. *Coretta Scott King.* Watts, 1991. 128 pp. Ill. (Impact Biographies)

MARTIN LUTHER KING, JR. (Civil Rights Leader)

Darby, Jean. *Martin Luther King, Jr.* Lerner, 1990. 112 pp. Ill. (Lerner Biographies)
*Many photographs add to this chronicle of King's life from childhood to death.

Faber, Doris and Harold. *Martin Luther King, Jr.* Messner, 1986. 128 pp. Ill. (In Focus Biographies)

Harris, Jacqueline L. *Martin Luther King, Jr.* Watts, 1983. 128 pp. Ill. (Impact Biographies)

Haskins, James. *The Life and Death of Martin Luther King, Jr.* Beech Tree, 1992. 176 pp. Ill.

Nazel, Joe. *Martin Luther King, Jr.: Civil Rights Leader*. Holloway House, 1992. 200 pp. Ill. (Black Americans)

Obaba, Al-Imam. *Dr. Martin Luther King, Jr.* African Islamic Mission, 1989. 43 pp. Ill.

Patrick, Diane. *Martin Luther King, Jr.* Watts, 1990. 64 pp. Ill. (First Books Biographies)
*This easy-to-read biography gives the reader an in-depth look at King's life as a civil rights leader.

Patterson, Lillie. *Martin Luther King, Jr. and the Freedom Movement*. Facts on File, 1990. 192 pp. Ill. (Makers of America)

Rowland, Della. *Martin Luther King, Jr.: The Dream of a Peaceful Revolution*. Silver Burdett, 1990. 128 pp. Ill. (The History of the Civil Rights Movement)

Schulke, Flip, editor. *Martin Luther King, Jr.: A Documentary ... Montgomery to Memphis*. Norton, 1976. 224 pp. Ill.

Yette, Samuel F. and Frederick W. *Washington & Two Marches: 1963 & 1983*. Cottage, 1984. Ill.
*With many striking color photographs, this book chronicles the two famous marches for civil rights in Washington.

BARTOLOME DE LAS CASAS (Political Activist)

Stopsky, Dr. Fred. *Bartolome de las Casas: Champion of Indian Rights*. Discovery Enterprises, Ltd., 1992. 64 pp. Ill.

ANTOINE LAVOISIER (Scientist)

Grey, Vivian. *The Chemist Who Lost His Head: The Story of Antoine Lavoisier*. Coward, 1983. 112 pp. Ill.

This intriguing title can be taken literally: Antoine Lavoisier was a chemist, and he did indeed lose his head--at the guillotine in 18th century France.

While his politics got him into trouble, Lavoisier always thought of himself as a scientist, first and foremost. His experiments transformed chemistry from a cacophony of fact and superstition into an exact science. By researching official records and talking with scientists and historians, Grey has pieced together an interesting description of Lavoisier's achievements, not only in science, but in agriculture, finance and social welfare as well.

Lavoisier's story also includes extensive references to his wife's capable support of the scientist's work.

ROBERT E. LEE (Military Leader)

===

Aaseng, Nathan. *Robert E. Lee.* Lerner, 1991. 112 pp. Ill. (Lerner Biographies)

We tend to trust biographers who dole out information about well-known folk with honesty and a sense of balance. Nathan Aaseng is such a biographer. From chapter one of *Robert E. Lee*, Aaseng demonstrates a grasp of his subject's human frailties as well as respect for his abilities, loyalty and integrity.

Through fascinating details, Aaseng offers insight into many aspects of Lee's character, including his strong sense of duty and his self-discipline. We learn that this military legend's belief in a just God affected his attitudes, which in turn affected his performance as the Confederate army's commander.

This is a captivating story that makes us wish we could have come face-to-face with this remarkable man.

Buchanan, Patricia. *Robert E. Lee: A Hero for Young Americans.* Winston-Derek Pub., 1990. 142 pp.

Commager, Henry S. *America's Robert E. Lee.* Cavendish, Marshall Corp., 1991. 128 pp. Ill.

Dubowski, Cathy E. *Robert E. Lee and the Rise of the South.* Silver Burdett, 1990. 160 pp. Ill. (The History of the Civil War)

Hogg, Ian. *Great American Generals: Robert E. Lee.* Longmeadow, 1992. 80 pp. Ill.

Weidhorn, Manfred. *Robert E. Lee.* Atheneum, 1988. 160 pp. Ill.

Reading a life story can inspire us, entertain us, sometimes amaze us. Weidhorn's book on Robert E. Lee can help us understand.

The author writes with respect for a man he describes as "a classic example of a decent and honorable man who somehow ends up on the wrong side."

Full of facts and much more information than the young reader of a history textbook would find, the book views the Civil War from the unique perspective of this prominent Confederate leader.

LEWIS AND CLARK (Explorers)

Moulton, Gary. *Lewis and Clark and the Route to the Pacific.* Chelsea House, 1991. 112 pp. Ill. (World Explorers)

Otfinoski, Steven. *Lewis & Clark: Leading America West.* Fawcett Book Group, 1992. 144 pp. Ill. (Great Lives Biography)

ABRAHAM LINCOLN (U.S. President)

Freedman, Russell. *Lincoln: A Photobiography.* Clarion, 1987. 160 pp. Ill.

Russell Freedman begins his Newbery Award-winning biography of Lincoln by focusing on the little things--how Lincoln spoke, how tall he was, his sense of humor. Perhaps Freedman is helping us relax with a legend, pulling down the walls of unapproachability that we often place around great people.

Freedman wants us to consider Abe's personhood as well as his accomplishments, and he gives us all the tools we need to do that. Well-written prose and many photographs provide images as solid as the logs that formed the walls of Abe's boyhood home. Freedman also treats us to a "Lincoln Sampler" of quotes attributed to the 16th President, and an overview of Lincoln-related historical sites.

Hayman, Leroy. *The Death of Lincoln: A Picture History of the Assassination.* Scholastic, 1987. 128 pp. Ill.

Lee, Andrew. *Lincoln.* Trafalgar Square, 1989. 64 pp. Ill.

North, Sterling. *Abe Lincoln: Log Cabin to White House.* Random House, 1987. 160 pp. Ill.

Sandburg, Carl. *Abe Lincoln Grows Up.* Harcourt Brace Jovanovich, 1975. 224 pp. Ill.

Shorto, Russell. *Abraham Lincoln: To Preserve the Union.* Silver Burdett, 1990. 160 pp. Ill. (The History of the Civil War)

Sloate, Susan. *Abraham Lincoln: The Freedom President.* Fawcett Book Group, 1989. 128 pp. Ill. (Great Lives)

Stefoff, Rebecca. *Abraham Lincoln: Sixteenth President of the United States.* Garrett, 1989. 128 pp. Ill. (Presidents of the United States)

CHARLES LINDBERGH (Aviator)

Lindbergh, Charles A. *Boyhood on the Upper Mississippi: A Reminiscent Letter.* Minnesota Historical Soc., 1987. 50 pp. Ill.

Lindbergh, Charles A. *Spirit of St. Louis.* Macmillan, 1984. Ill.

Randolph, Blythe. *Charles Lindbergh.* Watts, 1990. 160 pp. Ill. (Biographies)

DOUGLAS MACARTHUR (Military Leader)

Darby, Jean. *Douglas MacArthur.* Lerner, 1989. 112 pp. Ill. (Lerner Biographies)

*Many photos add to this concise biography of one of America's leading military men, whose accomplishments and failures are treated equally in this book.

JAMES MADISON (U.S. President)

Banfield, Susan. *James Madison.* Watts, 1986. 72 pp. Ill.

*A fine portrait of a great statesman and framer of the Constitution, with special emphasis on his philosophy.

Fredman, Lionel E. *James Madison: American President and Constitutional Author.* SamHar, 1974. 32 pp. (Outstanding Personalities)

Fritz, Jean. *The Great Little Madison.* Putnam, 1989. 160 pp. Ill.

James Madison, fourth President of the United States, spoke with a "weak voice" but a strong belief in his country and a powerful desire to be involved in forming its destiny. Jean Fritz sits us down by the fireside and chats awhile about this distinguished statesman's achievements and his personal life as well. She presents Madison as a voice of reason during the formulation of the U.S. Constitution. Complex historical issues become easy to understand, thanks to Fritz's conversational style.

Polikof, Barbara G. *James Madison: Fourth President of the United States*. Garrett, 1989. 128 pp. Ill. (Presidents of the United States)

MALCOLM X (Civil Rights Leader)

Davies, Mark. *Malcolm X: Another Side of the Movement*. Silver Burdett, 1990. 128 pp. Ill. (The History of the Civil Rights Movement)

Grimes, Nikki. *Malcolm X: A Force for Change*. Fawcett Book Group, 1992. 128 pp. (Great Lives)

Rummel, Jack. *Malcolm X: Civil and Religious Leader*. Holloway House, 1992. 200 pp. Ill. (Black Americans)

NELSON MANDELA (Political Activist/Leader)

Hoobler, Dorothy and Thomas. *Mandela: The Man, the Struggle, the Triumph*. Watts, 1992. 160 pp. Ill. (Biographies)

Hoobler, Dorothy and Thomas. *Nelson and Winnie Mandela*. Watts, 1987. 112 pp. Ill.

Stefoff, Rebecca. *Nelson Mandela: A Voice Set Free*. Fawcett Book Group, 1990. 128 pp. (Great Lives Biography)

WINNIE MANDELA (Political Activist)

Haskins, Jim. *Winnie Mandela: Life of Struggle*. Putnam, 1988. 180 pp. Ill.

Are women of courage born or made?

The question bears asking as we read this detailed biography of a woman whose story, at this writing, is still unfolding.

Using scores of anecdotes, author Jim Haskins takes us inside young Winnie's home and introduces her family. We witness the never ending struggles she dealt with as the wife and political disciple of Nelson Mandela. We feel her frustration and wonder at her strength.

Can someone learn the fortitude necessary to survive, and even to thrive in the face of adversity? Or must this kind of courage be woven into our personalities before we are born? Although she has generated her share of controversy, one cannot deny the inner strength that has kept Winnie Mandela a force to be reckoned with in South Africa.

THURGOOD MARSHALL (U.S. Supreme Court Justice, Civil Rights Leader)

Haskins, James. *Thurgood Marshall: A Life for Justice.* Galley, 1992. 154 pp. Ill.

Hess, Debra. *Thurgood Marshall: The Fight for Equal Justice.* Silver Burdett, 1990. 128 pp. Ill. (The History of the Civil Rights Movement)

Krug, Elizabeth. *Thurgood Marshall: Champion of Civil Rights.* Fawcett Book Group, 1993. 160 pp. (Great Lives)

Nazel, Joe. *Thurgood Marshall: Supreme Court Justice.* Holloway House, 1992. 200 pp. Ill. (Black Americans)

WILLIE MAYS (Athlete)

Burkhardt, Mitch. *Willie Mays: Baseball Player.* Holloway House, 1992. 200 pp. Ill. (Black Americans)

MARGARET MEAD (Anthropologist)

Ludle, Jacqueline. *Margaret Mead.* Watts, 1983. 118 pp. Ill.

Rice, Edward. *Margaret Mead: A Portrait.* Harper Collins Children's Books, 1979. 256 pp. Ill.
*This biography focuses on Mead's unconventional professional life, with details on each trip into the field.

GOLDA MEIR (World Leader)

Amdur, Richard. *Golda Meir: A Leader in Peace and War.* Fawcett Book Group, 1990. 128 pp. (Great Lives Biography)

Davidson, Margaret. *The Golda Meir Story.* Scribner, 1982. 228 pp. Ill.

This is, indeed, a story rather than a chronicle of events in the Israeli Prime Minister's life. The author's easy style sweeps us into Golda Meir's girlhood home. We live with her, discover fear and

injustice with her. We join her in building a Jewish homeland in
Palestine, and we are proud of her political efforts and successes.

This is a sensitively-written book that speaks in a language that
young people can understand. What an appropriate tribute to an
exceptional woman who wanted to share the message of peace with
the world.

MILTON MELTZER (Author)

Meltzer, Milton. *Starting from Home: A Writer's Beginnings.*
Viking, 1988. 160 pp. Ill.

Milton Meltzer is a master biographer; this time, the subject is
himself. His richly detailed autobiography demonstrates the author's
fascination with and respect for the past and what it can teach us.

Meltzer does not merely show us the world of his growing up. He
invites us in. We taste, smell and experience every moment. We
stand beside him at the penny candy store, feel his fear when he
learns of the Nazis and Hitler; suffer with him through the Great
Depression.

Starting From Home may encourage young readers to truly see
the specialness of their own lives for the very first time.

JULIA MORGAN (Architect)

Wadsworth, Ginger. *Julia Morgan: Architect of Dreams.* Lerner,
1990. 129 pp. Ill. (Lerner Biographies)

A woman in a man's world--that was Julia Morgan. This architect,
whose imagination gave birth to over 700 buildings, including the
Hearst Castle in San Simeon, California, was well respected by
those who worked with and for her. In this biography, Wadsworth
ably details Morgan's professional and personal lives, including her
closeness to her family and her desire to stay out of the limelight,
regardless of her accomplishments.

A great deal of the book is devoted to the incredible Hearst
castle. Many photographs help illustrate the scope of this jewel in

Morgan's professional crown. A directory of buildings designed by Morgan is provided.

GRANDMA MOSES (Artist)
Laing, Martha. *Grandma Moses: The Grand Old Lady of American Art*. SamHar, 1972. 32 pp. (Outstanding Personalities)

WOLFGANG AMADEUS MOZART (Composer)
Loewen, Nancy. *Mozart*. Rourke, 1989. 112 pp. Ill. (Profiles in Music)
Thompson, Wendy. *Wolfgang Amadeus Mozart*. Viking, 1993. 48 pp. Ill. (Composer's World)

JOHN MUIR (Environmentalist)
Wadsworth, Ginger. *John Muir: Wilderness Protector*. Lerner, 1992. 120 pp. Ill. (Lerner Biographies)

RALPH NADER (Consumer Advocate)
Celsi, Teresa. *Ralph Nader: The Consumer Revolution*. Millbrook, 1991. 104 pp. Ill.

EDITH NESBIT (Author)

Nesbit, Edith. *Long Ago When I Was Young*. Dial, 1988. 136 pp. Ill.

This gently written collection of memories expresses the viewpoint of a little girl who would one day grow up to be a famous writer. Edith Nesbit, nicknamed Daisy, tells us what frightened her, what amused her, what it was like to move from place to place as a youngster. Her book is an enchanting reflection of life in the mid-19th century. An interesting foreword by Noel Streatfield tells us more about Daisy and the wonderful children's books she wrote.

LOUISE NEVELSON (Artist)

Bober, Natalie S. *Breaking Tradition: The Story of Louise Nevelson.* Atheneum, 1984. 176 pp. Ill.

This biography of one of the finest American artists of our time begins with five-year old Louise's arrival in Maine from Russia. Even then, artistic talent lived within her, waiting for those around her to allow her to develop it.

Bober chronicles the course of Nevelson's personal and professional lives, including her penchant for unusual fashion, her shyness, and her need for self-expression.

While Bober's presentation of the artist's life and work is quite detailed, she points out that she does not attempt to interpret or criticize Nevelson's creations. Bober notes that she prefers to leave that to qualified experts.

RICHARD NIXON (U.S. President)

Larsen, Rebecca. *Richard Nixon: The Rise and Fall of a President.* Watts, 1991. 208 pp. Ill. (Biographies)
*This evenhanded biography of Nixon details his entire political career. Many photos add to this work.

Nadel, Laurie. *The Great Stream of History: A Biography of Richard M. Nixon.* Macmillan Children's Book Group, 1991. 144 pp. Ill.

Pious, Richard M. *Richard Nixon.* Messner, 1991. 144 pp. Ill. (In Focus Biographies)

Randolph, Sallie. *Richard M. Nixon, President.* Walker, 1989. 128 pp.

Stefoff, Rebecca. *Richard M. Nixon: Thirty-seventh President of the United States.* Garrett, 1990. 128 pp. Ill. (Presidents of the United States)

SANDRA DAY O'CONNOR (U.S. Supreme Court Justice)

Berwald, Beverly. *Sandra Day O'Connor: A New Justice, a New Voice.* Fawcett Book Group, 1991. 128 pp. Ill. (Great Lives)

JESSE OWENS (Athlete)

Gentry, Tony. *Jesse Owens: Olympic Superstar.* Holloway House, 1992. 200 pp. Ill. (Black Americans)

SATCHEL PAIGE (Athlete)

Humphrey, Kathryn Long. *Satchel Paige.* Watts, 1988. 128 pp. Ill.
You need not be a baseball fan to enjoy this engaging biography of one of the greatest pitchers who ever played the game.

Satchel Paige was a phenomenal talent who was relegated to playing in the Negro Leagues because discrimination kept all blacks out of the Majors. He threw the ball for 42 years, was eventually able to join a Major League team, and was named to the Baseball Hall of Fame in 1971.

Paige was a character. His unorthodox behavior sometimes caused his colleagues in the game to raise their eyebrows. But there was no denying his ability on the diamond and the hard work that kept him in the game at an age when most other players called it quits. In *Satchel Paige*, the author reveals much about the man and much about the social conditions of Paige's time.

THOMAS PAINE (Colonial American)

Buchanan, John G. *Thomas Paine: American Revolutionary Writer.* SamHar, 1976. 32 pp. (Outstanding Personalities)

QUANAH PARKER (Native American Leader)

Hilts, Len. *Quanah Parker.* Harcourt Brace Jovanovich, 1987. 160 pp.

Quanah Parker was a proud Comanche chief who led his tribe through a difficult period of history.

Author Len Hilts tells in detail the story of the chief's response to white encroachment on Indian land and lifestyle. His book is full of action and vivid description of customs and conflicts. At the center of it all is Quanah Parker, wanting to preserve his people's ways but realizing that compromises must be made.

Hilt's well-researched book is a valuable resource for those of us who seek to understand the historic relationship between whites and Native Americans and how it affects our dealings with one another today.

ROSA PARKS (Civil Rights Leader)

Friese, Kai J. *Rosa Parks: The Movement Organizes.* Silver Burdett, 1990. 128 pp. Ill. (The History of the Civil Rights Movement)

Siegel, Beatrice. *The Year They Walked: Rosa Parks and the Montgomery Bus Boycott.* Four Winds, 1992. 64 pp. Ill.

LOUIS PASTEUR (Scientist)

Newfield, Marcia. *The Life of Louis Pasteur.* Twenty-first Century Books, 1991. 84 pp. Ill. (Pioneers in Health and Medicine)

LINUS PAULING (Scientist)

White, Florence Meiman. *Linus Pauling: Scientist and Crusader.* Walker, 1982. 90 pp. Ill.

The life story of a man who has won Nobel Prizes in two different fields is bound to be awe-inspiring. After all, such a person must be exceptionally intelligent, versatile and dedicated.

Linus Pauling is indeed all of these things, and this biography includes impressive details of his professional life. But Florence White reaches beyond the accomplishments of the chemist and peace activist. She introduces us to the inquisitive child who worked hard and pursued knowledge while still doing the ordinary things that children do.

We learn that Pauling was an excellent teacher as well as a brilliant scientist. We witness his repeated attempts to bring international attention to the risks of nuclear weapons testing.

We learn that even Nobel Prize winners experience failure, frustration and simple pleasure. White reminds us that heroes are people, too.

ROBERT PEARY (Explorer)

Anderson, Madelyn Klein. *Robert E. Peary and the Fight for the North Pole.* Watts, 1992. 160 pp. Ill. (Biographies)

Dwyer, Christopher. *Robert Peary and the Quest for the North Pole.* Chelsea House, 1992. 112 pp. Ill. (World Explorers)

KING PHILIP (Native American Leader)
Cwiklik, Robert. *King Philip and the War with the Colonists*. Silver Burdett, 1989. 132 pp. Ill. (Alvin Josephy's History of the Native Americans)

PABLO PICASSO (Artist)
Lyttle, Richard B. *Pablo Picasso: The Man & the Image*. Macmillan, 1989. 192 pp. Ill.
Somer, Robin L., and Patricia MacDonald. *Pablo Picasso*. Silver Burdett, 1990. 128 pp. Ill. (Genius! The Artist and the Process)

MARCO POLO (Explorer)
Stefoff, Rebecca. *Marco Polo and the Medieval Explorers*. Chelsea House, 1992. 112 pp. Ill. (World Explorers)

BEATRIX POTTER (Author)
Taylor, Judith, Joyce I. Whalley, Anne S. Hobbs, and Elizabeth Battrick. *Beatrix Potter, 1866-1943: The Artist & Her World*. Frederick Warne, 1988. 244 pp. Ill.
Taylor, Judy. *Beatrix Potter: Artist, Storyteller and Countrywoman*. Frederick Warne, 1987. 224 pp. Ill.

RONALD REAGAN (U.S. President)
Devaney, John. *Ronald Reagan, President*. Walker, 1990. 137 pp. Ill.
Robbins, Neal E. *Ronald W. Reagan: Fortieth President of the United States*. Garrett, 1990. 128 pp. Ill. (Presidents of the United States)
Sullivan, George. *Ronald Reagan*. Messner, 1991. 128 pp. Ill.
*A thorough biography of Reagan through his years as governor and first term as President.

SALLY RIDE (Astronaut)
Hurwitz, Jane and Sue. *Sally Ride: Shooting for the Stars*. Fawcett Book Group, 1989. 115 pp. Ill. (Great Lives)

PAUL ROBESON (Singer, Actor)
Ehrlich, Scott. *Paul Robeson: Athlete, Actor, Singer, Activist*. Holloway House, 1992. 200 pp. Ill. (Black Americans)

Hamilton, Virginia. *Paul Robeson: The Life and Times of a Free Black Man*. Harper Collins, 1974. 224 pp. Ill.

Larsen, Rebecca. *Paul Robeson, Hero Before His Time*. Watts, 1989. 158 pp. Ill. (Biographies)

JACKIE ROBINSON (Athlete)

Reiser, Howard. *Jackie Robinson: Baseball Pioneer*. Watts, 1992. 64 pp. Ill. (First Books-Biographies)

Scott, Richard. *Jackie Robinson: First Black in Major League Baseball*. Holloway House, 1992. 200 pp. Ill. (Black Americans)

ELEANOR ROOSEVELT(Humanitarian, Diplomat, U.S.First Lady)

Jacobs, William J. *Eleanor Roosevelt: A Life of Happiness and Tears*. Grey Castle, 1991. 128 pp. Ill.

Roosevelt, Elliott. *Eleanor Roosevelt, with Love: A Centenary Remembrance*. Lodestar, 1984. 176 pp. Ill.

Biographies of Eleanor Roosevelt are many, but few are written with such warmth! Elliott Roosevelt tells of the strength and stamina of his famous mother with an insight uniquely available to an adoring son. Through countless anecdotes, he portrays his mother as a kind, intelligent woman with a love for adventure and a deep-seated idealism.

This is a captivating introduction to the public and private Eleanor.

FRANKLIN DELANO ROOSEVELT(U.S. President)

Cross, Robin. *Roosevelt and the Americans at War*. Watts, 1990. 64 pp. Ill. (World War II Biographies)

Devaney, John. *Franklin Delano Roosevelt, President*. Walker, 1987. 76 pp. Ill.

Greenblatt, Miriam. *Franklin D. Roosevelt: Thirty-second President of the United States*. Garrett, 1989. 128 pp. Ill. (Presidents of the United States)

Hacker, Jeffrey H. *Franklin D. Roosevelt*. Watts, 1983. 128 pp. Ill.

Larsen, Rebecca. *Franklin D. Roosevelt: Man of Destiny.* Watts, 1991. 224 pp. Ill. (Biographies)
*A thorough biography of the man who guided America through many crises.
Schlesinger, Arthur, Jr., editor. *Franklin D. Roosevelt.* Knowledge Unlimited, (no date listed) 128 pp.
Selfridge, John W. *Franklin D. Roosevelt: The People's President.* Fawcett Book Group, 1989. 128 pp. Ill. (Great Lives)
Sullivan, Wilson. *Franklin Delano Roosevelt.* Harper Collins Childrens Books, 1970. 154 pp. Ill.

THEODORE ROOSEVELT (U.S. President)
Musso, Louis, III. *Theodore Roosevelt: Soldier, Statesman and President.* SamHar, 1982. 32 pp. (Outstanding Personalities)

BABE RUTH (Athlete)
Berke, Art. *Babe Ruth: The Best There Ever Was.* Watts, 1988. 128 pp. Ill. (Impact Biographies)

SACAJAWEA (Native American Leader)
Bryant, Martha F. *Sacajawea: A Native American Heroine.* Council for Indian Education, 1989. 256 pp. Ill.
O'Dell, Scott. *Streams to the River, River to the Sea: A Novel of Sacajawea.* Houghton Mifflin, 1986. 191 pp.

ANWAR EL-SADAT (World Leader)
Finke, Blythe F. *Anwar Sadat: Egyptian Ruler and Peace Maker.* SamHar, 1986. 32 pp. (Outstanding Personalities)

Sullivan, George. *Sadat: The Man Who Changed Mid-East History.* Walker, 1982. 128 pp. Ill.
Understanding past and present conflicts in the Middle East is no easy task. But biographies like *Sadat* can clarify a complex collection of events by allowing us to view them through the eyes of a principal player.
In this detailed biography, Sullivan offers many personal details about Egypt's President Anwar Sadat, as well as solid, straightforward descriptions of life in Sadat's homeland. We learn that heroes

have heroes themselves; India's Mahatma Gandhi was a source of inspiration for Sadat.

Published in 1981, this book's final chapter does not speak of Sadat's assassination in October of that year. Our knowledge of his untimely death adds poignancy to the passages that recount his plans for a "Memorial to Peace" which was intended to be his final resting place.

ANDREI SAKHAROV (Political Activist)

LeVert, Suzanne. *The Sakharov File: A Study in Courage.* Messner, 1986. 128 pp. Ill.

So much has happened in the former Soviet Union since this book was published in 1986. That makes it all the more interesting to read.

Le Vert accomplishes several things in *The Sakharov Files*. She gives us an easy to understand overview of Soviet history and the principles of Communism; she presents, in detail, the life and courageous work of Andrei Sakharov, brilliant scientist and political dissident; and she helps us understand the Soviet atmosphere of secrecy and fear of dissent that forced Sakharov into exile when he publicly campaigned for human rights.

At the conclusion of *A Study in Courage*, Sakharov was still in exile in Gorky; his wife, Elena Bonner, was in ill health.

Today, of course, Sakharov is free, a symbol of the dissidents imprisoned for so long in the former U.S.S.R. Knowledge of current developments there certainly enhances the impact of this biography.

JONAS SALK (Scientist)
Sherrow, Victoria. *Jonas Salk.* Facts on File, 1993. 128 pp. Ill. (Makers of Modern Science)

MARGARET SANGER (Medical Leader)
Reynolds, Moira. *Margaret Sanger, Leader for Birth Control.* SamHar, 1982. 32 pp. (Outstanding Personalities)

Topalian, Elyse. *Margaret Sanger*. Watts. 128 pp.

Issues such as sex education and birth control are controversial today. Just imagine how they were regarded at the turn of the century when Margaret Sanger, the founder of Planned Parenthood, was beginning her work. In this very readable biography, Elyse Topalian reveals the personality of a woman motivated to revolutionize medical and social views on educating women about their bodies. She did this at a time when such activity was illegal and considered obscene.

We come to admire Sanger's courage in pursuing reform, and her ability to move mountains with the power of her own faith in what she was doing. Her story details the deeply personal experiences that led her to embark on this crusade.

ALBERT SCHWEITZER (Humanitarian)

Schweitzer, Albert. *Words of Albert Schweitzer*. Newmarket Press, 1984. 110 pp. Ill.

SEQUOYAH (Native American Leader)

Cwiklik, Robert. *Sequoyah and the Cherokee Alphabet*. Silver Burdett, 1989. 142 pp. Ill. (Alvin Josephy's History of the Native Americans)

WILLIAM SHAKESPEARE (Author)

Martin, Christopher. *Shakespeare*. Rourke, 1989. 112 pp. Ill. (Life and Works)

SITTING BULL (Native American Leader)

Black, Sheila. *Sitting Bull and the Battle of Little Big Horn*. Silver Burdett, 1989. 144 pp. Ill. (Alvin Josephy's History of the Native Americans)

HENRY STANLEY (Explorer)

Cohen, Daniel. *Henry Stanley and the Quest for the Source of the Nile*. Evans, 1985. 175 pp. Ill.

ELIZABETH CADY STANTON (Women's Rights Leader)

Cullen-Dupont, Kathryn. *Elizabeth Cady Stanton and Women's Liberty*. Facts on File, 1992. 144 pp. Ill. (Makers of America)

Griffith, Elisabeth. *In Her Own Right: The Life of Elizabeth Cady Stanton*. Oxford, 1984. 304 pp.

Kendall, Martha E. *Elizabeth Cady Stanton*. Highland, 1987. 72 pp. Ill.

Salsini, Barbara. *Elizabeth Stanton: A Leader of the Woman's Suffrage Movement*. SamHar, 1972. 32 pp. (Outstanding Personalities)

TECUMSEH (Native American Leader)

Shorto, Russell. *Tecumseh and the Dream of an American Indian Nation*. Silver Burdett, 1989. 136 pp. Ill. (Alvin Josephy's History of the Native Americans)

MARGARET THATCHER (World Leader)

Hole, Dorothy. *Margaret Thatcher: Britain's Prime Minister*. Enslow, 1990. 128 pp. Ill. (Contemporary Women)

Moskin, Marietta D. *Margaret Thatcher of Great Britain*. Messner, 1990. 128 pp. Ill. (In Focus Biographies)

HENRY DAVID THOREAU (Author)

Lawrence, Jerome, and Robert Lee. *The Night Thoreau Spent in Jail*. Bantam, 1983. 128 pp.

Miller, Douglas. *Henry David Thoreau*. Facts on File, Inc., 1991. 144 pp. Ill. (Makers of America)

HARRY S. TRUMAN (U.S. President)

Collins, David R. *Harry S. Truman: Thirty-third President of the United States*. Garrett, 1988. 128 pp. Ill. (Presidents of the United States)

Farley, Karin C. *Harry Truman: The Man from Independence*. Messner, 1989. 150 pp. Ill. (In Focus Biographies)

Libbey, Theodore W., Jr. *Harry S. Truman*. Childrens Press, 1987. 100 pp. Ill.

SOJOURNER TRUTH (Abolitionist)

Krass, Peter. *Sojourner Truth: Anti-Slavery Activist.* Holloway House, 1992. 200 pp. Ill. (Black Americans)

Ortiz, Victoria. *Sojourner Truth: A Self-Made Woman.* Harper Collins, 1986. 160 pp. Ill.

HARRIET TUBMAN (Abolitionist)

Bentley, Judith. *Harriet Tubman.* Watts, 1990. 144 pp. Ill. (Impact Biographies)

To call Harriet Tubman a "pillar of strength" is to understate the extent of her remarkable tenacity. Born a slave in 1821, Tubman labored in the fields. She survived a horrendous injury when, at 15, she tried to protect a runaway slave.

Tubman would never lose her passion for helping others in their quest for freedom. After escaping bondage herself, she brought family and friends north and eventually became the "Moses" of the Underground Railroad.

As Judith Bentley tells this amazing story, she invites Harriet to join in the telling. Through quotes and photographs, we see and hear her speak as she serves as a spy, a nurse, and eventually, a champion of women's rights.

Thanks to Bentley's skills and research, Harriet Tubman becomes such an imposing presence to the reader that we feel we can draw strength from her simply by reading her story.

Carlson, Judy. *Harriet Tubman: Call to Freedom.* Fawcett Book Group, 1989. 118 pp. Ill. (Great Lives)

Fitzgerald, Sharon. *Harriet Tubman: Civil Rights Activist.* Holloway House, 1992. 200 pp. Ill. (Black Americans)

McClard, Megan. *Harriet Tubman: Slavery and the Underground Railroad.* Silver Burdett, 1990. 133 pp. Ill. (The History of the Civil War)

Petry, Ann. *Harriet Tubman: Conductor on the Underground Railway.* Archway, 1983. 247 pp.

NAT TURNER (Abolitionist)

Bisson, Terry. *Nat Turner: Prophet and Slave Revolt Leader.*
Holloway House, 1992. 160 pp. Ill. (Black Americans)
Goldman, Martin S. *Nat Turner and the Southampton Revolt of
1831.* Watts, 1992. 176 pp. Ill. (Impact Biographies)

DESMOND TUTU (Political Activist/Leader)

Bentley, Judith. *Archbishop Tutu of South Africa.* Enslow, 1988.
96 pp.
Enter the frightening world of apartheid with author Judith
Bentley as she traces the life of Archbishop Desmond Tutu, South
African Archbishop of the Anglican Church.
Tutu questioned his world even as a boy in Klerksdorf, South
Africa. Intelligent, thoughtful and unable to ignore the injustice
around him, Tutu would go on to lead the anti-apartheid movement
and win the Nobel Peace Prize.
Of particular interest are some of Tutu's reflections in the closing
chapter of the book, written before anti-apartheid activist Nelson
Mandela was freed from a South African prison. For instance, Tutu
predicted that Mandela or another black leader would be South
Africa's prime minister by the end of the 1980's.
Although this did not come to pass, South Africa's struggle for
peace, justice and reconciliation goes on.

Wepman, Dennis. *Desmond Tutu.* Watts, 1989. 160 pp. Ill.
(Impact Biographies)

MARK TWAIN (Author)

Hassler, Kenneth. *Mark Twain: Dean of American Humorists.*
SamHar, 1975. 32 pp. (Outstanding Personalities)
Kane, Harnett T. *Young Mark Twain and the Mississippi.* Random
House, 1987. 176 pp. Ill.

Meltzer, Milton. *Mark Twain: A Writer's Life.* Watts, 1985. 120
pp. Ill.

Did you know that Samuel Clemens, a.k.a. Mark Twain, had a burning desire to be a riverboat pilot? That he once took singing lessons? That he loved inventions?

Morsels of information like these overflow from Milton Meltzer's *Mark Twain: A Writer's Life*. As usual, Meltzer has researched his subject well. He treats us to descriptions of Twain's many interests and careers, as well as excerpts from Twain's own writings. Meltzer's strong presentation of Twain's world include an account of Twain's involvement in the Civil War and detailed reports of his early work in newspaper.

Oh, and Meltzer also reveals the origin of Samuel Clemens' pen name. Interesting story!

LECH WALESA (Political Activist/Leader)

Stefoff, Rebecca. *Lech Walesa: The Road to Democracy*. Fawcett Book Group, 1992. 144 pp. Ill. (Great Lives Biography)

RAOUL WALLENBERG (Humanitarian)

Pangburn, Thelma I. *Raoul Wallenberg: Hero of the Holocaust*. SamHar, 1987. 32 pp. (Outstanding Personalities)

BOOKER T. WASHINGTON (Educator)

Neyland, James. *Booker T. Washington: Educator and Social Activist*. Holloway House, 1992. 200 pp. Ill. (Black Americans)

GEORGE WASHINGTON (U.S. President)

Boudreau, Allan, and Alexander Bleimann. *George Washington in New York*. American Lodge of Research, 1989. 275 pp. Ill.

Falkof, Lucille. *George Washington: First President of the United States*. Garrett, 1989. 128 pp. Ill. (Presidents of the United States)

Hilton, Suzanne. *The World of Young George Washington*. Walker, 1987. 112 pp. Ill.

McGowen, Tom. *George Washington*. Watts, 1986. 72 pp. Ill.

Meltzer, Milton. *George Washington and the Birth of Our Nation.*
Watts, 1986. 176 pp. Ill. (Milton Meltzer Biographies)

Is it possible that Milton Meltzer was a friend of George
Washington's in a previous life? That is the impression we get as
we read this wonderfully written biography.

Meltzer takes an inherently thrilling life story and raises it to new
heights. We are impressed with the phenomenal amount of detailed
information Meltzer has unearthed about someone who was born
in 1732. After all, there were no tape recordings or news footage,
only volumes of documentation produced over 160 years.

Meltzer uses all this research to turn an historical figure into a
person, with a childhood and a family, and the same dreams and
influences that motivate us today. Readers will feel as though they
are meeting George Washington for the very first time.

JOSH WHITE (Musician)

Siegel, Dorothy Schainman. *The Glory Road: The Story of Josh
White.* Harcourt Brace Jovanovich, 1983. 155 pp. Ill.

This story of black musician Josh White is, as the author explains,
"a combination of myth and hard fact." We learn that Josh was
born in 1914 and spent part of his boyhood serving as "eyes" for
blind, black, street singers traveling through small Southern towns.
We follow White's own career as a guitarist and a singer of blues,
folk songs and spirituals. His talent opened doors in New York
City, and earned him an invitation to Franklin Roosevelt's White
House. However, despite his abilities, Josh White struggled to
maintain his dignity as he faced the social and political obstacles
placed before black men during the 1950's and '60's.

The Glory Road is based largely on oral history, reminiscences
and recollections of White, and the abundance of dialogue in this
book includes many quotes from other performers.

FRANK LLOYD WRIGHT (Architect)

Murphy, Wendy. *Frank Lloyd Wright.* Silver Burdett, 1990. 128
pp. Ill. (Genius! The Artist and the Process)

Salsini, Paul. *Frank Lloyd Wright: The Architectural Genius of the Twentieth Century.* SamHar 1972. 32 pp. (Outstanding Personalities)

THE WRIGHT BROTHERS (Inventors)

Freedman, Russell. *The Wright Brothers: How They Invented the Airplane.* Holiday House, 1991. 128 pp. Ill.

This book does, indeed, tell us everything we could possibly want to know about how the Wright Brothers invented the airplane. Freedman gives us nearly every detail, every circumstance, every effort of Wilbur and Orville, as well as their forerunners in the world of aviation.

The volume contains a wealth of technical information, but Freedman softens the nuts and bolts approach by also focusing in on the brothers' personalities and ambitions. Thus, the book is appealing to the not-so-technically inclined.

The Wright Brothers also includes many original photographs taken by the famous pair, a list of "places to visit," and a helpful bibliography.

Reynolds, Quentin. *The Wright Brothers: Pioneers of American Aviation.* Random House, 1981. 160 pp. Ill.

Taylor, Richard L. *First Flight: The Story of the Wright Brothers.* Watts, 1990. 64 pp. Ill.

Welch, Becky. *The Wright Brothers: Conquering the Sky.* Fawcett Book Group, 1992. 144 pp. Ill. (Great Lives Biography)

ELIZABETH YATES (Author)

Yates, Elizabeth. *My Diary--My World.* Westminster, 1982. 188 pp. Ill.

A girl born into wealth is free to do whatever her heart desires. Or is she?

Elizabeth Yates provides a revealing look into life in a well-to-do upstate New York family. Daughters of privilege must live up to certain expectations; because of her social standing, Yates was not automatically free to follow the call of the writing life. She shares her struggle through diaries and journals she kept from ages 12 to almost 20. World-wide events touched Yates' life, but small things left impressions as well.

We get to know her family and the activities, priorities and formalities that dominated her everyday life. Yates eventually ventured out on her own and became an award-winning writer.

COLLECTIVE BIOGRAPHIES

One of the resources you won't find in this volume is a book known as a "collective biography." This publication is exactly what the label implies; it is a series of short biographical sketches about famous people who have something in common. For example, there are "collective biographies" of inventors, abolitionists, presidents, and so on.

So why aren't they included? Two factors guided our decision.

First, we want children and young people to read **books** about outstanding men and women, not just brief, fact-filled encyclopedia-type entries. Indeed, not all "collective biographies" fit that description. Some provide interesting stories, and we've reviewed six such books recommended by the National Council for the Social Studies to give you that perspective. All six are appropriate for the Intermediate and/or Young People age groups.

Secondly, in the *Index to Collective Biographies for Young People* by Karen Breen (R.R. Bowker Company, 1988), a total of 1,129 such books are listed. Even more are on the market today. Since this genre is so extensive and, in most cases, falls outside of our mission, we chose to exclude them.

Reviews

Outward Dreams: Black Inventors and Their Inventions. Jim Haskins. Walker, 1991. 128 pp. Ill.

The appendix in this book about black inventors lists hundreds of inventions developed by blacks between 1834 and 1900--not exactly a time when people of color were encouraged to be creative free thinkers. During part of that time, many blacks were not free at all.

213

Yet an individual's ingenuity can seldom be enslaved; thus, we have the plethora of original ideas described in this book.

The names we read in *Outward Dreams* are not household words, although most of us are familiar with George Washington Carver. However, these inventors' accomplishments revolutionized industry, medicine, agriculture and every other field they touched.

For instance, did you know that Jan Ernst Matzeliger's shoe lasting machine changed the shoe industry, created thousands of jobs, and cut shoe prices in half?

Thank you, Mr. Matzeliger!

Lives of the Artists. M.B. Goffstein. Farrar, 1983. 48 pp. Ill.

We open a book with such an ordinary title expecting to see a lineup of traditional biographies. *Lives of the Artists*, however, surprises us with prose that resembles free verse poetry, accented by color reproductions of the works of Rembrandt, Guardi, van Gogh, Bonnard and Nevelson.

Though not conventionally instructive, this unusual volume enriches the readers' experience of the artists' work. When used in conjunction with other biographical material, the book adds a new dimension to a child's introduction to the masters.

Dreams into Deeds: Nine Women Who Dared. Linda Peavy and Ursula Smith. Scribner, 1985. 160 pp. Ill.

The dreams of a child often bring the impossible into the realm of "perhaps." The dreamers in this book translated their dreams into lives of accomplishment.

The authors recreate incidents in the young lives of nine exceptional women, incidents that foreshadow the noteworthy paths their lives would eventually follow.

The role models featured in this volume are Jane Addams, Marian Anderson, Rachel Carson, Alice Hamilton, Mother Jones, Juliette Gordon Low, Margaret Mead, Elizabeth Cady Stanton and Babe Didrikson Zaharias.

The Changing Vice-Presidency. Roy Hoopes. Crowell, 1982. 192 pp. Ill.

U.S. vice presidents come and go, but unless they later win or inherit the presidency, they often disappear into the pages of history.

Roy Hoopes has rescued the second in command from obscurity by describing the duties, trips, speeches and other responsibilities of the vice president. Hoopes offers biographical sketches of each vice president through George Bush, including not only the famous, like Harry Truman and L.B.J., but the less than well-known, like Elbridge Gerry (James Madison's V.P.) and Daniel D. Tompkins (on the James Monroe ticket).

Take a Walk in Their Shoes. Glennette Tilley Turner. Cobblehill, 1989. 160 pp. Ill.

Here is a book that invites the reader to enter the lives of famous people--to "walk in their shoes." Each biographical sketch of 14 notable African Americans is accompanied by a brief skit in which the reader can act out an imagined scene from the hero or heroine's life.

All the selections in this book are brimming with anecdotes; the best chapters are those written chronologically.

The gifted individuals featured in this collection are Martin Luther King, Jr., Rosa Parks, Arthur A. Schomburg, Leontyne Price, Charles White, Garrett A. Morgan, Leroy "Satchel" Paige, Charles Drew, Frederick Douglass, Ida B. Wells, Oscar Micheaux, Mary McLeod Bethune and Maggie Lena Walker.

Indian Chiefs. Russell Freedman. Holiday House, 1987. 160 pp. Ill.

These are the voices of Native American leaders, trying to keep their tribal traditions and culture alive.

Striking photographs, strong description and thorough research combine to provide a dismaying portrait of Indians as prisoners in their own homeland. The six chiefs profiled in this book are all individuals. Each had his own way of dealing with white encroachment on the precious land and resources in the West. Each suffered at the hands of those who had come to conquer them at any cost.

The stories bring to mind the situation in the Amazon rain forest, where natives and nature are being displaced by "progress."

These chiefs, who led their people in times of crisis, are heard in this book: Red Cloud, Santana, Quanah Parker, Washakie, Joseph and Sitting Bull.

APPENDIX A

1993 List of "Notable Children's Trade Books in the Field of Social Studies" by the National Council for Social Studies (NCSS)

As *Hooray for Heroes!* was going to press, the NCSS released its latest listing of "Notable Children's Trade Books." We thought you might be interested in this additional information.

Books in our list cited by the NCSS:

Primary

Giblon, James Cross. *George Washington: A Picture Book Biography.* Scholastic, 1992. 40 pp. Ill.

Intermediate

Ayer, Eleanor H. *Margaret Bourke-White: Photographing the World.* Macmillan Children's Book Group, 1992. 112 pp. Ill.

Haskins, Jim. *I Have a Dream: The Life and Words of Martin Luther King, Jr.* Millbrook, 1992. 112 pp. Ill.

Porter, A.P. *Jump at de Sun: The Story of Zora Neale Hurston.* Carolrhoda, 1993. 88 pp. Ill.

Whitelaw, Nancy. *Theodore Roosevelt Takes Charge.* Whitman, 1991. 176 pp.

Young People

Goldman, Martin S. *Nat Turner and the Southampton Revolt of 1871.* Watts, 1992. 176 pp. Ill.

Haskins, James. *I Am Somebody! A Biography of Jesse Jackson.* Enslow, 1992. 112 pp. Ill.

St. George, Judith. *Dear Dr. Bell...Your Friend, Helen Keller.* Beech Tree, 1993. 96 pp. Ill.

Additional Books

Everett, Gwen. *Li'l Sis and Uncle Willie: A Story Based on the Life and Paintings of William H. Johnson.* Rizzoli, 1992. 32 pp. Ill.

Fritz, Jean. *George Washington's Mother*. Grosset, 1992. 48 pp. Ill.

Harrison, Barbara and Daniel Terris. *A Twilight Struggle: The Life of John Fitzgerald Kennedy*. Lothrop, 1992. 224 pp. Ill.

Hart, Philip S. *Flying Free: America's First Black Aviators*. Lerner, 1992. 72 pp. Ill.

Haskins, Jim. *Against All Opposition: Black Explorers in America*. Walker, 1992. 128 pp. Ill.

Haskins, Jim. *One More River to Cross: The Stories of Twelve Black Americans*. Scholastic, 1992. 160 pp. Ill.

Houston, Gloria. *My Great Aunt Arizona*. Harper Collins, 1992. 32 pp. Ill.

Levinson, Nancy Smiler. *Snowshoe Thompson*. Harper Collins, 1992. 64 pp. Ill.

McKissack, Patricia and Fredrick. *Madam C. J. Walker!: Self-Made Millionaire*. Enslow, 1992. 32 pp. Ill.

Meyer, Carolyn. *Where the Broken Heart Still Beats: The Story of Cynthia Ann Parker*. Gulliver, 1992. 192 pp.

Morey, Janet Nomura, and Wendy Dunn. *Famous Asian Americans*. Cobblehill, 1992. 192 pp. Ill.

Skira-Venturi, Rosabianca. *A Weekend with Degas*. Rizzoli, 1992. 64 pp. Ill.

Stevens, Bryna. *Frank Thompson: Her Civil War Story*. Macmillan, 1992. 144 pp. Ill.

Turner, Robyn Montana. *Mary Cassatt*. Little, Brown, 1992. 32 pp. Ill.

Van Steenwyk, Elizabeth. *Ida B. Wells-Barnett: Woman of Courage*. Watts, 1992. 144 pp. Ill.

Zindel, Paul. *The Pigman and Me*. Harper Collins, 1992. 160 pp.

SERIES INDEX

If a book listed in *Hooray for Heroes!* is part of a publisher's series, the series' name, in parentheses, is included in the listing and in this index. Here you will also find the names of additional individuals featured in each series but not listed as individual entries.

Primary Series

Art For Children (Harper Junior Book Group) 29, 39, 41, 42, 47

Marc Chagall	Frederic Remington
Albrecht Durer	Pierre-Auguste Renoir
Paul Gauguin	Henri Rousseau
Paul Klee	Henri de Toulouse-Lautrec
Henri Matisse	Diego Rodriguez de Silva
Raphael	y Velazquez

Best Holiday Books (Enslow) 26, 36, 37, 48
Biographical Stories (Raintree) 20-22, 24, 26, 28, 32, 33, 38, 40-42, 44-46, 48

Kit Carson	Casey Jones
Sam Houston	Richard the Lionhearted

Easy-to-Read Biographies (Dell) 25, 29, 34

Famous Children (Barron's) 22, 32
Famous People (Barron's) 27, 28, 30, 36, 39, 41, 45
First Start Biographies (Troll) 20, 26, 29, 34, 36, 38, 43, 47, 49

Gateway Biography (Millbrook) 20, 23, 24, 29, 31, 40, 42, 46

219

Black Elk
Lewis Carroll
Katherine Dunham

Elizabeth the First
John Philip Sousa

Step-Up Biographies (Random House)   26, 31-33, 36,
    37, 49
Stories of America (Raintree)   27, 34, 36, 44

The ValueTales (Oak Tree)   19, 21, 22, 24-30, 33, 34, 38-41, 43-45,
    47, 49
    Confucius (Honesty)   Cardinal Leger (Charity)
    Elizabeth Fry (Kindness)   Maurice Richard (Tenacity)
Today's Heroes (Harper Collins Children's Books)   20,
    24, 29

We the People (Creative Education)   21-24, 27, 28, 31,
    33, 34, 36, 39, 41, 42, 46, 47
    Buffalo Bill   Leif Ericson
    Jim Bridger   Ulysses S. Grant
    Kit Carson   Sam Houston
    Champlain   Chief Joseph
    Coronado   Lafayette
    De Soto   Francis Marion

Intermediate Series

Achievers (Lerner)   89, 112, 126, 165
    Neil Armstrong   Stephen King
    Isaac Asimov   Anne Morrow Lindbergh
    Lucille Ball   Oprah Winfrey
    Jane Fonda

Adventurers and Heroes (Troll)   104, 106, 123
    John Cabot and Son   Eric the Red &
    Vasco Da Gama   Leif the Lucky
    Francis Drake   Henry Hudson
                                Ferdinand Magellan
African-American Soldiers (Childrens Press)   146
    Benjamin Davis, Jr.   Daniel "Chappie" James

American Heritage Jr. Library (Troll) 115, 125, 132, 161
American Indian Stories (Raintree) 118, 139, 142, 155, 157, 164
    Plenty Coups   Wilma Mankiller
    Hole-in-the-Day   John Ross
    Ishi   Maria Tallchief
American Women in Science (Equity Institute) 147
    Elma Gonzalez   Nancy Wallace
    Dixie Lee Ray
American Women of Achievement (Chelsea House)
    91-95, 97-101, 110, 113, 117, 119, 122, 125, 128, 137, 139, 141,
    149, 152, 155, 163, 165
    Ethel Barrymore   Clare Booth Luce
    Isadora Duncan   Barbara McClintock
    Mary Baker Eddy   Louise Nevelson
    Helen Hayes   Beverly Sills
    Lillian Hellman   Gertrude Stein
    Anne Hutchinson   Gloria Steinem
    Jeane Kirkpatrick   Edith Wharton
    Emma Lazarus

Baseball Legends (Chelsea House) 90, 103, 118, 136,
    137, 142, 148, 152
    Grover Cleveland Alexander Walter Johnson
    Johnny Bench   Sandy Koufax
    Yogi Berra   Christy Mathewson
    Ty Cobb   Stan Musial
    Dizzy Dean   Brooks Robinson
    Joe DiMaggio   Frank Robinson
    Bob Feller   Willie Stargell
    Jimmie Foxx   Ted Williams
    Bob Gibson   Carl Yastrzemski
    Rogers Hornsby   Cy Young
Black Americans of Achievement (Chelsea House) 90,
    92-97, 99, 101, 107, 111, 115, 121, 123, 124, 126, 131, 136,
    142, 146, 148, 152, 158, 159, 161
    Josephine Baker   Lena Horne
    James Baldwin   Jack Johnson
    Amiri Baraka (LeRoi Jones) James Weldon Johnson
    Count Basie   Barbara Jordan
    Romare Bearden   Lewis Latimer

Charles W. Chesnutt
Paul Cuffe
Father Divine
Charles R. Drew
Katherine Dunham
Ralph Ellison
James Farmer
Ella Fitzgerald
Marcus Garvey
Dizzy Gillespie
Alex Hailey
Prince Hall
Chester Himes
Billie Holiday

Joe Louis
Ronald McNair
Elijah Muhammad
Eddie Murphy
Charlie Parker
Sidney Poitier
Adam C. Powell, Jr.
A. Philip Randolph
Nat Turner
Denmark Vesey
Alice Walker
Madam C.J. Walker
Walter White
Richard Wright

Changing Our World Biographies (Dell)   146
Childhood of Famous Americans (Macmillan Children's
      Book Group)   89, 91, 94, 103, 107, 114-116, 118, 122, 125,
      128, 129, 131, 132, 134, 142, 147, 149, 151-153, 157, 158, 160,
      162, 165
Crispus Attucks   Knute Rockne
Mary Todd Lincoln
Colonial Profiles (Enslow)   91, 120, 144
Cornerstones of Freedom (Childrens Press)   92, 94, 95,
      97, 100, 106, 115, 119, 129, 133, 143, 153, 155, 161, 165
Creative Minds (Carolrhoda)   95, 99-101, 110, 113, 115,
      129, 137, 139, 146, 149, 153, 158, 159, 162, 163
Pearl Buck   Jan Matzeliger
George Gershwin   Maria Mitchell
Johann Gutenberg   Ellen Richards
Alice Hamilton   Lucy Stone
Scott Joplin   Levi Strauss

Discovery Biographies (Chelsea House)   91, 95-97, 100,
      107, 110, 111, 113, 115-117, 119, 123, 124, 125, 127, 129,
      132-135, 140, 141, 147, 151, 158, 161-163, 165
Jim Bridger   Samuel F.B. Morse
Henry Clay   Ringling Brothers
Mary Todd Lincoln

Young People Series

DESCRIPTOR INDEX

HEROES INDEX

ABOUT THE AUTHORS

DENNIS DENENBERG (D.Ed., Pennsylvania State University; Phi Beta Kappa, The College of William and Mary) is an Associate Professor and Coordinator of Field Experiences at Millersville University of Pennsylvania. He is a former high school social studies teacher, elementary school principal and district assistant superintendent. The author of *Toward a Human Curriculum: A Guide to Returning Great People to Classrooms and Homes* (Trillium Press, 1991), he has written and spoken extensively about heroes.

LORRAINE ROSCOE (B.A., Cabrini College) is a freelance writer and the full-time mother of two. She specializes in topics related to education and mental health issues, and served as an advisor to Dr. Denenberg in the writing of *Toward a Human Curriculum. Hooray for Heroes!* is her first book.